A PENNY
FOR THE
GOVERNOR

Income Taxation

in Washington

SEATTLE AND LONDON

A Penny for the Govern

a Dollar for Uncle Sam

$A DOLLAR FOR UNCLE SAM

PHIL ROBERTS

UNIVERSITY OF WASHINGTON PRESS

LIBRARY OF CONGRESS CATALOGING-IN-PUBLICATION DATA

Roberts, Philip J.

A penny for the governor, a dollar for Uncle Sam : income taxation in Washington/Phil Roberts.

p. cm.

Includes index.

ISBN 0-295-98251-9 (acid-free paper)

1. Income tax—Law and legislation—Washington (State)—History. I Title.

KFW475 .R63 2002

343.79705'2—dc21   2002072441

CONTENTS

Preface *vii*

Acknowledgments *xi*

1   Setting the Stage *3*

2   Civil War Income Tax *7*

3   Civil War Income Tax in Oregon:
      A Comparative Assessment *26*

4   Consensus I: Federal Income Tax and
      Washington's Reaction, 1894 *37*

5   Consensus II: Washington Ratifies
      the Federal Income Tax, 1911 *47*

6   The Background for Tax Reform, 1914–1931 *56*

7   The Washington Income Tax of 1931: Veto and Response *73*

8   Electoral Success, Judicial Defeat *86*

9   Attractive Alternatives to an Income Tax, 1933–1940 *100*

10   Income Tax Efforts after World War II *119*

Notes *127*

Comment on Sources *182*

Index *187*

PREFACE

" *Taxes are the bedrock of government,* necessary for building roads and schools, for fostering new industry, and for providing care
for people. Taxation is also about wealth redistribution. Through politics,
economic interest groups do battle over which groups have to pay and which
groups are "subsidized" with lower rates or exemption. If there is change
in a society, it often comes with a cost. Ultimately, if voters want change,
they also must decide who will pay for it. By following the public debates
over taxes, one gains an understanding of the priorities that society holds
about the place of government in relation to other institutions and the role
government should play in the economic lives of its citizens. More important, an examination of taxation can demonstrate the relative influence of
interest groups on the political process over time. "

Some historians would agree with William E. Leuchtenburg that "war
between the country and the city had been fought for decades," while others dispute the significance of such a construct.[1] An evaluation of the role
of urban-rural conflict in such developments as the rise of the Ku Klux Klan
and the adoption of Prohibition indicates that other cultural or economic
factors seem to have had greater importance. Local studies of the Klan in
Colorado, for instance, have demonstrated that it was not simply a prod-
uct of the countryside.[2] Similarly, studies of the 1928 presidential election—
previously viewed as the classic electoral battle between "country" (drys)
and "city" (wets)—have shown that the line between the opposing forces
cannot be so neatly drawn.[3]

This book is the first to test the existence of urban-rural conflict by examining that most fundamental of political issues, taxes—who decides, who pays, and how much. Economic self-interest is not the only factor in tax decisions. Assumptions about economic development, social responsibility, and government influence over business and property shape tax systems. Cultural assumptions and political philosophies have roles as well. This book explores that complex mix by closely examining how citizens of one state dealt with tax questions and how they responded to taxes that had been formulated nationally. Were there significant differences in how rural people and urban residents responded to taxation? If so, can differences be ascribed to fundamental urban-rural conflicts? If such conflicts have any appreciable significance, they should be obvious in any examination of tax policy. By formulating the debate in terms of urban-rural conflict (and, of course, taking into account class), one may gain an increased understanding of how taxation politics influenced (and were influenced by) the economic and cultural forces in the United States from the days of Lincoln to the New Deal.[4]

The questions about taxation policies can be tested by examining the state of Washington, typical as any state during the period. It was neither a farm state nor an urban center (in 1930 Washington was the second most urbanized state in the West). Although the state had a reputation for political radicalism (the Seattle General Strike, for example), it had been dominated by Republicans from territorial days to 1932, a pattern not unlike those found in many Western and Midwestern states during the same period. Economic conditions in the urban areas had improved until the Great Depression, while conditions on the farms eroded. In this respect, too, Washington reflected the national trend. The state's population was relatively homogenous, with few ethnic, religious, or racial groups living in the urban areas. In the seventy years from the Civil War to the Great Depression, Washington was a typical developing state, mirroring the national mood and experience in nearly all respects.[5]

This book also explores the connections between politics and tax policy by analyzing how citizens of the state of Washington reacted to federal tax policy, responded to national debates over tax issues, and opted for particular forms of taxation for themselves and their property. The governors, legislatures, and courts were important players in the drama, but average citizens also participated directly through the initiative process. This direct democracy allowed rural and urban groups to take tax policy directly into law. It is difficult to compare the evolutions of taxes levied by various states, particularly when many states lacked the initiative process. In Washington, the initiative was commonly used, thus allowing identification of the political forces driving tax policy.

But the forces were not just in Washington. They were present everywhere in the country. To remind the reader that tax debates can take very divergent turns—even in places with similar populations, geography, and industry—this study includes occasional references to tax debates in Oregon, Washington's neighbor to the south. Such comparisons shed light on the twists and turns in tax politics that took the citizens of two very similar states down very different roads.

As this book demonstrates, there was an intersection between class and geography in the tax debates in Washington. In the few instances when rural interests joined with the urban working class, they could control the tax debates. When that union did not occur, because of either economic conditions or cultural divides, urban dwellers set the tax agenda even when they did not control the legislative process. Whether or not this proves that "urban" and "rural" describe polar differences, the Washington example shows that the concept of a dichotomy still has value when examining how a consensus was reached on that most crucial of political issues, tax policy.

Early on, frontier citizens had experience dealing with the tax man. At the same time that law enforcement had barely taken hold in a far-flung, lightly populated territory, tax collectors were on the scene assessing and gathering federal taxes. Whether or not an individual paid generally depended on what region of the country he had come from. New Englanders, for instance, made up a disproportionate number of taxpayers. Even in cases where they earned less income than natives of other regions, New Englanders paid their taxes, either out of patriotism or a general sense of duty.

As an initial inquiry into understanding the development of tax policy in Washington, this book examines how the federal government was able to set up a tax-collecting system on the frontier while the Civil War was raging in the East. These initial encounters created perceptions about taxation among both urban and rural residents. The residue framed future tax debates.

Readers should notice that this book is not about the American roots of income taxation nor is it about other aspects of taxes such as taxation of real property or natural resources.[6] Instead, it is limited to the narrower issue of how income taxes were applied or resisted in the Pacific Northwest.

ACKNOWLEDGMENTS

In the course of writing a book, one accumulates many debts. I want to acknowledge a few of the many people who helped me in so many different ways over the years.

Thanks to Otis Pease, my dissertation chair at the University of Washington Department of History, for his guidance as well as for suggesting the topic of this study; William Rorabaugh, mentor and friend, for sharing his knowledge about the main issues covered in this book; the late Robert Burke for suggesting the urban-rural divisions and his expert critique of the original manucript; Dauril Alden for his valuable suggestions and critique of earlier drafts; and the late Aldon Bell for his insights on state politics.

Thanks to the librarians and archivists at Suzzallo Library, University of Washington; the Washington State Archives; and the National Archives, Seattle Branch. I also thank the many people whom I interviewed about taxation questions, especially Charles Hodde and Congressman Jim McDermott. I am grateful to Joyce Justice, National Archives, for bringing the assessment roles to my attention; to Lewis Saum and Carol Zabilski of *Pacific Northwest Quarterly,* who published a portion of an earlier version of the Civil War chapter; to John McClelland of *Columbia,* who published an earlier abridged version of the state income tax chapter; to Terry Willis for letting me cite an early draft on her work on the Unemployed Citizens League. I benefited greatly from critical readings and other assistance from Richard Kirkendall, John Findlay, Jon Bridgman, Suzanne Young, Richard Johnson, Thomas Pressly, and the late Arthur Bestor and Vernon Carstensen.

Special thanks to the University of Washington Press, particularly Julidta Tarver, who never lost faith in this project, and the Press's copy editors, production staff, and referees, anonymous to me, who provided valuable suggestions, particularly on style and organization. Thanks, too, to the College of Arts and Sciences, University of Wyoming, for providing a portion of the funding for the completion of this work.

I am indebted to my colleagues and mentors at the University of Washington and to my colleagues in the Department of History, University of Wyoming, for helping make this book possible. In this venture, however, I alone am responsible for any errors and, of course, for all interpretations and judgments.

My greatest debt is to my wife, Peggy, who introduced me to Seattle and the Northwest and who supported me as I changed careers from law to history.

PHIL ROBERTS
June 2002

A Penny for the Governor,

a Dollar for Uncle Sam

1 Setting the Stage

At last, an income tax. Farmers, reformers, and labor organizers pushed it through in the state of Washington in 1932. But it lasted barely a year. What happened? If it existed such a short time, why did it pass to begin with? Why did such a popular measure fail after it had gained the approval of more than 60 percent of the voters in 1932? The answer lies in an intriguing blend of politics, economics, and a tradition of urban-rural conflict that was not unique to one state in the far northwest of the United States.

The income tax was popular with farmers and reformers throughout the country in the first part of the twentieth century. In the depression years, it also gained support from labor and the urban poor. In the election of 1932, Franklin D. Roosevelt led a Democratic sweep nationally, and in Washington, the Democrats won control of both houses of the state legislature for the first time in history. Five voter initiative measures passed comfortably. The one that authorized a state income tax surpassed all of the rest—even repeal of the state's "bone-dry" law. Seventy percent of Washington voters cast ballots for the income tax; 62 percent favored bringing back beer; 61 percent approved a property tax limitation.

Many income tax proponents failed to realize, however, that the ballot victory did not necessarily ensure the act's implementation. Determining its constitutionality would be up to the nine elected justices on the Washington State Supreme Court.[1] In accordance with constitutional rules on initiatives, Initiative 69 became law thirty days after passage. Nonetheless,

3

the law required that the governor sign the proclamation. The lame-duck governor, Roland Hartley, a victim of the Democratic landslide in 1932 who had vetoed an income tax bill in the previous year, reluctantly signed the proclamation December 8, 1932.

The state's economy worsened during the winter.[2] Some politicians believed that the income tax would provide relief once it took the burden off real and personal property the next year. Reformers rejoiced at the prospect of progressive taxation at last. Government officials were pleased, too, at the thought of a predictable revenue source. But lawyers and legislators were well aware of the constitutional flaws in the tax initiative.

Plaintiffs mounted legal challenges to the law in Thurston County Superior Court the day after the governor signed the proclamation. The tax commission, though, went ahead and prepared the machinery for tax collection. While members hoped that such efforts would not be rendered futile by unfavorable court rulings, the commission staff struggled to ensure that the tax would pass constitutional muster.

Meanwhile, the leadership of the Washington State Grange, an organization of farmers with a long record of support for the income tax, congratulated members for the hard work they had put into the income tax campaign.[3] It was a major victory for rural Washington, Grange officers believed.

In urban areas, the tax met with little enthusiasm. Many still-employed Seattleites knew that it had passed because of the combination of farmers and working-class people, many of whom were jobless with no incomes to tax. Soon after the initiative passed, two groups of Seattle businessmen prepared lawsuits to challenge the constitutionality of the measure. Insurance agency operators and auto dealers were heavily represented among the litigants. The suits were brought in the names of William M. Culliton and Earl McHale, prominent principals in the two occupations.

Thurston County Superior Court Judge D. F. Wright consolidated the two cases for trial in the winter of 1932–33. The legislature was still in session when Wright announced his decision. He entered a decree permanently restraining the commission from enforcing the act. The income tax, in his view, was "wholly unconstitutional."[4]

The State Tax Commission appealed the decision to the Washington State Supreme Court. The nine-member, elected court heard oral arguments a few months later. Both sides were wary, unsure how the court would rule.

After the hearing, the court announced that a decision would come down sometime in early fall.

An informal vote indicated that the court would uphold the income tax. Nonetheless, state officials were alarmed by the probable magnitude of the revenue shortfalls if the decision were to go the other way. With such prospects in mind, a sales tax bill had been introduced in the 1933 legislative session.

In early August 1933, ill health forced the resignation of a known antitax supreme court justice. Less than a week later, Governor C. D. Martin, who had ridden to victory with the income tax initiative the previous year, announced that he was appointing a close political ally to the seat—James M. Geraghty, who had served briefly as the governor's director of efficiency. Geraghty came from Eastern Washington, where he had been a longtime political advisor to the governor. Income tax proponents must have been comforted by Geraghty's appointment, because he was known to be supportive of the income tax.

The Washington State Tax Commission was cautiously printing income tax forms, but officials were unsure how many would be needed. The federal Internal Revenue Bureau figures showed that approximately 50,000 Washingtonians earned sufficient incomes in 1931 to file federal returns. The Washington tax exemptions and brackets varied so significantly from the federal ones that officials found it difficult to estimate how many people would have to file state tax returns. As a tax expert advised in the *Seattle Times* in late March of 1933, state tax returns "must be filed by a large number of people who have never paid income taxes before." As a result of this peculiarity, the tax commission mailed forms to far more than 50,000 households. In fact, the forms went to nearly everyone in the state, including farmers and wage laborers earning far less than the minimums subject to taxation. Forms were even sent to persons in occupations exempted from paying the tax. Newspapers statewide printed what apparently had been only an informal response to a reporter's question: "If you received an income tax return form in the mail, you must fill out the return and file it regardless of the amount of your income."

The chief justice scheduled a rehearing on the case in late August. On September 8, 1933, the state supreme court announced its decision: in a 5–4 decision, it struck down the state income tax as unconstitutional. Tax supporters, including Grange members, were stunned. Geraghty surprised neither the governor nor income tax proponents. Nonetheless, his vote to uphold the tax statute did not turn out to be pivotal. Instead, a justice who had favored the tax in June changed his position by September. Reporters speculated on who had switched sides. Did one justice receive the complicated tax form in his mailbox between the two dates?

The majority opinion said that the income tax was unconstitutional because it violated the 14th amendment to the state constitution, which required that all direct taxes be uniform on all categories of property. Even though the income tax had been an initiative, that fact was "of no controlling importance." Also irrelevant were similar phrases in constitutions in the adjoining states of Oregon and Idaho, where income tax statutes had withstood constitutional challenges.

Legal scholars criticized the tortured reasoning in the decision. But tax opponents were delighted with the court's ruling. In their view, the state of Washington had suffered a far too close brush with income taxation. Farmers watched as a hard-fought victory was snatched away by those whom they viewed as urban opponents.

More than a half-century later, the state of Washington is one of only eight states without a state income tax.[5] In the first decade of the new millennium, more than a century after statehood, local governments in Washington still rely on real property taxes for their revenues. A statewide sales tax has funded a significant part of the state government budget since it was adopted in 1935. In fact, the pattern of taxation has changed very little from 1935 to the present. In an era when income taxes are practically institutionalized in other states, the barest mention of such a tax in Washington seems to elicit wide public outcry.[6]

Urban-rural conflict over taxation was not always clear cut. The tax question went through four distinct phases: voluntary compliance (1862–72); consensus (1873–1911); urban-rural conflict (1912–32); and the attractive alternatives phase (1933–40). During the first two periods, discussions involved federal taxes; during the second two, they concerned choices of forms for the support of state government. Though Washington is used in this study, the phases should be observable in all other nonindustrial states, the time periods dependent on each state's level of development.[7]

2 Civil War Income Tax

A month after the battle of Antietam in Maryland, the bloodiest engagement of the Civil War, Union tax notices appeared in newspapers around the North. By passing a comprehensive tax bill, one small part of which was a tax on personal income, Congress conceded that the Civil War would cost far more than any member had hitherto expected. On October 25, 1862, some 2,500 miles west of the battlefields, the inhabitants of Washington Territory first encountered the new income tax in the *Walla Walla Statesman* and in Olympia's *Washington Standard*, and for the next decade, they approached it with trepidation and ambivalence.[1]

Newspapers of the period do not record how the territorial residents, who numbered fewer than the soldiers killed on each side at Antietam, initially reacted to modern taxation. From a territory exempt from army conscription, not to mention the ravages of war, the Union asked a modest financial sacrifice.[2] The law required payment only from those persons making in excess of $600 per year. For those accustomed to tithing, the tax rate was a bargain, a modest 5 percent for all taxpayers, regardless of income.[3]

When Congress passed the Civil War tax law in the summer of 1862, it put into operation the first national tax in America geared to a person's income. Several states, at various times, taxed income.[4] Southern states experimented with income taxes even during the Civil War.[5]

Leaders of the industrialized North felt the pressures of a war economy. Prior to the Civil War, the federal government relied on customs duties and land sales to finance its operations. Except in 1836, when land sales surpassed customs duties by one million dollars, the duties usually contributed in excess of 80 percent of federal revenue.[6] Consequently, neither the Mexican War nor military expeditions against Indians in the West caused any real need for "internal revenue." In fact, during the Jackson administration, the federal debt was liquidated, and Congress debated the hot political issue of how to dispose of the surplus.[7] The depression of 1837 settled the matter by wiping out the federal surpluses, just as the economic crisis forced abrupt halts to state improvement projects.[8]

The panic of 1857 caused a series of budget deficits from 1858 on that totaled some $50 million by the end of the fiscal year 1860. Despite vigorous loan and tariff policies, the federal government was unable to stem the massive withdrawal of bank deposits following Southern secession.[9]

The U.S. Treasury was almost empty when Lincoln took office on March 4, 1861. The administration, in the opening months of the war, resisted tax increases. Secretary of the Treasury Salmon P. Chase tried to raise sufficient revenues from the sale of government bonds. When Congress met in July 1861, leaders recognized that higher taxes were the only alternative, despite Chase's objections. Two days after the disastrous Union defeat at Bull Run, a tax bill calling for $20 million to be raised from the states was introduced in Congress.[10] The proposal was hardly novel. It was modeled after the direct tax that the federal government had used to finance the War of 1812, and it consisted of a set quota for each state to be assessed against real property.[11]

Because the states would assess the tax primarily against real estate, many congressmen, particularly those from agricultural states, opposed it. Representative of this view are the remarks of Indiana congressman Schuyler Colfax: "I cannot go home and tell my constituents that I voted for a bill that would allow a man, a millionaire, who has put his entire property into stock, to be exempt from taxation, while a farmer who lives by his side must pay a tax." Congressman Thaddeus Stevens of Lancaster, Pennsylvania, the committee chairman, claimed that the Constitution made illegal any tax that was not applied proportionately among the states and territories. He argued that the states should determine what would be taxed to raise the required revenues.[12]

The Colfax point of view gained considerable support. A provision was added to decrease the direct tax by one-third, making up the difference with a tax on income. Before the full House, one proponent explained that such a tax could raise twice the revenue of the old direct tax on land alone. The new tax act, including the provision for income taxation, passed the House on July 29, 1861, by a vote of 77–60. The Senate passed the measure on August 2. The income tax section of the law, set to take effect June 30, 1862, set a flat rate of 3 percent on all income above $800 per year. The direct tax took effect immediately, and states and territories had to meet the collection quotas, applied proportionally by population. The law required each state to collect its quota and also made the states responsible for collection of the income tax, from which they could deduct 15 percent for administrative costs.[13]

Washington Territory's direct tax quota was the curiously unrounded sum of $7,755.33. The territorial auditor, R. M. Walker, predicted that Washingtonians would pay the direct tax enthusiastically. "The Citizens of this Territory have expressed their gratification in being afforded an opportunity of contributing their quota in sustaining their government and strengthening its hands in putting down the present gigantic and monstrous rebellion," he wrote Secretary of State William Seward, enclosing a copy of the legislative act assuming the debt and apportioning the territory's share among the counties, based on the assessed valuation of property in each county.[14]

The auditor's optimism, however, failed to translate into money for the war. Almost six months after Congress assessed the levy, Washington Territory had raised only $600, not even 10 percent of its quota. The territory never did pay the assigned amount. Washington collectors managed to raise only $4,268 of the $7,755 quota. The territory was not alone. Utah Territory failed to pay a cent. Colorado Territory, the only other northern delinquent payer, came within $800 on a $22,200 quota. Ten states still owing money in 1888 were all part of the Confederacy, assigned quotas under the law despite their secession.[15]

The income tax provision of the 1861 act was never put in force. The law authorized the secretary of the treasury to collect the tax, but he took no steps to do so. A few months later, Congress began work on an even more extensive income tax measure, necessitated by the already spiraling war costs. The new tax was to be levied for three years, beginning in July 1863.

When President Lincoln signed the act into law on July 1, 1862, this more comprehensive tax code reduced the exemption to $600 per year. The 3 percent rate was retained but only for annual incomes of less than $10,000. Higher incomes would be taxed at 5 percent. Individuals were taxed for incomes earned during the calendar year, but returns were not due until May 1 of the following year.[16]

Perhaps the most important aspect of the new tax law, absent from the 1861 act, was the change in collection procedures. Congress created the Bureau of Internal Revenue to carry out provisions of the 1862 act.[17] No longer would tax collecting be left to the individual states and territories. Even though its relative value for revenue raising proved insignificant during this period, the tax provided the structure of the modern-day collection system. In July 1862, only a tax commissioner and three clerks made up the internal revenue staff. By January 1863, almost 4,000 people were on the payroll throughout the Union, including the Far West.[18] Each of the 185 collection districts in the United States was headed by a district collector and aided by a district assessor. Both positions were presidential appointments, although each had the power to choose his own assistants. The collector's job amounted to little more than a sinecure for political friends, but the assessor's duties required good judgment, honesty, and a commitment to fairness if the tax system was to work properly.[19]

When Congress began debate on the provisions of the 1862 tax, the nation was more occupied with news from the battlefields.[20] Future taxpayers in Washington Territory learned of the law's passage from a wire report buried among the long dispatches from the battlefield. Steilacoom readers of the *Puget Sound Herald*, for instance, were given a terse one-line summary of the vote on final passage, three weeks after the event had occurred.[21] Not until October did a territorial newspaper print the entire text of the law, though its provisions had been summarized throughout the summer and early fall.[22] Readers following the controversy in Congress over the excise tax portions must have recognized the humor in an August article in the *Washington Standard* and the *Walla Walla Statesman* poking fun at the long list of transactions and items subject to the new tax. The papers printed a bogus list of taxes: "Kissing a pretty girl $1; homely one $2. . . . Old bachelors over 30 are taxed $10; over 40, $20; over 50, $50 and sentenced to banishment to Utah. . . . Each pretty lady is to be taxed from 25 cents to $25. She is to fix the estimate on her own beauty. It is thought that a very large amount will be realized from this provision."[23]

The humor was not addressed to the income provision alone but more particularly toward the numerous duties placed on articles and products and the annual license fees imposed on bankers, auctioneers, cattle brokers, photographers, lawyers, physicians, and even jugglers. Peddlers, livery stable keepers, soap makers, and brewers were also assessed, and hotels and taverns had to pay yearly license fees depending on their gross receipts. Bowling alleys and billiard rooms paid on the number of alleys and tables, while circuses had to pay $50 per year, and theaters, $100.[24]

In August 1862, President Lincoln appointed Major H. A. Goldsborough of Washington, D.C., to the collectorship in Washington Territory, a relatively insignificant post given the remoteness and tiny population of the area. Goldsborough, whose father had served for decades as chief clerk in the Navy Department, was politically well connected. His brother, Commodore Louis M. Goldsborough, commanded the Atlantic Blockading Squadron and was married to the daughter of William Wirt, former attorney general and Anti-Masonic party presidential candidate.[25]

The second important tax position in the territory, district assessor, went to John G. Sparks, a native of Indiana.[26] Sparks's responsibility included explaining the tax and coaxing or coercing people to comply with its terms. Goldsborough was charged with collecting the revenue and forwarding it to the Treasury Department in the nation's capital.

The occupation licenses, according to the law, had to be paid effective September 1, 1862, but due to the distance from the national capital and the poor communications, official notices of that fact did not appear in Washington newspapers until late October. Goldsborough, the collector, did not arrive in the territory until October 9, making the trip across Panama, by steamship to Steilacoom, and by stagecoach to Olympia. Sparks set up housekeeping in Walla Walla and met the collector in Olympia, where they planned immediately to begin tax collections.[27]

From the beginning, the new federal taxes counted on taxpayers' willingness to pay, and the newspapers in the territory furnished encouragement. The humorous jibes of August did not reappear. The first official notice of the occupation tax appeared in territory newspapers in late October. The *Walla Walla Statesman* editor wrote of the official notice: "We bespeak for the government requirements upon industry and wealth of the citizens of Washington Territory a cheerful and prompt response."[28] Newspaper editors reminded territorial residents—so delighted to be given "an opportunity of contributing their quota" to the earlier tax—that they still owed a significant amount of that bill. The *Standard* editor, in the same issue with the new tax notice, reported that Kitsap County had paid more than $500 of "her proportion of the direct tax" and, additionally, county residents had "contributed about $4,000 to the Sanitary Fund" for Union soldiers. Elsewhere in the same issue he told taxpayers that the tax burden was even more onerous in the South: "The rebel tax law takes 20 percent of value of all real and personal property in Dixie."[29]

Not every newspaper editor believed that the income tax was an effective way to raise federal revenues. The editor of the *North-West* in Port Townsend agreed with Paul K. Hubbs, a Portland lawyer who had asserted that "collecting the direct and income tax in Washington Territory . . . will cost the government $274 more than the gross sum to be collected." The newspaper did not amplify on Hubbs's figures or their precision, even though Congress and Treasury Department officials themselves apparently had little idea of how much revenue the tax would raise.[30]

By late fall Sparks had appointed six assistants, each in charge of a division made up of one or more counties. Assistant assessors and deputy collectors were not on the federal payroll. They were employees of their principals, who paid them varying wages.[31] John Denny, a sixty-nine-year-old Seattle pioneer, headed Division 1, made up of King, Pierce, Snohomish, and Whatcom counties. A forty-eight-year-old bookkeeper, E. S. Dyer, assessed in Division 2—Kitsap, Jefferson, Island, and Clallam counties. Dyer, a native of Maine, lived at Port Townsend, where he boarded with a local merchant. Sparks named D. R. Bigelow, a horticulturist, to assess in Thurston, Lewis, Sawamish (Mason), and Chehalis (Grays Harbor) counties. No biographical data are available for the assistant assessors in the other three districts: Edwin L. Dole of Vancouver, L. J. Rector of Walla Walla, and S. F. Ledyard, address not stated. Ledyard's area of responsibility was "Eastern Washington," then consisting of Shoshone, Nez Perce, and "Idahoe" counties in Idaho, Missoula County in Montana, and Spokane County in Washington. Goldsborough employed only three assistants, but all were prominent in their respective areas. The businessman W. W. Miller of Olympia was in charge of the Puget Sound District; A. R. Burbank of Monticello was named to collect revenues along the Columbia River; and the Walla Walla lawyer and banker D. S. Baker was to handle the chore in the eastern part of the territory.[32]

Sparks had a monetary incentive to maximize the number of taxpayers. The law provided payment of $1 for every 100 taxable persons on the assessor's list. Additionally, each assessor received $3 per day while "instructing his assistants" and $5 per day while "hearing appeals, revising valuations and making out the lists." Goldsborough and other collectors looked to receipts for their wages. A collector received a commission of 4 percent on the first $100,000 in taxes he brought in and 2 percent for everything above that amount, not to exceed $10,000 per year.[33]

Just before Christmas, Sparks moved his office from Walla Walla to Olympia in order to coordinate more closely with the collector.[34] In the meantime, each of the assistant assessors advertised his presence for 15 days at a central location in the district where he expected to receive comments on assessments.[35] Once the assessment had been made and validated, the collection process began. "Deputy collectors will be appointed in due time," Goldsborough promised in a January 1863 newspaper notice. By February, his appointees were notifying the public about where to bring assessment sheets and tax payments.[36]

Unlike the assessors, the collectors did not visit individual businesses or taxpayers' homes. In the month before the final payment deadline, each collector spent from one to two days in each county seat. The notice for Pierce County is typical: "Taxpayers Attention! . . . The U.S. Tax Collector will visit Steilacoom on Friday, the 20th inst., and hold a levee at Galliher's hotel on that and the following day. Gentlemen will please to walk up to the captain's office and settle, nor leave it till the accepted time is past."[37] Even if payment were but ten days late, 10 percent would be added to the tax, Goldsborough's assistants warned.[38]

As further encouragement for prompt payment, newspapers reported that President Lincoln intended to pay tax on his income even though, as a government employee, he was exempt from the law's provisions.[39] Lincoln's example was not enough to allay tax officials' fears of wholesale tax avoidance, possibly through public ignorance of the law. In a sentence long enough to show that he had a talent for serving in the new federal bureau, Sparks issued an exhortation with a veiled threat.

It will be observed that the law does not intend to lay a duty upon what a man necessarily consumes in living, it therefore is wisely provided that $600 shall be exempt from this tax, yet it is equally clear that if a man chooses to live extravagantly, or otherwise consume or expend treble that amount, or the entire amount of his gains, profits, or income, he is still liable to pay a tax on all over $600.

The assessor warned late payers that "after 30 days, and ten days after levied by the collector, five percent will be added," contradicting the collector's notice of the previous month, which threatened a 10 percent late charge.[40]

Meanwhile, Goldsborough had financial troubles, perhaps from extravagant living or maybe because of the speculations he made on town lots in Olympia during his term as tax collector for the territory.[41] Although the exact nature of the debt is not clear, the district court issued a judgment to M. R. Tilley on March 19, 1863, against Goldsborough's Olympia property for payment of the $1,507.07 Tilley was owed. Included were 12 town lots and an entire city block, and in December 1863, the sheriff seized the property and sold it from the courthouse steps to satisfy the judgment.[42] Once the sale was held, Goldsborough quit the collector's post, left Olympia, and returned to Washington, D.C.[43]

He was replaced by Philip D. Moore, an ambitious forty-year-old New Jersey native who had been Victor Smith's assistant in the Port Angeles customs office in 1863. A former editor of a Newark, N.J., newspaper, Moore was in Washington, D.C., at the time of his appointment. He took the long Atlantic voyage to Panama, crossed the isthmus of Panama, and boarded the steamer *Moses Taylor* for the last leg of the journey. He brought with him to San Francisco more than one million dollars in legal tender notes and $50,000 in revenue stamps, both items in short supply in the West.[44]

Newspapers in the East frequently noted fraud charges brought against collectors and assessors, but despite Goldsborough's troubles and Moore's close connections to the controversial Smith, Washington newspapers made no mention of any problems in the revenue offices of the territory. Distant officials enjoyed no such immunity. The *Oregonian* in nearby Portland railed against a "Third Auditor of the Treasury," in charge of the Oregon Indian war debt, and indirectly defended local officials: "[His] only idea of Oregon seemed to be that it was a nest of sharpers and thieves, when in fact, he was better skilled at corruption and more adroit in roguery than all the rascals of this coast together."[45]

Sparks seemed sensitive to such possibilities by publicly warning his assistants of the serious consequences of breaking his rules. If an assistant failed to comply with them, he "shall be discharged from office and fined $200 and costs," Sparks wrote.[46]

Regardless of official conduct, the tax collections continued. Several of the seven newspapers serving the fewer than 7,000 residents of the territory began printing tax information in January 1864 for the upcoming collections in April and May. The rates did not change, but for the first time the published notices of tax assessments included specific information on what income qualified for taxation, what was exempt, and what expenses could be deducted. Taxpayers could deduct such now familiar items as state and local taxes, business expenses, costs of property repairs, and farm operations. Sparks's notice in the Olympia newspaper stressed the need for taxpayers to "prepare their accounts . . . [so as] to expedite the business; and when called upon by the assessor, with the assistance of the forms and blanks which will be furnished them, will be able to render satisfactory accounts to themselves and the Assessor."[47]

As in the previous year, the assessor visited businesses, while the collector or his assistants waited for taxpayers to come to them. For instance, in the summer of 1864, Moore or his assistant spent one day in each of eight towns. They were in Seattle on June 28 and Port Townsend on July 2. The total assessment for "internal revenues" in the territory in 1864 came to $22,409, only $7,000 of which came from income taxes. The greater sum came from the license fees and duties.[48]

The rates for 1864 leaped upward because of the escalating costs of the war. Taxpayers earning income up to $5,000 paid taxes of 10 percent; from $5,000 to $10,000, 12.5 percent; and above $10,000, 15 percent. Nationally, enthusiasm for the tax was fading, and tougher penalties had to be applied for evasion.[49]

Early in 1863, the commissioner issued instructions that individual returns were private and none of the information would be divulged except to revenue agents. His ruling sparked a national newspaper debate in which editors argued that they should be allowed to publish incomes as a check against possible fraud and collusion between agents and taxpayers. The commissioner, eyeing the increases in reported tax evasion, reversed his position in 1864, agreeing that publicity might aid the collectors.[50]

Even in lightly populated Washington Territory, Sparks faced, if not outright evasion, at least willful delay in tax payments. In a letter he wrote to the Olympia newspaper, he explained why the government felt compelled to assess a late payment penalty against a popular Monticello man, Dr. A. Ostrander, a forty-five-year-old, New York–born physician. "I felt convinced that in some instances, the failure [to file] was unintentional, but I finally came to the conclusion that [the penalty] would work less hardship and expense than to subject the parties in distant parts of the territory to the expense of attending an examination before the Assessor."[51]

Nothing further is known of the Ostrander case. Apparently, the doctor paid the tax and the penalty, but Sparks's letter revealed the growing political discontent with the tax. He pointedly noted, "I will pass over the comments of the Democrats on what the editor pleases to term the imposition of onerous taxes, as the object of such statements is apparent." Although it is not known to which editorial he was replying, Sparks indicated the editor's hostility toward taxation of incomes: "I trust . . . that the income of [the editor's] toil will not be 'violently wrested' from him or any other citizen, either by the 'enactment of political legislation or the hands of the assassin,' by which term he means, I presume, the Assessor or his assistants."[52]

The federal tax officers faced an open challenge the next month in Washington Territory, when Alex S. Abernethy, a prominent Cowlitz County lumberman, apparently became one of several Washingtonians caught failing to file in 1865.[53] Sparks noticed his nonpayment and sent notice that the lumberman owed the tax plus a 50 percent penalty for failing to file. Instead of challenging the ruling in court (or complaining to the delegate in Congress), Abernethy angrily wrote an open letter to the editor of the *Standard*. He flatly accused Sparks's assistant of failing to deliver the four-page tax form. Abernethy claimed that he had paid, but since he had not received the form directly, he did not pay the tax collector who came to town to accept the returns. Instead, he had mailed the payment. It was not his fault that it was lost in the mail, Abernethy argued, becoming the first Washingtonian on record to make the claim.[54]

Sparks's reply may not have been the first of its kind in internal revenue history, but it reflected the increased appeals to voluntarism while it also warned of dire consequences if the tax bills were ignored. "Blank forms are furnished by assistant assessors and I cannot too earnestly urge prompt and full compliance with the requirements of the law, and by so doing it will not become necessary to inflict the penalties provided for a neglect or other cause." He concluded that it was Abernethy's responsibility to meet the deadline regardless of whether or not he had been given a form. "I hope I have cleared up the issue and removed the impression that [taxpayers like Abernethy] have experienced either 'unfair' or 'unjust' treatment at my hands."[55]

At the close of the war, the federal government needed every dollar it could collect. The federal deficit—only $25 million at the end of the first year of the war—amounted to nearly $1 billion at the war's end. The national debt, a mere $90 million in 1861, stood at $2.7 billion four years later. Even though the federal budget needed revenues more than ever, the patriotic calls for payment that had been popular during wartime lost much of their appeal. Nonetheless, assessors continued to use patriotic slogans to encourage compliance with the largely self-enforcing tax code. The federal tax, by this point, collected income only from those who were willing to proclaim publicly that they had earned incomes high enough to be taxable. By 1866, the number of such willing souls stood at 460,000.[56]

The war was over, so economic expansion, not patriotism, was the theme of Governor William Pickering's enthusiastic report to the Washington territorial assembly in January 1866. Of the more than $76,000 in federal revenues collected in Washington in the fiscal year 1865, $20,719 came from income taxes, more than double the amount from income taxes the previous year.[57] Pickering also revealed that the federal assessor expected in the next year to collect more than $60,000 in Washington Territory, even though Idaho was no longer a part of the Washington tax district. The Republican-appointed governor took issue with political opponents by pointing out that the cost of assessing and collecting the revenue was only about $16,000 per year, far less than the amounts raised.[58] He ended his tax report on an optimistic note: "It is gratifying to know that the United States taxes are cheerfully and promptly paid, and the large and steady increase of revenue indicates a highly prosperous condition of the business and industrial interests of the country."[59]

Once the war ended, the income tax, occupation licenses, and the taxes on the long list of manufactured items met with increasing opposition. In 1866 Congress voted to eliminate the progressive rate structure and apply a uniform rate of 5 percent on all incomes above $1,000. Previously, the threshold had been $600.[60] In Washington Territory, Governor Marshall F. Moore (no relation to the collector Moore) expressed a common view in his address to the legislature in December 1867: "The immense debt incurred during the recent war necessarily makes the weight of taxation oppressive to all. With strict economy in the administration of government, an increasing development of our natural resources, and with a full revival of the industrial interests of the entire country, we will find nevertheless, that our 'burden is not greater than we can bear.'"[61]

The governor failed to mention, however, that the territory had extra incentive to encourage compliance that had nothing to do with paying back the debts accrued from the war. In January 1867, Congress voted to set aside the net proceeds of internal revenue raised in Washington Territory to June 30, 1868, to build a new penitentiary at a cost of up to $20,000. By the time the site was chosen in 1869, however, the $20,000 set aside for the project proved insufficient, much to the disappointment of local officials.[62]

Two years later, the internal revenue commissioner sent notice to Congress, reminding the members that the income tax law was to expire on April 30, 1870. Congress, after all, had always viewed the tax as a "temporary measure."[63] As a result, the tax renewal question became a hotly debated political issue nationally and in Washington Territory. As an observer wrote years later, many critics of the tax concluded that the collections continued after the war not because the revenues were sorely needed by that point but because it was hoped that the tax [would] bring "within reach of the . . . law great numbers who had hitherto avoided giving in their receipts at all, or had made imperfect or fraudulent returns in order to escape the excessive tax."[64]

Few Washingtonians earned incomes sufficient to be liable for income taxes, but nearly everyone paid higher prices for goods because of the excise taxes. Thus, most of the local debate concerned not the tax of incomes but the duties on various products. "The [Democrats] believe that taxes should be levied to raise revenues, and not to regulate morals or control the laws of demand and supply," the *Washington Standard* declared. "The burden of taxes upon beer, whiskey and tobacco is paid by the poor. . . . Rich men, as a class, do not spend their money on luxuries; they save and invest it in bonds, or whatever will pay them the best," the newspaper added.[65]

The *Standard* made no mention of the law requiring payment of 5 percent taxes on all income over $1,000, perhaps because most of the populace was exempt.[66] On the day before Independence Day, however, the Olympia paper published a list of all taxpayers in Western Washington.[67] The next week, it published the list and incomes for taxpayers living elsewhere in the territory.[68] Only 305 Washington residents paid income taxes for 1868.

Despite the territory's population increase over the following two years, the number of income tax payers actually declined. Congress raised the exemption in 1869. A tax was owed only on income in excess of $2,000 per year. At this point, the number of taxpayers nationwide dropped to 74,000.[69]

The personnel in the territorial tax offices changed considerably after the Civil War. Sparks was removed in a political dispute with the Johnson administration in 1866. In 1870, however, the Grant administration appointed him territorial auditor.[70] Sparks's former position was given to Samuel D. Howe, a thirty-seven-year-old Kentuckian living in Olympia and working as a merchant at the time of his appointment. He served only to the end of Johnson's presidency; when Ulysses S. Grant became president, Howe was removed and the assessor's job went to Edward Giddings. Trained as a civil engineer, Giddings had served in various New York state offices under his friend and former president, Millard Fillmore. Giddings came west in 1849, and by the early 1860s, he was a clerk in the Washington territorial surveyor's office. He was deputy surveyor at the time Grant appointed him to the tax assessor's position. In 1875, he became the revenue collector for the territory; while serving in that position in 1876, Giddings died.[71]

Collector Moore, also removed by Johnson, was replaced in 1868 by Hazard Stevens, son of the former territorial governor Isaac Stevens, who had been killed in the Battle of Chantilly. Moore returned to practicing law and retained his prominent role in Republican party politics. He was keynote speaker at the 1870 state Republican convention.[72]

The assistant collectors and assessors positions experienced rapid turnover during the period. Usually, the assistant assessors were clerks, often in their thirties or younger. For example, J. D. Laman, the assistant in Walla Walla, was thirty-nine and the father of five young children. Ross G. O'Brien, the Olympia assistant assessor, was twenty-eight, a Civil War veteran, and single. Both Laman and O'Brien remained with the tax assessor's office for some time, but the young men who worked as assistants in the Vancouver-Columbia River area seem to have stayed but a few months.[73] Little information is available on the collector's office staff during this period, although it is apparent that they were often well-established businessmen with bookkeeping experience—and some political connections.

Who Were the Washington Taxpayers?

The assessors' lists for Washington Territory before 1868 have been lost, thus making it impossible to ascertain the identities of taxpayers during the Civil War years. The 1869 list, comprising names of taxpayers from the previous calendar year, lists 305 taxpayers; the 1870 list provides the names of 254 people who paid for the calendar year of 1869. Even though the latter list contained fewer names, the 1870 roll is more useful to study because it was compiled in June, at almost exactly the same time the 1870 census was taken. All but 33 names on the tax list also appear on that year's federal census.

Some assumptions about the typical taxpayer can be made by comparing the 1870 assessment roll with the 1870 census, even though shortcomings in the quantity and quality of the data are obvious. The census listed a variety of data for each person, including name, age, sex, occupation, and— important for this study—an estimate of the value of his real and personal property. Obviously, the estimates were highly subjective. Some estimates may have been far too high, others too low. Nonetheless, some tendencies can be observed. For instance, if the assessment rolls are a true measure of ability to pay an income tax, then the majority of taxpayers should exceed the average real and personal property levels of nontaxpayers. Further, if two people share common census characteristics in a given community, the names of both should either appear or not appear on the tax rolls. For example, if a farmer in one census district paid a significant tax, his neighbor, who responded in a like fashion to the census questions, should appear on the assessment roll, too. Finding such correlations requires a careful analysis of the census data for all 254 people who paid income tax in 1870 as well as random samples of those citizens who paid no taxes. One of three assumptions can be made, for example, if the neighbor listed far higher amounts of personal and real property, the rest being equal, and yet he paid no tax while his less well off neighbor did: (1) the census estimates are in serious error; (2) the tax assessments were not evenly administered; (3) the non-taxpayer, for one reason or another, avoided paying the tax.

The 221 taxpayers whose names appear on the census (87 percent of the people paying taxes in 1870) accounted for $13,946 (92 percent) of the total income tax collected in the territory.[74] With one exception, all taxpayers were male and white. The woman was also the only black taxpayer: Rebecca Howard, operator of a hotel in Olympia. She was forty at the time of the census, and both she and her fifty-two-year-old husband, listed as a white farmer, had been born in Massachusetts.[75]

The average age of the Washington taxpayer was 39.7 years. The twenty-year-old Seattle merchant J. Franenthal was the youngest taxpayer. Only 28 men over the age of fifty paid any tax. The eldest was a seventy-four-year-old Port Madison lumberman, a Portuguese citizen who was also the only taxpayer listed on the census as unable to read or write English. Six of the 65 foreign-born taxpayers are listed on the census as noncitizens—the one Portuguese, three Canadians, a Scottish blacksmith, and an English butcher.

The census takers asked each citizen to estimate the total value of his personal property. Census estimates of personal wealth have been proven to be highly unreliable.[76] Nonetheless, some inferences may be drawn about the amount of earned income and, therefore, of tax liability. For instance, from among those who paid, a taxpayer declaring to the census taker that he owned $1,000 in personal property could expect a tax bill of around $15. In the general population, farmers owned significant personal property but rarely met income minimums under the tax law. The tax law in 1867 was changed to favor farmers by requiring tax payment only on sales of livestock, not on its increasing value if it was not sold. Nationally, few farmers had incomes sufficient to surpass the $1,000 exemption, so few actually paid the taxes before 1867 anyway.[77]

When census information is compared to the number of taxpayers, the data suggest that tax avoidance in Washington Territory was widespread. This conclusion is hardly surprising, given the factors of distance, uneven enforcement, and novelty of such a tax. Tax avoidance is especially apparent in several areas.

Several counties registered no resident taxpayers. None of the 270 voting-age males in Stevens County paid income taxes, nor did any of the 238 Cowlitz County male residents over twenty-one years old. No tax returns were filed by residents of Yakima (143 male voters), Snohomish (334), or Clallam (149) counties. No assistant assessors lived in those counties, and possibly those assigned to assess there did not believe it to be cost effective to do so. More than 36 percent of all taxpayers lived in Walla Walla County. Although it was the state's most populous county in 1870, only 20 percent of the territory's population of voting-age males lived there. Thurston County also had a high ratio of taxpayers per population. Assessors were resident in both counties. However, the highest proportion of taxpayers to population was in tiny Skamania County. There the 11 taxpayers accounted for more than one-eighth of the county's voting males.

More than a fifth of all taxpayers were merchants, and another 5 percent described themselves as retired merchants. The age-occupation breakdown indicates that many of the taxpayers in their late thirties were merchants. Farmers made up the second highest occupational group, with 22. Just 13 lawyers, 7 doctors, and 1 banker paid any income taxes in the territory in 1870. Nine workers in lumber mills and 7 mill owners paid taxes, as well as 12 bookkeepers. These figures suggest that relatively few members of high-status occupations paid the tax. Census figures show that there were 43 lawyers, 36 doctors, and 4 bankers in the territory who did not file an income tax return. For example, the banker Dexter Horton of Seattle paid no income tax even though he held real property worth $20,000 and personal property amounting to $6,000. The Walla Walla farmer Philip Ritz declared almost the same holdings in real and personal property; he, however, paid a tax of $41.65.

New England natives, less than 7 percent of the territory's total population, accounted for 30 percent (66) of all taxpayers. Maine natives showed the highest per capita incidence of tax-paying. Twenty-nine of the 221 Washington taxpayers (or 13 percent) were born in Maine, yet only 3.5 percent of the total population came from the Pine Tree State. And Maine-born taxpayers were not more heavily represented among high-income occupations than those from elsewhere. While almost a third of Maine-born taxpayers were merchants, more than half of the Ohioans who paid taxes were engaged in that occupation, as were almost 35 percent of New Yorkers and 40 percent of Massachusetts natives. On the average, Maine taxpayers declared to census takers less personal property ownership, for example, than those from the other three states. This finding suggests that, regardless of occupation or wealth, Maine natives had a greater tendency to pay taxes than persons of the same occupation and equal wealth from other states.[78]

Another 30 percent of the taxpayers were foreign born, although in the territory they made up 20 percent of the population. Three-eighths of all tax-paying merchants were foreign born, and three of the five saloon keepers listed on the tax roll had been born abroad. Seven of the 22 farmers were born in foreign countries, including fifty-two-year-old, Irish-born Joseph

Petrain of Vancouver, who paid the least of any taxpayer—five cents on taxable income of one dollar!

Thirty-two taxpayers listed birthplaces in the Midwest. Nearly 22 percent of the territory's residents were born in Midwest states, yet natives of the region amounted to but 14 percent of those paying taxes. Although many Midwest natives in the total Washington population might have been farmers, Midwest-born merchants accounted for almost 22 percent of taxpayers who were natives of Midwest states. (With one exception, all were born in Ohio.) Five Midwest-born farmers were taxpayers in 1870, but four natives of that region paying an income tax worked in communications (newspaper and telegraphy).

The 13.6 percent of Washington taxpayers born in the Northeast states amounted to a slightly higher proportion than Northeast-born people in the total population. Nearly half of the persons paying over $100 in taxes were New York natives, including the Olympia merchant D. B. Finch, who paid the most taxes of any Washingtonian—more than $1,300 on income in excess of $26,000. For the census, Finch set the value of his personal property at $65,000.

More than half of the Northeast natives were between forty-one and fifty years old, and only one was under the age of thirty. In general, greater tax liability (reflecting greater wealth) results from greater accumulation as a result of experience and corresponding increased earning power. More than one-fifth of New England-born taxpayers were thirty years old or younger; only 15 percent were over fifty-one. In fact, the 66 New Englanders were fairly evenly divided among the age groupings. This is not the case with natives from other regions. Only 15.6 percent of Midwest natives were under thirty and 6 percent over fifty-one.

Just fifteen Southern-born Washington residents paid income taxes in 1870, 6 percent of the total taxpayers, but Southerners also made up 6 percent of the territory's population. Only three, at the most, might have served in the Confederate army. Nine of the fifteen Southern-born taxpayers came to Washington prior to the Civil War and before the income tax law took effect. At least two of the others were probably too old to have served.[79]

Length of residence in the territory could be determined for only 60 percent of Washington taxpayers. Of those born in New England, 38 percent came before 1863, indicating that as a group they were the most recent arrivals. More than half of the Northeast natives were longtime Washington residents. Of the 60 people who paid more than $50 in taxes, 25 of them had moved to the territory before the Civil War's end, while only 11 had resided in Washington less than seven years. Only one of the seven people who paid in excess of $400 in taxes had moved to the territory since the Civil War.

Natives of the border states (Maryland, Kentucky, and Missouri), 8 percent of the population, accounted for just 6 percent of the taxpayers. Three lawyers, one of whom served as United States Land Office receiver, were born in border states. Only one other region, the Northeast, showed a greater number (one more) of lawyer-taxpayers.

New Englanders, as a group, had no higher incomes than natives of other regions. Nonetheless, they were more likely to declare their tax liability. Determinations of wealth in Washington Territory in 1870 are beyond the scope of this chapter, but the fragmentary evidence from the census report and the tax record does suggest that New England natives were not necessarily the wealthiest in the territory. New England natives with modest incomes and average amounts of real and personal property tended to pay the tax, while only the more well-to-do individuals born in other regions paid.

In light of the distances and sparsity of population, it is worth noting that more than 250 Washingtonians paid federal income taxes in 1870, despite the tax's unpopularity and the relatively high exemptions. The territory equaled the nation in terms of proportion of the population obeying the tax law. For Washington Territory, the 254 taxpayers accounted for approximately the same proportion or 1 percent of the total population of 23,955. Many Washingtonians, like residents in the Northeast and elsewhere, met their tax obligations despite the myriad excuses for and means of evading them.

In this first phase of federal income taxation, the Civil War tax was met with general unconcern. In some respects, paying it was viewed as making a voluntary contribution. The administrative apparatus, both nationally and in Washington, was inefficient and largely ineffectual against evasion. In Washington Territory the tax collectors and assessors tended to be aspiring young politicians who had less familiarity with accounting principles than with steering through the shoals of political intrigue. When critics blasted these bureaucratic shortcomings, the tax itself inevitably became tarred by the same brush.

Even though this period can be characterized as one of voluntary compliance, the problems with tax enforcement foreshadowed future tensions. The relatively small number of taxpayers in the 1860s and early 1870s principally were in business and professional occupations. When the income tax became a national issue in the early 1890s, it was not surprising that many supporters of the measure were farmers who were untouched by the Civil War tax, and opponents were merchants and urban professionals who in some cases felt its full effects or avoided paying it.

The income tax in Oregon met with similar problems, but the administration and payment of taxes there seemed more orderly and, at the same time, more controversial. The period of "voluntary compliance" in Washington Territory was a time of more efficient enforcement and greater participation in federal tax-paying in the neighboring state of Oregon.

3 Civil War Income Tax in Oregon
A Comparative Assessment

An earthquake shook Portland and northwestern Oregon on October 7, 1862. The early morning rattling was the "severest felt here since February, 1856," according to a local newspaper.[1] An earthshaking event of the financial variety gained notice in the next day's news. The most influential newspaper in the state, the *Oregonian,* started running on the front page the Internal Revenue Act—all 117 sections of it. The act was so lengthy that even set in small type the contents took up the entire right column (and often the two right columns) of the broadsheet paper for the next two weeks.[2]

The tax came as no surprise to Oregon residents. Congress had passed the act three months earlier, and since then news about the national tax bill had shared column space with stories about the war. As early as August, the *Oregonian* had given readers a "synopsis" of the law furnished to it "by Eastern papers."[3]

Confederate sympathizers made up a sizable proportion of the young state's population, particularly in the southern counties.[4] Jackson County, the fourth most populous in the state, caused Unionists the most concern.[5] It was there that the hotly debated 1858 slavery article to the state constitution had received support from the highest percentage of voters.[6] In 1860, Oregon's favorite son Joseph Lane was nominated in Baltimore to run with John C. Breckenridge on a slave-code presidential platform. The ticket gained strong support in Lane's home state—particularly in Jackson County—but Lincoln won the state's electoral votes.[7]

Even elsewhere in Oregon, support existed for the Confederacy. At least four Oregon newspapers expressed prosecessionist views, and in October 1862, three of the four were suppressed as "treasonous sheets" on the order of General Wright, the West Coast army commander headquartered in San Francisco.[8] Sometimes fistfights broke out among neighbors holding opposing views, but few cases of violence seem to have occurred, certainly fewer than the frequent clashes reported at the time in California. Secessionists recognized early that they were a distinct minority in Oregon.[9]

During the summer months of 1862, while Union forces in the East took on Stonewall Jackson's troops at the Second Bull Run, the Oregon Democratic party, which had ruled the state for a dozen years, found itself locked in what seemed ever more likely to be a referendum on secession. The governorship, held for a decade by Democrats, seemed in jeopardy. The thirty-seven-year-old Republican candidate, Addison C. Gibbs, unabashedly linked Republican victory to support for the Union.[10] Until then, the Democrats, led by Senator Lane, the defeated vice-presidential candidate, had done their best to play down the crisis in the East. In a feeble attempt to counter Gibbs's attacks, the party again endorsed its state's-rights position, which included opposition to federal taxes as encroachments on state authority. Not only did they declare the tax act a usurpation, but Oregon Democrats also criticized its length and complexity. They carefully pointed out that the issue had nothing to do with the war.[11]

The voters apparently believed the Republicans on this issue as they did on most others, and Gibbs was elected decisively. In his inaugural address in September 1862, the new governor equated tax-paying with loyalty. "A great majority of the people of Oregon are loyal men—willing to pay their taxes, aid in the circulation of U.S. Treasury notes without a murmur—to do any act prompted by the spirit of our fathers," he reportedly told the crowd.[12] Later in the day, Gibbs addressed a joint session of the legislature and again linked tax-paying to loyalty.[13]

Pro-Union newspapers continued to hammer home the importance of taxes to provide sufficient revenues to put a rapid end to the war. "In raising such a force, the President should understand that so far as taxation becomes necessary to a vigorous and successful prosecution of the war, and so long as its fruits are faithfully applied to that purpose, the people will not hesitate at any amount, for they mean this rebellion to be destroyed and the Constitution sustained, cost what it will or come what may, and in comparison with these results, they will disregard the dangers and bloodshed and expenses of the war," wrote the editor of the *Oregon Statesman*.[14]

Some papers tried to keep the issue alive as a political one even months after the Democrats had lost the governorship. "Democrats" was still a synonym for "tax evaders." When several residents of Lane County objected to paying the initial tax assessment, the *Oregonian* labeled them disloyal, contending that by not paying they were saying that "they did not respect Abe Lincoln or his laws." They would see the light, however, "when they have to pay a heavy fine and have their property confiscated," the *Oregonian* editor concluded.[15]

In 1864, supporters of the presidential candidate and former army general George B. McClellan tried to use the tax issue against the Republicans, but Lincoln partisans were quick to point out that the increases were not caused by anything they had done. If the South (and the Democrats, by implication) had not tried to destroy the Union, income taxes would have been unnecessary.[16]

Despite the best efforts to couch the onus of taxation in patriotic slogans, even Oregonians of Union stripe did not greet the assessors with smiles and open purses. Aaron Bushwiler reported encountering immediate trouble preparing his annual Portland city directory the first year of the tax. "He says he has to answer more questions than he asks, as many who have not previously heard of him seem anxious to know if he has anything to do with the tax-gatherer, an individual much dreaded nowadays."[17] Nonetheless, taxpayers were told how much worse citizens of secessionist states had it. The Confederates were planning to demand a full "one-fifth of income" for taxes. Even the few Oregonians who made sufficient incomes to pay the income tax faced a lighter burden than that.[18]

Although some newspapers asserted to the contrary, many observers believed that the tax act was difficult for most nonlawyers to understand. Not only was its length intimidating, but the language was confusing and details often seemed contradictory. Oregon papers continued to run long columns written by Internal Revenue Commissioner George Boutwell in which he tried to explain peculiar aspects of the law such as "what constitutes taxable silver plate."[19] Oregon's U.S. District Judge Mathew Deady wrote a column attempting to explain some of the numerous legal terms dotting the act.[20] Although editors cautioned law-abiding citizens that the act would require careful record-keeping and standardized accounting systems, it is doubtful that many of them had themselves adopted such measures. Some book dealers advertised the availability of self-help manuals. S. J. McCormick, a Portland bookseller, offered the *Citizens' Edition of the New National Tax Law.* The book, according to a newspaper ad, "is one that may be very useful to the businessman for reference."[21]

Despite the confusion, pro-Union papers countered that the supposed difficulties were imaginary. The provisions "are easily understood, and the Secessionists cannot evade them," the *Oregonian* editor wrote. "He may be determined never to fight against his own people, but the law will at least compel him to pay his fair proportion of the expenses of those who are not so squeamish on the subject."[22]

In Oregon, patriotic exhortation continued to fuel support for the income tax throughout the war. Once the war ended, another reason had to be found for paying the income tax. The duties of the collectors and assessors, appointed during the war, became more difficult when it was over. Throughout the life of the income tax, just one man served as district assessor in Oregon. Such continuity was absent in Washington Territory.

In 1862 President Lincoln appointed two Portland men to head the collection and assessment "district of Oregon."[23] Both were "politically reliable" Republicans who were experienced in the realm of public finance. The assessor, fifty-year-old Thomas Frazar, had served a term as Multnomah County assessor prior to his appointment. His biography contrasts sharply with that of Washington's assessor, who gained his appointment before ever setting foot in the state.[24]

Frazar came to Oregon from his native Massachusetts in 1851 as an agent for his brother, Captain Amherst Alden Frazar, a wealthy Boston trader. Unlike many of the '48ers, Frazar made the trip via the Isthmus of Panama, not by wagon across the continent. In May 1851, he built a two-story house in Portland, using the bottom floor for his trading business. Later in the year, he followed the mining boom to Jacksonville, where he opened a merchandise branch of his Portland business. Two years later, he returned east to Boston for his wife and five daughters, arriving with them in December 1853, after a long voyage around Cape Horn. Mrs. Frazar, the daughter of a New Hampshire sea captain, helped establish Portland's first school.[25]

Frazar sold his interest in the Portland business in 1857 and bought a farm near the city, where he became a charter member of the Oregon Agricultural Society, which endeavored to promote fruit-growing and other endeavors. The sudden death of a seventeen-year-old daughter in school and the deaths of two others from diphtheria in 1862 caused him to abandon farming and return to Portland, where he took on the duties of his new post. Like many of his fellow Republicans, Frazar was a former Whig, and at the time of his appointment, he was considered a pioneer in the party of Lincoln.[26]

A Portland attorney, Lawrence W. Coe, was appointed to the collector's position. Like the notorious Goldsborough in Washington, Oregon's collector also had a military title. Unlike Goldsborough, however, Coe was locally well known and respected as a man who exercised prudence in his personal financial affairs. He was commissioned and appointed lieutenant colonel of the First Regiment, Third Battalion, Oregon Volunteers, in 1863, but he retained his collector's post as well.[27]

On October 4, 1862, after his appointment was ratified, Frazar announced division of the state into ten assessment districts. "As soon as possible I shall appoint one Deputy in each District, and furnish them with their necessary papers," he informed the public through a newspaper notice.[28]

His first problem did not involve the income tax. When Congress passed the tax act, included were provisions requiring stamps on many legal documents. Frazar's first public announcement indicated the problem with the stamps: "No stamps have yet been received in Oregon. When received notice will be given."[29] The problem continued. By February 1863, the stamps still had not arrived. The commissioner of internal revenue suspended the requirement for them on the Pacific Coast until March 1, 1863, but it was not until mid-March that the revenue service finally got stamps to Portland.[30] The incident points out the increasingly confusing state of tax collection in an area so remote from central administration.

Frazar continued to supply the state's newspapers with notices on tax rulings. Some were simple statements such as a warning that revenue stamps could not be used for postage.[31] Others were complex statements of how bonds and bank receipts were to be assessed for tax purposes.[32] Coe's collection duties were restricted to receiving license and excise tax monies, which were collected throughout the year. Most taxpayers waited until near the May 1, 1863, deadline to make payment. Even then, the government allowed a 30-day grace period before collection had to be made.[33]

Despite the confusion, contradictory reports, and untested quality of the new tax-collecting structure, the first year of income taxation in Oregon ended with few reported problems. The excise tax caused the most difficulty. "Mr. Graves, the deputy collector of U.S. taxes for the district of Oregon, has placed in the hands of the justices of the peace of this city, complaints against certain persons who have neglected and refused to pay the U.S. license and taxes assessed against them," the *Oregonian* reported in January 1863. "Two or three were yesterday put through for delinquency and it is the intention of the officer charged with the duty of collecting to proceed without further delay to enforce the provisions of the law."[34] It was not until the war ended that incidents of income tax evasion appeared in the papers.

Frazar announced the names of his appointees for nine of the ten districts in November 1862. The tenth was not named until the following month.[35] Biographical data can be found for eight of the ten assistant assessors. None lived in Oregon at the time of the 1850 census, but neither had the longtime resident Frazar, who came the next year. The assistant assessors' most obvious similarity was in their ages. Like their counterparts in Washington Territory, most were in their thirties; the oldest was forty-two, the youngest, twenty-five. None seems to have had significant formal education. None was a native of the West, but three had been born in Ohio, the home state of Treasury Secretary Salmon P. Chase. Two of them, Charles W. Savage and William A. K. Mellen, retained their positions until the income tax law was repealed. H. A. Coulson resigned from the lucrative Multnomah County district in November 1863, following his election as county clerk. He was replaced by William Grooms, who stayed in the revenue service position until the tax expired. In fact, the longevity of the appointments is striking compared to the rapid turnover in Washington Territory.

Demographically, the assessors in 1867 bore noteworthy similarities to the men who had held the positions during the war. Savage in Jacksonville, Mellen in Monmouth, and Grooms in Portland retained their wartime jobs. They were joined by six new colleagues. All were Republicans; at least two had held commissions in the Oregon militia.

Who Were the Oregon Taxpayers?

Federal tax revenues raised in Oregon during the first year of the new tax amounted to $108,843.23. The totals by district indicate that Portland had overshadowed all rivals in economic prosperity.[36] "We learn the pleasing fact that, from Multnomah County alone, is derived nearly one-half of the entire amount of United States tax collected throughout the state of Oregon," the *Oregonian* editor announced. "This fact will give persons abroad some idea of the importance of Portland as a place of business."[37]

The tax revenues collected in Oregon continued to climb as tax rates increased, as incomes rose due to wartime inflation, and as collection practices became more efficient. After the war, as rates declined, the Oregon collections remained fairly constant. Curiously, the 1868 total was almost exactly the amount raised in 1863.[38] The 1869 total, again, was close to $108,000 statewide, with the Multnomah County share climbing to more than five-eighths of the state total.

Portland's share of the federal income tax in 1870 was greater than its proportion of the state's population. The 1870 census showed the Rose City with nearly 8,000 people, just 9 percent of the state's total population of 91,000.[39]

Of the 1,272 people paying federal income tax in Oregon in 1870, 655 were residents of Multnomah County.[40] These residents—slightly more than 51 percent of all taxpayers—contributed more than 67.6 percent of income tax revenues. The average Oregon taxpayer paid $67.64 each in 1870, but the Multnomah County average was $88.80 each, significantly higher than that in any other district. The four largest tax bills in Oregon were paid by Multnomah County residents. The transportation magnate J. C. Ainsworth paid $7,336.15 in federal income taxes in 1870, while the banker W. S. Ladd's bill was $3,203.45. The merchant and banker C. H. Lewis paid more than $2,300 in taxes, while Henry Failing, another Portland merchant, contributed more than $1,000 to Oregon's total. The rest of the Oregon taxpayers paid an average of but $56.89 if these four huge bills are removed from the total. Even then, however, Multnomah County's average is well above that of other areas of the state.

Typically, Oregon taxpayers in 1870 were urban residents (in Portland, the only urban area in the state, with a population of a bit more than 8,000). Many were merchants and lawyers; a few were manufacturers, owners of lumber mills, or steamship proprietors. Tradesmen were well represented. In Portland, even church pastors' names are found on the tax rolls, and physicians are also among those listed.

A closer analysis of residents of two areas reveals the demographic patterns of taxpayers: District 1, an area encompassing Clatsop and Columbia counties in the far northwest corner of the state; and District 6, Jackson and

Josephine counties, traditionally an area not favorable toward the federal government. (Douglas County was in District 6, too, but was omitted from this analysis.)

The population of Clatsop and Columbia counties numbered 2,118 in 1870, when about 2 percent of residents paid federal income taxes. Birthplaces for thirty-six of the forty taxpayers in District 1 could be identified. Nine were foreign born (five in England, three in various areas of Germany, one in Italy). Eight were New York natives, the most for any one state. Three each came from Vermont and Massachusetts. Two were from Maine. Southerners outnumbered Midwesterners: two Virginians and an Alabama-born lumberman to one each from Ohio and Illinois. Most of the New Englanders were employed in sea-going activities, while three of the New York natives were government officers, and the rest a scattering of merchants, a carpenter, and a river pilot. The oldest taxpayer was a sixty-five-year-old Kentucky merchant; the youngest, a thirty-one-year-old Canadian-born owner of an Astoria mercantile house. The average age was a bit under thirty-six.

An analysis of the male population of the two counties indicates that Midwesterners were underrepresented among taxpayers. Many, however, were employed in agricultural pursuits. Nonetheless, Southerners were a bit overrepresented, there being few natives of that region among the populations of Clatsop and Columbia counties. Nearly all of the Clatsop and Columbia residents who identified themselves as merchants to the census taker also appeared on the tax roll. This consistency contrasts sharply with the situation in Washington Territory, where the names of numerous merchants are absent from the tax record. This finding suggests that tax collecting was more uniform and efficient in Oregon than in Washington Territory, but it may simply indicate that Oregon merchants, as a class, were relatively more affluent, earning enough to meet the income minimum in the tax code.

Jackson and Josephine counties, however, present a quite different picture. In 1870, the two counties were home to 5,947 people, including 5,001 whites, 2,968 of whom were male. (There were 872 males listed as "colored" in both counties, 238 of whom can be identified as Chinese workers, and only 74 "colored" females.) At the same time, only 23 Jackson and Josephine residents paid taxes. This group amounts to less than four-tenths of 1 percent of the total population. Even if only the white population is considered, the number still does not reach .5 percent of the population. Birthplaces for all but one of the taxpayers can be identified. Only three were foreign born, two merchant brothers from Bavaria and an Irish-born farmer. Four were New York natives; three came from New England and two more from other states in the Northeast. Three came from border states (one each from Delaware, Kentucky, and Maryland). Four Southerners, two from Virginia and two from Tennessee, paid taxes. Just as in Clatsop and Columbia counties and Washington Territory, only three taxpayers came from the Midwest (two from Ohio and one from Illinois).

Again, as in the case of the other areas examined, New Englanders were overrepresented among taxpayers compared to their number among all workers. Just 65 of the 1,298 persons whose occupations were listed in the census for Jackson County were born in New England. New Englanders made up about 5 percent of the population. Eighty-nine New York natives lived in Jackson County, 6.9 percent of the working population. Another finding consistent with the other studies is that Midwesterners, as a group, were less represented among taxpayers than their numbers in the general population would have suggested. In Jackson County, 346 workers listed birthplaces in the Midwest, 26.7 percent of the total persons who listed occupations. (An analysis was made of the personal and real property declarations made to the census taker, but these statements were not considered in this study when it was found that Charles Savage, the income tax collector, also served as Jackson County census taker!)

$$$

In many respects, Oregon's experience with the federal income tax seems similar to that of Washington. Both areas were far from the battlefields of the Civil War, neither had reliable communications with the East, and both were sparsely populated compared to the developed states and territories elsewhere in the country.

But in several ways, the differences are striking. First, Oregon was a state. Admitted to the Union February 14, 1859, two years before the war began, Oregon did not rely on the federal government to subsidize government services. Elected legislatures set taxation policies without having to submit such laws for approval by the federal agency responsible for regulating the territories.[41] State officials answered to the populace. They were not subjected to the incompetence often accompanying the presidential appointments of faithful party workers to territorial governorships, secretaries' posts, and judicial appointments. Presidents cared little whether or not western appointments were popular as long as their reputations did not cause embarrassment in states where electoral votes were at stake.[42]

A second important difference, linked to the first, was the injection of the tax issue into politics. In Washington, the only territorywide election was for the single, nonvoting delegate seat in Congress. All other races were local, and consequently, national issues seldom dictated campaign themes. Further, the territory was in its infancy at the beginning of the Civil War, and the Democratic party, already badly shattered nationally by the beginning of the 1860s, never enjoyed the electoral success that it had gained in Oregon. In fact, throughout the life of the Civil War income tax, Washington remained firmly in the hands of the Republican party.

Third, Washington's administration of the tax was given over to outsiders. The first collector, the first assessor, and several other tax officers in Washington received their appointments without having lived in the territory or knowing anyone who resided there. In Oregon, the appointments were universally made from local men, many of whom had held county or state offices or were active in local Republican party politics.

The well-developed Oregon economy contributed to a much more efficient tax bureaucracy than existed in Washington. Even as early as the 1860s, Portland merchants dominated trade eastward to Walla Walla and held their own against rival merchants in Salem, Corvallis, and Jacksonville. The commerce centers were well established and transportation between them was far less difficult than the tortuous trails over mountains, across rivers, and through uncut forests that linked the far-flung villages of Eastern Washington with the few populated areas along the waterways in the West.

Despite the numerous differences caused by politics, administrative efficiencies, and local control, the percentage of citizens who paid the federal income tax in Oregon was not significantly different from that in Washington. For example, in the census year of 1870, when the number of taxpayers had declined somewhat from earlier years, almost 1,300 Oregonians in a population of 91,000—1.4 percent of the population—paid the tax. Similar patterns of payment within the state among residents in different counties are apparent in Oregon. For instance, Jackson County residents were less likely to pay than their Portland counterparts. In Oregon, as in Washington, place of birth correlates with tax-paying. New England natives were most likely to pay their taxes, regardless of their wealth. In contrast, Midwesterners tended to avoid paying, even when their declarations of financial worth to the census taker suggest that they were liable.

Merchants were more numerous and earned higher incomes in Oregon, on average, than in Washington. In both Oregon and Washington, the biggest taxpayers were men holding extensive interests in transportation facilities. In Oregon, just as in Washington Territory, the urban resident was more likely to be assessed for taxes than residents in small towns or rural areas.

Washington and Oregon provide interesting contrasts not only in views toward taxation, but in their respective stages of development and in the residents' opinions on the role an individual should play in financing government activities. Oregon residents, faced with better administration and the threat of effective enforcement, were outwardly motivated to pay federal income taxes. For Washingtonians, the income tax was little more than a minor annoyance that one could either respond to or ignore. In the Territory of Washington in the Civil War period and immediately after, payment of federal taxes depended on voluntary compliance.

4 Consensus I: Federal Income Tax and Washington's Reaction, 1894

Numerous issues, ranging from Prohibition to municipal ownership of utilities, divided Washington voters during the Gilded Age and into the Progressive era. Oddly, income taxation did not become a divisive issue in the state. Most people wanted the federal income tax because of the benefits it seemed to imply for a state in which income levels were relatively low and ownership of major industries was absentee.

Taxation did not become a partisan issue in Washington until the Populist party's national platform in 1892 offered it as one solution to the plight of farmers who were weighed down in debt, victimized by declining farm prices, and subjected to the unfavorable terms of Republican protective tariffs. The income tax plank appealed to many farmers. Passage of a national income tax by Congress in 1894 raised little controversy in Washington, although the state's congressional delegation, who voted against the legislation, seemed at odds with the majority of the electorate on the issue. When the U.S. Supreme Court struck down the federal tax as unconstitutional, few Washingtonians expressed strong feelings on either side of the issue. When the state legislature passed the Constitutional amendment making a federal income tax possible, the nearly unanimous vote for ratification reflected the broad consensus. It was the proposal of state income taxation that brought conflict.[1]

Washington was on the verge of major economic expansion when the Civil War income tax expired in 1873. The federal government, through territorial officials, provided Washingtonians with free, relatively honest administrations. Taxes were not a burning issue, especially in those sessions in which there was regional competition for government facilities such as a prison or a college and for railroad land grants and transportation monopolies. The tax questions that did arise involved the continuing problems of property taxation arising from local school districts and counties assessing property owners to maintain local services.[2]

In local communities and in the territorial legislature, no one seriously challenged the property tax system. But on this issue and many others, the quiescence of the territorial period did not continue beyond statehood in 1889. Nonetheless, when it came to federal income taxation, there was broad consensus.

Washington became a state on November 11, 1889, but by admission day, conflicts between farmers and businessmen, many resulting from grievances against the railroads, were already clearly evident.[3] At the state constitutional convention, delegates from farming areas demanded stronger controls over railroads through an elective state rail commission. As one Eastern Washington delegate said: "The railroad makes a canvass of our county and figures on what a man makes, the number of children he has, and they find how much it takes for their bare support, and leave enough to put in another crop and they take the rest."[4]

The antirailroad proposals were swept aside, but neither side admitted defeat.[5] Antirailroad delegates were angry. One labor delegate refused to sign. Farmers along rail routes around Washington were alarmed by what seemed to be a prorailroad document. (Ironically, one concession to the antirailroad group was the addition of a clause in the state constitution requiring all property to be assessed equally without regard to class of property. Forty years later, the state supreme court used the clause to overturn the state income tax.) As a result, they revived the Washington State Grange.

The first Washington chapter of the Patrons of Husbandry—the Grange—was formed in Waitsburg in 1873, but it apparently did not survive.[6] The new Grange reorganized during the summer of 1889 when 16 units were formed representing more than 400 farmers in Clark, Skamania, and Klickitat counties. Its primary aim was to fight against the proposed state constitution drafted the previous month. Soon, the organization spread to Eastern Washington. The Grange gained a strong following, but in terms of numbers it was not as successful as the Farmers' Alliance, an organization with a more militant agenda.[7]

The battle against ratification of the state constitution failed, but the organizations shifted to other goals. Farmers, once integral parts of particular geographic regions of Washington, became more unified as a group. It became obvious to farmers in the Vancouver area, for instance, that they had more in common with wheat farmers in the Palouse than they had with townsmen in their area. Not only did they organize as a means of making changes in state and local legislation, but they also saw the implications of injecting their views into the national debates on tariffs and taxes.[8]

Nationally, Congress debated silver purchases, the tariffs, and currency legislation.[9] Many congressmen, representing constituencies containing large numbers of economically distressed farmers, believed that increased silver coinage would inflate the currency and make farm debts less onerous. In the 1890 session, Republican congressmen, primarily from the Northeast, agreed to support silver legislation if farm and silver-state representatives agreed to support a new protectionist tariff bill. Consequently, Congress passed the Sherman Silver Purchase Act in the summer of 1890 and, soon after, the McKinley tariff. The tariff, named for William McKinley, then chairman of the House Ways and Means Committee, raised duties on manufactured articles to an average of about 50 percent, the highest to that time. In addition to the silver compromise, the protectionists offered sops to agriculture within the tariff bill. One section provided for high duties on some agricultural products, while another gave the president authority to raise duties on several more as a means of pressuring other nations to reduce tariffs on American imported products. The sponsors of the bill put sugar on the free list but, as a concession to Southern congressmen, offered federal subsidies to sugar manufacturers who might suffer damage.

Republican supporters of the tariff, including both senators from Washington, believed that the measure would be acceptable to farmers. In the end, it satisfied few congressmen from the Midwest and South. The extent of the measure's unpopularity became apparent in the congressional elections later in 1890. The Democrats campaigned against the measure, gained a majority in the House, and narrowed the Republican margin in the Senate to just eight.[10]

When the national economy seemed about to collapse in June 1893, the Democrats had the misfortune of having their standard-bearer, Grover Cleveland, in the White House. But those caught in the economic tailspin awarded some of the blame to the Republicans, the gold standard, and high tariffs. Banks failed in numerous Washington towns—14 in Tacoma, 5 in Spokane. In Everett, a town built around the timber industry and lumber mills, three of the five banks closed and wages fell about 60 percent.[11] The Northern Pacific Railway went bankrupt in August. The Great Northern tottered, managing to be one of two transcontinental railroads escaping bankruptcy. By 1894, the depression was severe, and much of the electorate was frightened by the violence of the Pullman strike and Coxey's army. Despite identification of the strikers with the Populists, Washington voters elected 23 Populist legislators in 1894. Their elections came at the hands of the Democrats, who were all but eliminated from public offices in the state.[12]

Two Republican congressmen represented the state of Washington in 1893. The eastern district representative, John L. Wilson of Spokane, was a native of Indiana who had served in the Civil War as a messenger for his father, Colonel James Wilson (later an Indiana congressman). President Chester Arthur appointed the younger Wilson to a patronage job in 1882 as receiver of public lands at Colfax, Washington. Wilson moved to Spokane when the land office was moved there three years later. Grover Cleveland ousted Republicans from federal posts in the territory following the presidential election of 1884. Wilson, who was among those replaced, opened a law office and practiced until 1889. In that year, he won election as Washington's first congressman. A Republican party loyalist, he had little sympathy for income taxes.[13]

Neither did his House colleague from Washington, William H. Doolittle of Tacoma. A Pennsylvania-born Civil War veteran, Doolittle practiced law in New York and Nebraska before coming to Colfax two years earlier than Wilson. In 1888, he moved his practice west of the Cascades to Tacoma. When the 1890 census allowed Washington an additional House seat, Doolittle was elected from the western part of the state.[14]

Watson L. Squire of Seattle represented Washington in the U.S. Senate. Like the two congressmen, Squire was a Civil War veteran and lawyer. Employed by Remington Arms Company, Squire left the Connecticut firm in 1876 and purchased large tracts of land in Washington. He moved to Seattle in 1879, and five years later he was appointed territorial governor. The organizer and president of Union Trust Company of Seattle, he was the wealthiest member of the Washington delegation and the most closely connected to the Stalwart wing of the Republican party, made up of those who resisted Populist and Progressive measures. While Wilson was closely affiliated with Hill, Squire was associated with Henry Villard, another rail magnate.[15]

The second Washington seat in the Senate was vacant from March 1893 until Wilson was elected to it in January 1895. The original holder, John B. Allen, had been elected to the four-year term when the two senators were chosen at statehood. When he came up for reelection, the legislature, deadlocked regionally and politically, adjourned without confirming him and so the U.S. Senate refused to seat him.[16]

In 1894, when key votes over the tariff, income tax, and currency reform came before both Houses of Congress, not one of the three Washington congressmen voted with the coalition of Westerners and Southerners sworn to fight the Northeast on such measures. The 1894 income tax is one example.

The Populist party platform in 1892 contained a plank on the income tax, declaring that it was needed because the "fruits of the toil of millions are boldly stolen to build up the fortunes for a few."[17] President Grover Cleveland, who believed in the general justice of such a law, did not endorse it, but in 1893 he did speak in favor of taxing income that was derived from corporate revenues. It was a long step in the direction of an income tax.[18]

When Congress opened in 1894, the majority of Democrats on the House Ways and Means Committee favored an income tax.[19] The committee attached it to the tariff reform bill designed to overhaul, if not completely overturn, the provisions of the McKinley tariff and bring it into accord with the Democrats' liking. There were huge splits among Democrats, but with a coalition of Midwestern and Southern Populists and major compromises with the Republicans, House Democrats were able to pass a new tariff bill in February 1894 with the income tax provision still attached.[20] The vote on final passage was 204–140, with 8 not voting. Washington's two congressmen voted with the losing side. So did both congressmen from Oregon and Idaho's single representative.[21]

The income tax was not designed to affect all wage earners. Only incomes above $4,000 per year would be taxed, and then at a flat rate of just 2 percent. The proceeds of rents, interest, dividends, salaries, and earnings from any trade or business had to be figured into income, and corporations had to pay a tax.

The tax stayed in the bill even after Northeast congressmen made impassioned arguments about its "socialist" tendencies. The House, on a roll call vote just before final passage of the entire bill, retained the income tax provision. In fact, the section appears to have been one of the most popular in the entire bill. It passed 182–48, with 122 not voting. Just as they had done on final passage of the compromise tariff, Washington's Wilson and Doolittle voted against retaining the income tax.

The bill went to the Senate, where, after a rancorous debate, it passed with amendments July 3, 1894, by a vote of 39–34, with 12 not voting. Again, Watson Squire, Washington's solitary senator, voted against it.[22]

Squire joined an unlikely coalition of opponents that included silver-state Republicans (angry with Cleveland for repealing the silver purchase act) and Northeasterners from both parties. Senator David B. Hill, a New York Democrat, summarized the opposition to the bill when he called it "a rag-tag production—it is a crazy-quilt combination—it is a splendid nothing." He concluded with the prophesy, "I believe the income tax feature as a whole and many of its details to be unconstitutional." Squires did not participate in the debate; he apparently offered home state newspapers no comments on the income tax issue.[23]

The *Seattle Times, Tacoma Daily Ledger,* and other state papers provided lengthy coverage of the debate over the tariff and the income tax provision. The influential dailies did not support either the tariff measure or the income tax provision attached to it. When the Wilson-Gorman tariff bill finally passed, an editor summarized the prevailing attitude among Washington Republican observers: "The Democratic tariff bill, under the manipulation of the trusts and tariff committees, is a ring-streaked and speckled freak of the first water. It is neither fish, flesh, fowl nor good red herring— neither free trade, protection nor tariff reform." He correctly predicted, "It will please neither the East, West, North or South," but he made no mention of the income tax.[24]

Wall Street grumbled and some legal scholars remained skeptical of the legality of a tax on personal income, but to most observers, the tax applied to few wage earners, and even for them, the rate was a pittance. Some opponents carped about its seeming socialist tendencies, while others worried about the added power it was sure to give to government. One writer used both arguments. "The inquisitorial methods contained in the tax, as well as the arbitrary power given to the United States officers, are, perhaps, more distasteful to the American citizen than the socialistic tendencies of a measure to raise revenue at a time when neither war nor any other extraordinary circumstance renders an act of this kind necessary," wrote a commentator for the *Albany Law Journal*, a publication subtitled "A Weekly Record of the Law and the Lawyers."[25] Another writer, a Wall Street attorney, dismissed passage of the tax as the result of "the desires [*sic*] of leading members of the Democratic Party in Congress to curry favor with the Populists and throw a sop to the Socialists," yet he warned, "It is a measure of purely socialistic tendency."[26]

Meanwhile, the weekly *People's Advocate* in Chehalis began a series of articles on banking titled: "History of Banks—Have Always Been Arrogant Oppressors of the People." The theme was the inevitable defeat of the income tax.[27]

Despite the grumbling of Wall Street attorneys and the worries of Washington Populists, legal scholars knew (and the bill's opponents conceded) that the U.S. Supreme Court had upheld a similar measure, the Civil War income tax, in an 1881 case.[28] That decision, written by the Lincoln appointee Justice Noah H. Swayne of Ohio, concluded that an income tax was not a direct tax. "Whenever the government has imposed a tax which it recognized as a direct tax, it has never been applied to any objects but real estate and slaves," Swayne wrote.[29]

The government proceeded to put into place a revenue-collecting apparatus modeled after the Civil War–era system. Collection began in the spring of 1895. "Income tax returns are coming in far beyond the expectations of officials," noted an article in the *Tacoma Weekly News*, datelined Washington, D.C., in early April. "To save time and avoid complications, collectors were instructed to certify and send returns the 10th of each month and therefore no reports have been received of a date later than March 10. Nevertheless 10,000 returns have already been received and are being verified and recorded," the story added, pointing out that, nationally, the tax was expected to bring in "at least $20 million" by June 1, the close of the fiscal year. The filing deadline was April 15, but time was provided for late payment. In the same article, the writer announced that, thus far, taxpayers had had little difficulty completing the forms. "All things considered the work is going forward with very little friction."[30]

Fewer than 300 Washingtonians filed returns the final year of the Civil War, but in 1895, the government received forms from nearly 2,500 Washington individuals and corporations.[31] The increase seems impressive until one examines the context. The total population of Washington had grown from 23,955 in 1870 to 357,232 in 1890—and that figure does not include the influx during 1891 and 1892. If the 2,500 people who filed were the only Washingtonians who were liable under the tax law, then they represented a mere .7 percent of the state's total population.[32] The figure is not extraordinary, given the low average wages, the poor economic condition of Washington agriculture and industry, and the relatively high exemption of $4,000. Nonetheless, it indicates the slight impact the 1894 income tax had on Washington residents. Nonetheless, newspaper stories revealed that tax opponents were planning to defy the law by not filing. "The millionaires are the anarchists and the people are finding it out," the People's Advocate responded to the report.[33]

But there were not many millionaires in Washington, apparently. Just three Washingtonians submitted returns showing incomes in excess of $50,000. Like its predecessor, the 1894 income tax was "a rich man's tax" affecting few Washingtonians.

A Seattle Times writer did not suspect that Washingtonians liable for the tax were evading payment, but he pointed out that some taxpayers had filed "under protest," adding, "Mr. Gleason [deputy U.S. Collector of Internal Revenue] says that he knows of no person or corporation that he considers liable who has not made return, but he may yet find some, through information not yet before him."[34] Many Washington taxpayers did file at the eleventh hour. "Yesterday Mr. Gleason had to handle above 300 income returns, that being the last day for those subject to the tax to make return," a Seattle Times story noted on April 16.[35]

It is not known how many additional returns were filed. Even if it had been 500 more, the percentage of taxpayers still would not have reached the 1870 level, one of the lowest in the Civil War tax's existence. Washington Territory ranked near the bottom in population in 1870, but as a state in 1890, it was 34th in population among the 44 states. Nonetheless, it is doubtful that Washington's share would have been less in 1890 than it had been in 1870.

In this context, the positions taken on the issue by Washington's congressional delegation and the editorial opposition to it by the Seattle newspapers are curious. The population favored the tax, while the representatives and press did not. Perhaps, as Lawrence M. Friedman puts it, legislators and reporters saw the tax as "the opening wedge for a major transformation of American society."[36] Populists in Washington viewed the actions of these representatives less charitably, however. To the *People's Advocate* and others, it was additional proof that the political leaders were allied with the bankers and capitalists of the East—the opponents of economic justice who had caused them great misery. The *People's Advocate* editor castigated lawyers and other public officials for blatant supping at the public trough. It referred to the Washington congressional delegation and other elected officers as "the precious officials," in the sense that it cost a precious penny to keep them in office.[37]

Wall Street lawyers associated with the nation's largest firms brought the income tax case to the U.S. Supreme Court. William D. Guthrie raised money for the suit among his clients, found a willing litigant (a Massachusetts shareholder named Charles Pollock), and brought suit in the U.S. District Court for the Southern District of New York.[38] Guthrie argued that the income tax was unconstitutional because it violated the constitutional requirement that direct taxes be apportioned according to population.[39] Joining Guthrie was Joseph Choate, another famous Wall Street attorney.[40] Because final payment date for the tax was July 1, 1895, and neither party wanted the decision delayed beyond that date, the case rapidly made its way to the Supreme Court. Oral argument was set for five days in March 1895. Guthrie and Choate faced the U.S. Attorney General Richard Olney. Newspapers around the nation gave the story front-page coverage.[41] The *People's Advocate* editors wrote of some of their Northwest competitors: "The Republican press is clamoring . . . on the ground that if [the income tax] is allowed to go to the statute books, it will do away with the necessity of a tariff." The editorial concluded that "our Supreme Court has come to a pretty pass, when party necessity and feeling can control it. . . . It is well known that if the income tax was submitted to the people today, nine out of every ten would vote in favor of it."[42]

The parties in the case were not satisfied with the first decision rendered by the court in early April. One justice was ill and unable to participate, and on the crucial issue of the constitutionality of the tax, the court deadlocked 4–4. Olney suggested that the court rehear the case and it did so later that month. The second round of oral arguments took up 227 pages in the printed record.

The result was a stunning defeat for income tax proponents. Chief Justice Melville Fuller, writing for the majority, called the income tax a "direct tax" that violated the Constitution. Justice John Harlan, in a stinging attack on the majority's logic and reading of past precedents, warned that the case would require a constitutional amendment.[43] Harlan wrote in an angry dissent, "[The majority decision] strikes at the very foundations of national authority, in that it denies to the general government a power which is, or may become, vital to the very existence and preservation of the Union in a national emergency, such as that of war with a great commercial nation."[44]

Most newspaper editors in the Northeast were delighted with the result, while publishers of some Northwest papers concealed their satisfaction and reported the decision without comment. Populist partisans were livid. The *People's Advocate* called for impeachment of the judges, dismissing Harlan's suggestion for a constitutional amendment. "No matter how much we amend the Constitution, the corrupt justices will always declare in favor of the rich," the editorial concluded.[45] The former governor of Oregon, Sylvester Pennoyer, wrote an open letter to a national law journal echoing the *Advocate*'s position. He argued for impeaching the "nullifying judges for their usurpation of legislative power."[46]

The argument raged in newspapers and legal periodicals throughout the year. Populists used the decision to win important election victories and build coalitions with Democrats and progressive Republicans in some states. The income tax had not been supported by the Washington congressional delegation nor by the leading state newspapers. Nonetheless, after the Western outcry over the Supreme Court decision in Pollock and the seeming smugness with which the "Eastern interests" greeted it, the issue was cast in terms of the West versus the East. When Washington had another chance to participate in the national debate over a federal income tax, the result would be derived from a broad consensus in favor of such a measure.

5 Consensus II: Washington Ratifies the Federal Income Tax, 1911

The 1911 legislative session in Washington represented the high point of progressive reform in the state.[1] It was the session in which the initiative, referendum, and recall were instituted. It was also the session that passed the Federal Income Tax Amendment to the U.S. Constitution. The passage itself is not surprising and certainly not unique in its nearly universal support. What is most unusual about Washington's ratification is the almost complete absence of debate over the issue, both in the legislature and in the media. In other states, positions on the issue divided along class lines. Debates were often rancorous and highly partisan. In Washington, little rhetoric was invoked in favor of the amendment and nearly none against it.[2]

This fact indicates that Populist propaganda since Pollock seemed to have an impact on framing the issues of debate over the income tax. This time around, the debate did not center on patriotism as had the discussions over the Civil War income tax. Nor did the sides divide along class lines. Washingtonians, according to a Populist-Progressive spokesman, should support the income tax as a means of throwing off the yoke the Northeast had on the American (and, in particular, the Western) economy. In a sense, the tax would redistribute wealth by taxing high incomes in the East, incomes viewed by Westerners as "spoils" gained from the resources of the West. Also, the income tax revenues would lessen the need for other taxes. In the view of both farmers and businessmen in Washington, income taxes would not hurt the local economy. In fact, the revenues gained from it might be used to build coastal defenses or lower tariffs, both conducive to Western profit.

When the state had the opportunity to speak out on federal income taxation, the 1911 Washington legislature voted for ratification of the Federal Income Tax Amendment during the first weeks of the session. The vote in favor was overwhelming in both the state senate and the house of representatives. The handful of Democrats in each body voted with the majority of Republican progressives who were responsible for the passage of ratification.[3] Even the so-called Taft Republicans largely supported the measure, although their reticence on the issue mirrored the reluctance of their national leader in the White House to place much political capital into its passage.[4]

The legislative history of the income tax amendment in Washington illustrates the amendment's almost universal acceptance. Senator James W. Bryan, a thirty-seven-year-old former Bremerton city attorney, introduced Senate Joint Resolution Number 1, the ratification measure. He moved that it be considered as a "special order" (not subject to normal intervals between first, second, and third readings) on January 18.[5] Bryan, a Yale graduate who had worked as a printer prior to gaining his legal education, practiced law and, at the same time, published a Bremerton newspaper, the *Navy Yard American*. The shipyard town of Bremerton, in fact, was the largest town in his 23rd District, which also included Island County, mostly agricultural, and Mason County, home of several large logging operations.[6]

The legislature did not act on the measure immediately. J. A. Falconer, the senate president, moved that it be sent to the Committee on Public Revenue and Taxation. The bill went to the committee, which sent it back on January 17 with the recommendation that it be placed on general file. On second reading, only minor amendments were inserted, for instance, the singular form of "income" and a comma. Senate President Falconer set consideration under a special order for January 25.[7] Following the third reading, four Republican senators moved for final passage. The vote was an overwhelming victory for ratification. Only five senators, all five "Old Guard" Republicans, voted against the bill, while 32 senators voted for it. Five members were absent.[8]

The progressive agenda put forth by proponents of the income tax ratification bill was popular with Washington voters all over the state. The opposition, small and unorganized, represented all corners of the state.

None of the five senators voting "no" came from the same region. In fact, the "standpatters" represented widely different constituencies. Two were from principally urban areas while the other three came from small-town districts.[9]

None of the five opponents seems to have spoken openly against ratification. Even though one, John L. Roberts, chaired the committee to which the amendment bill was referred, apparently he did not attempt to bottle up the measure there, and the opponents represented no groundswell from their districts. The reasons for their vote seem to have been personal, and any common thread can be gained only by inference. Their only obvious common characteristic was their Republican party affiliation, which they shared with the overwhelming majority of their colleagues. Like nearly all legislators in Washington's early history, they were primarily from the relatively comfortable upper class.[10] Another commonality, at least for four of them, was their political fate. Of the five men who voted against ratification, only one was still serving in the legislature in 1913. Although the tax vote was not an issue in any of their unsuccessful campaigns, their pattern of opposition to progressive measures was not popular in most of Washington in 1912.

The five who voted against ratification could have shared the label given to one of their number, the Ellensburg banker and merchant John Smithson, state senator representing Kittitas and Chelan counties, who was described in his legislative biography as "a merchant by calling and a gentleman from inheritance."[11] From a largely rural district in north central Washington, the fifty-two-year-old Smithson was first elected to the legislature for one term in 1893. His senate tenure was to prove equally transitory. Elected in 1908, he lost his seat after one term. His defeat, however, came not at the hands of the Democrats but to another Republican in the Progressive-Stalwart showdown, the 1912 primary.

John L. Roberts, too, epitomized Washington's Republican Old Guard. The oldest member of the senate, he was chairman of the Committee on Public Revenue and Taxation, the committee to which the bill had initially been referred. He was the only member of that group to vote "no" on final passage. The Welsh-born Roberts emigrated to Wisconsin in 1867, to Oregon the next year, and to Walla Walla in 1880. After serving five terms as mayor of Walla Walla and two terms in the state senate from there, Roberts moved to Tacoma and established the Puget Sound Iron and Steel Foundry.

His legislative biography proudly described his extensive land ownership in and around Tacoma.[12] His committee chairmanship reflected Roberts's long senate tenure. First elected in 1892 for one term, he had served continuously since 1905. Like the first-termer Smithson, however, Roberts's reelection bid in 1912 was unsuccessful.

Another tax opponent, A. B. Eastham, a Vancouver dentist, also came to the legislature as a comfortable small-town Taft Republican. Eastham's election to the legislature capped a long career in public office. Just before the turn of the century, following two terms on the Vancouver City Council, he was elected to five consecutive mayoral terms. Born in Oregon in 1858, he represented Clark County in the senate.[13]

Arvid Rydstrom, a railroad contractor from Tacoma, had been active in Republican party politics for more than a decade even though he had been in the senate only since 1909. Rydstrom, born in Sweden, was fifty-four years old. His legislative biography noted that he lived "on Knob Hill" in Tacoma, which meant, in those days, that he "had arrived."[14] The votes he cast in the 1911 session reflect his strong ties to the railroads.

The only senator to vote against ratification of the amendment and still gain future reelection was Ralph D. Nichols, a King County Republican. The Iowa-born lawyer, at thirty-six, was the youngest tax opponent. A graduate of the University of Washington, Nichols represented the University District in Seattle. Throughout the early part of the century, the district remained one of the most conservative in the state. It was a district populated by the new upper-middle-class professionals and merchants who had moved to homes in the streetcar-created suburbs of the state's largest city. Nichols's reelection, however, might be because—unlike the other opponents of the income tax amendment, who were "holdovers" from the 1908 election—he did not have to run in 1912.[15]

The measure was sent to the house where the featured battle was going on between "wets" and "drys" on the proposal to prohibit local-option liquor legislation during the session. The vote was close—53 "wets" to 41 "drys." Legislative committees were assigned on the basis of the members' stands on liquor. Party affiliation hardly mattered, given the paucity of Democrats (just 12 in the lower chamber).[16]

Nonetheless, on the day most legislators were still quarreling over the speaker's arbitrary committee assignments, the speaker, State Representative Hugh C. Todd of Whitman County, joined with J. A. Ghent of King County's

44th District, to cosponsor House Concurrent Resolution Number 3, the house version of the senate bill. The bill was introduced on January 12, the fourth day of the session. Just as in the case of the senate bill, the house version was referred to a committee chaired by a Republican "standpatter," Phil S. Locke of Chehalis. Like his Senate counterpart, Locke voted against the measure on final passage. Although such action might have been possible, he did not try to hold the measure up in his Committee on Constitutional Revision. Within days of its referral, the bill was out of committee and on the floor for second reading, during which time the identical senate version, having already passed that body, was substituted. Speaker Todd and Representatives Edward Brown of Whatcom County, A. S. Ruth of Thurston County, and Daniel Landon of King County moved for passage. The house vote was 80 for and 1 against—Representative Locke.[17]

Although Locke was the only representative who voted against the bill, 15 house members were absent at the time of final passage. Only four, however, had been absent during a vote just before the tax measure came up for consideration, and they were the only four who did not vote on a bill that came up just after the tax amendment's passage. Because there is no recorded debate on the measure, and newspapers were silent as to opposition, nothing can be extrapolated from the other nine's curious absences. Were they conducting other duties or were they making a statement? Whichever, most of the absent members, politically and demographically, resembled the senators who had voted "no."[18]

The bill was sent to Governor Marion Hay on February 1, 1911, who forwarded notice of ratification to Congress. The federal income tax was one state closer, with Washington bringing the amendment halfway to the three-fourths of the states required for ratification.

Washington newspapers paid scant attention to the passage. In fact, few newspapers informed readers of the amendment's progress. The *Seattle Times*, for instance, buried a terse two-line paragraph on Bryan's introduction of ratification in a story summarizing all legislative activities for the day. During the week the tax ratification resolution was reported to the floor of both houses, the *Times* printed an interview of State Tax Commissioner J. E. Frost. In it, Frost seemed to criticize the "state system," which, he said, "imposes the heaviest burdens upon those least able to bear them and at the same time, has allowed the predatory interests of huge size to escape legitimate taxes." The *Times* article concluded: "To change this unjust

discrimination a constitutional amendment is necessary and is to be introduced at the present session of the legislature. It should be adopted."[19] Was
the reference to the ratification of the federal income tax amendment or to
state taxes on property or business? There is no evidence that any amendment on taxation, least of all state income taxes, was either proposed or
offered in the 1911 session.

The confusion points out the relative lack of interest the press had in
the issue locally, even though ratification by other distant state legislatures
often gained newspaper mention. In the *Seattle Times*, which ignored final
passage of ratification in the Washington legislature, stories appeared about
the tax's passage in Oregon and Ohio as well as about prospects for the
amendment in New England states.[20] If there is no conflict, there is no story.
Newspaper editors must have believed that by 1911 there was near universal consensus on the need for a federal income tax.

Besides, statewide, other local items seemed far more newsworthy in
January and February of 1911. In Seattle, Mayor Hiram Gill was fighting
attempts to have him recalled in a mid-February election. The Gill recall
stories pushed the legislative activities off the front pages of the *Times*, the
Star, the *Post-Intelligencer*, and the *Argus*. Tax amendment stories amounted
to no more than a few sentences.[21] Legislative ratification of the tax amendment was history by the time the mayor lost to George W. Dilling by 6,214
votes (the Socialist candidate, Dr. E. J. Brown, polled 4,690 votes, 11 times
as many as the Socialists had in the previous municipal election). Enough
grist existed for the newspapers' mills on those issues that the consensus on
the income tax ratification hardly seemed newsworthy. The editors apparently thought, in light of the consensus the tax held among the public, Why
try to pretend there was any controversy—or news—about it?[22]

Harold R. Hindley, the able legislative reporter for the *Spokane
Spokesman-Review*, reported most news from Olympia in great detail, but
not the tax amendment ratification. When the resolution was introduced
in the legislature, Hindley's report the next day in the *Spokesman-Review*
buried the news deep within a summary story on the legislature. The single
sentence on the tax read: "Bryan of Bremerton introduced the income tax
amendment to the federal constitution, in which the legislature must vote
at this time, also bill No. 10, to prevent courts from issuing restraining orders
which would interfere with an officer doing the duty enjoined on him by
law."[23] The day after the resolution was reported out of committee—one

of the first pieces of legislation to make that step—Hindley reported the fact in one sentence at the end of a story headlined: "State Confirms Backus as Regent of UW."[24]

If Chehalis's *People's Advocate* had been publishing, or if the conditions had been the same as in 1895, Bryan might have been extolled as a hero. As it was in 1911, the *Bremerton Searchlight*, published in Senator Bryan's hometown, paid scant attention to the senator's role in introducing the tax ratification resolution. A single line, buried among reports of his committee assignments, carried the news of Bryan's action on the tax amendment.[25] As further evidence of the paper's attitude toward the ratification, the week the resolution passed, the Bremerton paper's legislative story was titled "Legislature Passes Unimportant Bills."[26]

To members of the press, the tax amendment must have seemed as dull as the 1911 legislature's election of Washington's U.S. Senator. "The election," according to the *Anacortes American*, "was notable for its brevity and lack of interest."[27]

After the session ended, in its recapitulation of the legislative session, the same paper did not compliment what others have called one of the best legislatures in the state's history. "In spite of the fact that the recent session of the legislature will probably stand for ages with a record for sensational non-achievement," local legislators performed well. In "Senator Bryan's Record," a minutely detailed account of the legislative achievements of their district legislator, the paper failed to even mention the tax resolution.[28]

If newspaper writers, legislators, and the general public were not interested in the federal income tax amendment, high school debaters paid close attention to the issue. The national debate topic for 1910–11 was: "Resolved, that an income tax should be part of a federal system of taxation, provided that the constitutionality of such a tax shall not be raised."[29]

By March, when legislatures of Washington and 15 other states had ratified the amendment, the public support of the issue was clear. So was the pattern of victories in high school debates. "The affirmative side has the popular phase of the question," one Washington newspaper noted, saluting its hometown team who lost arguing the negative against a rival high school.[30]

The progressive "insurgents" in the Washington legislature dominated both house and senate, and the session is recognized as probably the most significant for reform in the state's history. In the glow of progressive success in passage of a workers' compensation measure, an eight-hour work-day for women, and establishment of an insurance commission, the federal income tax amendment seemed of little significance. After all, punitive federal government operations were distant, for the most part. Nearby federal facilities provided needed jobs and payrolls.

As insignificant as the tax might seem in the short run, many Washingtonians recognized that in order to maintain (and expand) the navy yard at Bremerton and build stronger coastal defenses along Puget Sound, the federal government needed a sounder tax base. The benefits promised to far outweigh the minor disadvantages to the relatively few prosperous income earners in the state who might find themselves subject to the tax.

As a Washington newspaper editor wrote in a story calling for "national preparedness" against the ever-growing Japanese empire: "Much is done for the East; far too little for the West."[31] In Western states like Washington, with modest financial resources and huge tracts of absentee-owned lands, further development depended on federal government spending. A federal income tax, even a modest one, had promise of keeping military posts open, constructing federal buildings in rapidly growing cities, and providing the resources for what Western progressives viewed as the country's least developed region.

Only a few "standpatters" in the Washington legislature—themselves probable taxpayers because of their high-income occupations—harbored (mostly silent) doubts. In the progressive tide of 1911, they were hopelessly outnumbered. When the state became the taxing authority, standing to benefit from an income tax, the arguments in favor were less compelling to citizens in well-developed regions, who saw little need for state services. Further, with a state income tax, the prospective taxpayers promised to be less affluent and more numerous. But those issues were still another generation into the future. For the moment, Washington yawned its way into ratifying federal income taxation.

Conclusion

Fifty years after the income tax first came to Washington, the state's legislature ratified its incorporation into the U.S. Constitution. Residents of the sparsely settled state, most of whom had come from elsewhere, seemed to react to the tax on the basis of where they had come from. The rapid influx of population in the final quarter of the nineteenth century, the changes wrought in agriculture, and increasing industrialization caused Washington residents to look at taxes, in particular federal income taxes, in a different light. The Populist credo that two factors "control the nation—money and education" ushered in an era in which many issues had bases in class and, secondarily, of region. By 1911, the idea of a federal income tax had become almost universally accepted as a means of gaining back from the East what had been taken in the form of interest on bonds and bank deposits, in raw natural resources, and from favorable trade balances with the less developed states of the West.

During the entire fifty years, however, the debate was over federal income taxation. But the ratification of the federal income tax amendment brought an end to the era of consensus on income taxation. In a state where income levels were relatively low and wealth was widely distributed, there had been little debate on taxing incomes on a national level. Despite the storms over other political issues, and income taxation in the early years, the period ended with public consensus on the issue.

Federal Income Taxation:

· Wanted to maintain + expand navy yard + build stronger
 coast defenses + protect against Japan - needed
 Federal gov. spending

· Few Washingtonian's would be affected / have to pay   relatively low wealth
  - viewed as way for East to pay back
    what was taken from int. on bonds + bank
    deposits, in raw & natural resources, + from
    trade balances w/ less developed W. states

 = public consensus in WA on fed taxation

6 The Background for Tax Reform, 1914–1931

Hard economic times came to Washington in the 1920s and 1930s. Many observers believed that the dips in the business cycle were inevitable and that only time would cure the distresses. Others believed that government policies could mitigate these peaks and valleys.

These contrasting beliefs translated into two opposing views on the nature of state taxation. Since only time would cure the problems, said the first group, the role of government was to reduce the tax burden but otherwise remain aloof from meddling in the economy. A Washington Taxpayers' Council press release summarized this view in 1922:

> The purpose of government is just what the word implies—to govern the people, to protect the citizen's life, liberty and property rights—literally, to promote honesty, maintain safety and minimize crime. Every departure from the actual functions of government weakens government and adds unnecessary expense to burden the people. Every person, not a beneficiary of government, has a vital interest in curtailing unnecessary expenditures of government.[1]

Proponents of the second view called upon the more comfortable individuals in society to recognize their debt to the general good. Tax policy, in good times as well as bad, should be used as an instrument to promote economic equality. A graduated income tax was one device by which this could be accomplished. Between those extremes were individuals who viewed taxes

56

as simply a means of funding essential government services. Most Washingtonians in the 1920s shared this neutral view of tax policy.[2]

Strong campaigns began for tax reform in Washington, and in 1931, the legislature passed an income tax bill. The governor vetoed the measure. By contrast, agitation for an income tax in Oregon had been successful in 1923. When the Washington legislature finally enacted an income tax law, the Oregon tax had been reinstated following repeal a few years earlier.

Even though the Washington legislature ratified the 16th Amendment with nearly unanimous support, legislators saw no need to adopt a state income tax in 1911. Property taxes maintained government services in Washington, and the tax burden was not heavy. It amounted, for example, to just 1.4 percent of the market value of taxed property in 1910, well below the national average.

Despite the relatively low taxes in Washington, some residents believed that local levies were excessive. "While the state is an inviting field for economic study, it is in the lower forms of government and district administration that the greater waste is to be moderated," pointed out a 1916 pamphlet titled "The TaxEater Will Get You if You Don't Watch Out."[3]

In another 1916 pamphlet, Vanderveer Custis, a University of Washington economics professor, recommended reform of the state tax system. In his view, no one tax was preferable to any other. "If it were necessary to rely on one tax exclusively, an income tax would doubtless be the best," he argued. The federal income tax posed both advantages and disadvantages to a state tax, in Custis's view. Advantages were in "efficiency of assessment and convenience to the taxpayer," but a high rate, necessary if both state and federal government were to use the same tax, was a serious disadvantage. He concluded that a state income tax would be best if it could act as a partial substitute for the general property tax.[4] For the next decade, opinions such as this guided tax reformers.

Until World War I, income taxes were viewed as "rich man's taxes." With the steep federal income tax increases brought about because of the war, such a description seemed less accurate. The number of Washingtonians who paid federal income taxes illustrates the effect of the increases as well as the state's prosperity. In 1918, more than 95,000 residents filed tax returns and paid a total tax bill of $9.7 million on net income of $266 million. More than 9,600 people filed but did not pay tax on incomes between $1,000 and $2,000. The most numerous taxpayers were those who made between

[handwritten margin notes: low income 1-2000; pz-2 yr; +2 yr's; pr't; of taxes; st.]

$2,000 and $3,000. These 22,198 people paid $914,858 in taxes, the most of any income group. Just 15 people made over $100,000 and 10,513 indicated incomes in excess of $4,000.[5]

A year later, almost 20,000 more people filed federal income tax forms in Washington, and the total net income jumped to $326 million. Thirty-two Washington residents made more than $100,000 during 1919—more than twice as many as the previous year. The number earning more than $4,000 also increased dramatically, to 16,131. Nonetheless, the largest total tax, $969,447, was paid by the 44,224 people in the $1,000 to $2,000 income bracket.[6]

Congress reduced tax rates in 1920. Nonetheless, 148,067 Washingtonians, 10.9 percent of the population, filed returns on a total income of more than $375 million. The total tax collected in Washington decreased more than $2.5 million from 1919. Again, the 56,468 taxpayers with incomes of $1,000 to $2,000 paid the largest total tax, $1.1 million. This group made up 4.2 percent of the total population of Washington, but they paid, as a group, nearly 3 percent of the total income tax collected in the state.[7] The federal income tax may have affected few people in 1870 and in 1895, but by 1920, 10.9 percent of the population filed returns. There was increasing skepticism about income taxes, particularly in urban areas where wages rose rapidly during World War I. Other forms of taxes worried farmers and property owners.

[handwritten margin notes: 1920; (0.9%; of population]

Real property taxes had nearly doubled in a decade by 1920. Much of the increase came from local school districts dependent on property assessments for operating expenses and as a revenue base from which to pay back bonds floated for new construction projects. Tax hikes were not responsible for all of this increase, however. Some of the sharp rise resulted from inflationary increases in property values that made prewar assessed valuations seem parsimonious. Some observers believed that there was a simple solution—maintain the same mill levies, but increase the sizes of exemptions. A few others argued for statewide equalization, but they often found themselves drowned out by residents of richer districts who felt such equality would mean reducing the quality of education for their children.[8]

The 1917 legislature strengthened the independent State Tax Commission charged with overseeing the collection of the state's tax levies. The three tax commissioners also served on the State Board of Equalization along with the state auditor and the commissioner of public lands. Each September, the board took testimony around the state on tax rates and advised county auditors on valuation practices. Their most important duty, however, was to assess the property value of railroads and street railways. The tax commission also collected inheritance taxes and gross earnings taxes from express companies operating in the state.[9]

Previously, county officers had sole authority over collecting the tax along with county assessments, and except for railroad property in multiple counties, the commission's role was primarily advisory. The change, according to supporters, would promote equalized taxation throughout the state, but when commission members clashed with state and local officials over collection practices, the commission was abolished by the 1921 legislature. The agency duties were taken over by a director of taxation and examination in the executive branch.[10]

With legislative authorization, Governor Louis F. Hart appointed a blue-ribbon committee to look into taxation problems in the state. The nine members appointed from throughout the state held 12 public meetings in Seattle, Tacoma, Aberdeen, Chehalis, Vancouver, Yakima, and Spokane. Governor Hart appointed all nine members on June 17, 1921. They were Nathan Eckstein and Robert H. Harlin of Seattle, George M. Elliott and Frank D. Oakley of Tacoma, D. W. Twohy of Spokane, W. W. Robertson of Yakima, Alex Polson of Hoquiam, Peter McGregor of Hooper, and S. B. L. Penrose of Walla Walla.[11]

The overriding concern of taxpayers, according to the committee's report, was "too much money being spent by the taxing bodies in the state." The group suggested improvements in standardizing and administering existing taxes, the most important of which was a call for equalization of all assessments. The committee recommended a 3-cent-per-gallon gasoline tax, increases in filing fees and annual license taxes on corporations, and establishment of "a highway tribunal" to secure "more vigorous action against those who violate the highway law."[12]

The Hart committee endorsed "the principle of personal income tax under suitable conditions," but concluded that it "would be unwise to introduce the income tax at this time."[13] The average return would be low because the average wages were low, the committee reasoned, noting that the tax "is distinctly an urban tax."[14] "If the income tax could be applied to the cities alone," the commission report pointed out, "it would be fairly productive. But its administration must be statewide to be effective."[15] A state sales tax "is not a proper tax to be used in the state of Washington," the report added.[16]

Powerful railroad interests and timber firms, arguing that stripping them of generous exemptions would mean lost jobs, opposed equalizing assessments of their properties with those of other taxpayers. The 1923 legislative session took no action on the equalization issue, but valuations rose on farm property and urban homes. Taxes on real property continued to increase in most Washington counties. Some increases from 1912 to 1925 were dramatic. The Cowlitz County levy in 1912 was 38.5 mills, but it had reached 87.19 by 1925. The smallest increase from 1912 to 1925 was seven mills in Douglas County. Some counties had lower rates in 1925 than in 1919 and 1920, but in all counties, there was an upward trend from 1912 to 1925. A four-page pamphlet published by the Seattle-based Washington Taxpayers' Council demanded action from the 1923 legislature: "The 1921 legislature resisted the enormous pressure then exerted to effect the sorely needed tax revision, only by begging time to study the problem and promising to effect reform in its next meeting."[17]

Educational institutions were squeezed in the early 1920s by revenues that failed to keep pace with escalating costs. In 1924, when legislative support for education was not forthcoming, the Washington Education Association (WEA) and other education groups gathered sufficient signatures for an initiative calling for a $4 million state bond issue to finance schools. At the same time, some property owners, weary of all kinds of increases, put their own measure up for voter approval. These taxpayers were less certain that prices would stabilize, and they opposed any measure smacking of state control of local education, including state funding. They favored a constitutionally mandated limit on the mill levy any property owner could be assessed. These taxpayers, represented most vocally by Seattle realtors but including many farmers, argued that without these limitations government spending and taxes would continue to mount. The Voters' Information League, an organization formed by leading Seattle businessmen, published a newsletter demanding limits on mill levies. The newsletter carried a story about another group known as the "40 Mill Tax Limit League."[18]

In 1924, the loose coalition of disgruntled landowners gathered sufficient signatures to place an initiative on the ballot that would limit the total tax levy of all governmental units to 40 mills. In its first electoral outing, the 40-mill limitation failed by a vote of 128,677 in favor to 211,948 opposed. (A similar measure gained the ballot two years later, but it failed, too, even though it had broad support from business and property owners.) The WEA-sponsored bond issue was also defeated, in a 99,090 to 150,030 vote.[19]

Nonetheless, the 40-mill limitation was to become a fixture on the Washington ballot during the 1930s. Indeed, as the next chapter will demonstrate, passage of the initiative in 1932, and in the next three general elections, contributed to the defeat of the income tax by lessening the tax crisis for landowners. With a threat of higher property taxes, such taxpayers might have looked at other revenue sources as a means of limiting tax pressures on real property. For them, the issue was made irrelevant once an upper limit had been placed on real property assessments.

The ongoing debate over taxes brought about by tax hikes and the proposals offered by Governor Hart's blue-ribbon committee caused a resurgence of interest in the State Federation of Taxpayers' Associations, an organization formed before World War I to lobby for tax relief. The organization, revived and reorganized in 1922, gained instant success when it joined in the defeat of the WEA-sponsored bond initiative. Within the next two years, the federation boasted 28 county organizations throughout the state. The trustees of the organization included small businessmen from small Eastern Washington counties, a few lawyers, and representatives of several important trade associations. M. F. Gose of Pomeroy, a former supreme court justice, served as state president. A Spokane businessman, Lester M. Livengood, was first vice-president and editor of the association's newsletter.[20]

Early in its existence, the taxpayers' association allied with the Republican party. In April 1924, its newsletter announced the executive committee's endorsement of the 1924 Republican state platform.[21] The Seattle Real Estate Board joined with the association to work for passage of the 40-mill property tax initiative later in 1924. Consistent with the association's sympathies with industry was its opposition to the public power initiative the same year.[22] From these coalitions would come the opposition to the income tax in the next decade.

Rural areas generally lined up in favor of a property tax limitation, but also in favor of income taxes and public power. The most vocal organization on tax issues was the Washington State Grange. The Grange had a long record of involvement in state politics. Many of the leaders in the 1920s and 1930s had held positions in the organization for many years. The highest officer, Albert S. Goss, was elected to the top post of master in 1922.[23] He had moved two years earlier from Eastern Washington to manage the Associated Grange Warehouse Company in Seattle. Fred W. Lewis of Thurston County had served continuously as secretary of the statewide organization since 1907. In the following decade, the organization became the leader of proponents for income taxation.[24]

$$$

The Republican Roland Hill Hartley gained the governorship in 1924 by allying with anti-union forces and endorsing tax savings through governmental retrenchment, a position popular with the business community. A controversial governor who had his own ideas on government and taxes, Hartley clashed with members of his own party as well as with other state officials.[25]

Soon after Hartley was inaugurated, he announced to the legislature that he would ask for appropriations for state institutions for only one year, during which time he would survey the needs of the state agencies. At the end of that time, he would call a special legislative session to appropriate the funds for the next year based upon his recommendations. Hartley's first target was the University of Washington and its president, Dr. Henry Suzzallo, a longtime Hartley foe. Hartley criticized Suzzallo's "excessive" spending on such projects as the new university library, under construction at a cost in excess of one million dollars.[26]

Along with his demands for tax savings, Hartley asked the legislature to reconstitute the State Tax Commission along the lines recommended by the Hart committee. The 1925 legislature authorized it and taxpayers' associations endorsed it, believing that an independent tax commission would be less susceptible to the will of state bureaucracy.[27] The three members were to serve six-year terms with one term expiring every two years. Governor Hartley appointed the three initial members on April 1, 1925, to staggered terms. Donald McInnes, a Port Angeles banker and dairy farmer, drew the two-year appointment while the Spokane businessman Fred K. McBroom received the four-year term. S. H. Chase of Seattle was appointed for the full six years.[28] When McInnes accepted the $6,000-per-year post, he told a reporter: "I am absolutely in sympathy with Gov. Hartley's efforts to reduce taxation and will work to that end religiously."[29] He was described in the article as the "heaviest individual taxpayer in Clallam County." He owned four dairy farms and intended to remain active as vice-president of the First National Bank of Port Angeles during his term.

It was widely believed that all three men were Hartley loyalists who would never deviate from the governor's policies. But Hartley discovered that he did not always get what he expected from his appointees. In the summer of 1925, he lost patience with the gubernatorial-appointed University of Washington Board of Regents and ordered them to fire his old nemesis, President Suzzallo. When the board refused, Hartley removed members favorable to the college president, and the new regents succeeded in ousting Suzzallo in October 1925. The dispute continued for several months in 1926, and throughout the year, supporters of Suzzallo and the university tried in vain to gain the 97,576 signatures required to hold a recall election. Reports indicated that the recall petition fell far short.[30]

Even though the recall did not succeed, many public officials and newsmen were critical of Hartley's high-handed leadership. Some complained about how the spoils system had returned to higher education. Others criticized Hartley for actions such as making unauthorized purchases without legislative approval.[31]

Hartley had reined in his regents by late 1925, but his appointees to the State Tax Commission did not help his administration's popularity. In November 1926, the tax commission ordered an increase in the valuation even though the previous legislature had reduced the mill levy by 1.488 mills statewide. The revaluation would cost taxpayers in King County more than $1 million and in small rural counties, an average of about $100,000 annually. Experts estimated the change would lead to an increase of $661,000 in tax receipts during the following year.[32]

Editors, already suspicious of Hartley because of the spending stories and his disputes with Suzzallo and others, were outraged at the tax commission's action. The commission passed a de facto tax hike while "[Hartley] spent $2,757 for draperies and $430 for new mirrors," complained the *Centralia Chronicle* editor, adding that state government needed spending restraints, not increased valuations of real property. The governor who had ridden into office on the claim that he would reduce spending proved himself to be a big tax spender, the paper concluded. His tax commission obediently raised the funds.[33]

Hartley defenders countered that such frivolities as attempting to recall the governor were bigger wastes of taxpayer money. As the editor of the pro-Hartley *Everett News* observed, a recall election would cost the state $300,000. Who were the legitimate protectors of the public purse?[34]

Hartley survived the recall attempt, but demands for property tax relief continued. The economy seemed strong in much of Washington in the early 1920s, but not all businesses were satisfied with the tax climate. Some businessmen worried that the increasing state and local taxes would discourage investment in the West. Dr. Carl C. Plehn, a University of California finance professor, told 600 businessmen at a December 1925 meeting of the Western Division of the U.S. Chamber of Commerce in Seattle that state and local taxation had risen from "$16 per capita before the war to $40 now." He warned that the rate had to stabilize or decline if businesses in the West were to remain economically competitive.[35]

The legislature provided little leadership on the issue. Except for the unsuccessful introduction of a bill in the special session of 1925 to outlaw the inheritance tax, the legislature did not answer the demands for tax reform. Senator E. J. Cleary of Whatcom County introduced "An act relating to and prescribing certain laws which may never be passed and providing for an amendment to Section 23, Article 1 of the State Constitution." The Republican lumberman's bill was aimed at forbidding introduction of inheritance taxes. When the bill was referred to the constitution revision committee, the members voted a "do not pass" recommendation and the measure died.[36]

Pressure for reform mounted during the next two years, particularly from rural areas already feeling the effects of economic depression. The 1927 legislature finally acted on the classification problem. Both the house and the senate passed a constitutional amendment to be submitted to the voters in November 1928 that would change the constitution's definitions and allow the legislature to reclassify property for tax purposes. Included along with homes and office buildings for the first time would be "intangibles" such as bonds. The house passed the measure by a vote of 73–20 with four absent. The senate voted for it 41–0 with one senator absent.[37]

The measure had the strong support of the State Grange, the Washington Education Association, the Washington Parent-Teacher Association, and the Washington Realty Boards.[38] Many bond holders, railroad officials, and bankers opposed the amendment, but few did so openly, preferring to allow friendly newspapers to question the need for such a change. In Eastern Washington, the *Spokane Spokesman-Review* and the *Spokane Chronicle*, both owned by the conservative publisher William H. Cowles, opposed the amendment. Cowles's agricultural newspaper, the *Washington Farmer*, raised doubts among its rural readers. All three publications argued that passage of the amendment would be costly for taxpayers.[39]

West of the Cascades, a small Seattle tabloid, the *Business Chronicle*, led opposition to the amendment. Two of the major dailies, the *Times* and *Post-Intelligencer*, also were unfavorable but less stridently.[40] Yakima newspapers, owned by the Hart commission member W. W. Robertson, editorialized against the classification amendment.

Rural newspapers criticized urban opposition to any kind of tax reform. "Seattle Dodges Taxes—Others Must Pay" read a typical headline in the summer of 1928.[41]

The *Grange News* called the *Business Chronicle* editor Edwin Selwin "a genius" in a tongue-in-cheek editorial. The writer pointed to a widely publicized poll taken just before the election by Selwin's newspaper that showed strong opposition to the measure. With little advertising and few paid subscribers, Selwin's paper had been able to "blossom into one of the largest newspapers in the state" immediately before the election, the *Grange News* writer noted. Nearly every farmer received copies, particularly the issue published the week before the election in which Selwin "ranted" against the amendment in several columns, but "no one paid a cent for the paper." Certainly, Selwin's newfound prominence was due to the behind-the-scenes funding provided by Seattle banks and railroads, the writer concluded.[42]

The measure lost 131,126 to 140,887.

Farm representatives bitterly accused the "interests" of lying to the voters in order to defeat the bill. "Led by the mysteriously financed Tax Payers' Economy League," the newspapers were either willing partners or had been duped, the *Grange News* writer charged.[43]

Defeat of the measure brought calls for passage of an income tax. "Opponents of the proposed tax amendment suggested that an income tax would be preferable to the classification amendment during the recent campaign," the *Grange News* editorialized. "This was merely a subterfuge—or 'camouflage'—to divide the vote of those who want the wealthy to pay their just share of the tax burden." Since it had been suggested, however, the editor recommended that the legislature comply with the request and pass an income tax.[44]

In the 1929 session of the legislature, Senator F. J. Wilmer of Whitman County introduced a bill to authorize a state income tax. Wilmer was a sev-

Grange supports income tax

enty-year-old Rosalia banker. A native of Wisconsin, he had been elected to the senate for the first time in 1921. Whitman County, an agricultural county in Eastern Washington, had a strong Grange membership.[45] The measure gained broad support from rural senators and passed the senate with only eight votes against it. When the measure went to the house, however, it was referred to the House Rules Committee where it remained bottled up until the final day for consideration of senate bills. When it was time for the day's calendar to be presented, the tax measure had been left off.[46]

blocked by urban legislators

Income tax proponents were outraged. "I never knew of one [legislature] so firmly roped and hog-tied by the big interests as the one just closed in Olympia," complained Representative J. W. Lindsay of Clallam County.[47] "The dog tax in Seattle pays more than the '$750 million' in foreign bonds tucked away in Seattle safe deposit boxes," the *Grange News* editorial pointed out.[48]

At least one attempt at tax reform drew little support outside Seattle. Charles G. Heifner, a King County Democrat (and "investment official"), introduced a bill to establish a state sales tax. A senate committee, dominated by urban senators in the overwhelmingly Republican body, gave the bill a "do pass" recommendation, but rural senators kept the measure from reaching the top of the senate calendar.[49] The urban-rural differences on tax methods were to continue in this vein for another decade, with urban legislators generally favoring the sales tax and rural representatives pushing for income taxation.

sales tax *tax blocked by rural leg*

The House Rules Committee did more than simply kill the income tax measure. On March 20, 1929, the house passed a "franchise privilege" tax applied only to banks and financial corporations, the effect of which was to decrease taxes of the large urban banks but hurt the small mutual savings banks by denying them similar exemptions.[50] Although it was not specifically an "income tax," the act imposed a flat 5 percent tax on net income of those organizations. The provisions were borrowed from a similar bill then pending in the California legislature but differed from that act in two significant respects. The Washington bill did not include individuals, partnerships, or firms, and though banks were allowed to deduct interest, the Washington bill would allow no such allowances to savings and loan institutions. Neither geography nor party seemed to determine support for the measure. Senate passage was by a vote of 30–11, with one senator absent. Five King County Republicans voted against the bill along with Heifner,

pro big banks anti mutual savings banks

the only King County Democrat. Others voting "no" were two Spokane County senators, and one each from Pierce, Whatcom, and Jefferson counties.[51] Predictably, the State Bankers' Association favored the bill, and Governor Hartley signed it into law on March 20.[52]

The Hartley administration needed no additional controversy. As a means of calming the waters and heading off what many critics thought were dangerous income tax bills, the governor followed Hart's example from 1921 and asked for legislative approval to appoint a blue-ribbon group to examine the tax issues.

On the same day he signed the bank tax law, Governor Hartley signed the bill authorizing a tax investigation committee. The bill passed the house by a vote of 80–14, with three absent. The only opponents were representatives from King County and the only three Democrats in the house: Knute Hill, a fifty-two-year-old Prosser schoolteacher and active Granger; Pearl Wanamaker, twenty-nine, a Coupeville teacher; and O. H. Olson, thirty-eight, publisher of a Pasco weekly. The legislation provided that the body submit its findings to the governor at least six months before the legislature reconvened in 1931.[53]

Before Governor Hartley had time to appoint his blue-ribbon committee members, the banking tax law went to court. In fact, the day after the bill became law, the first of four suits was brought in the Superior Court of Thurston County challenging it on various grounds. Two of the four suits were brought by investment bankers, and a third was filed on behalf of 63 savings and loan institutions in the state. Washington Mutual Savings Bank, for itself and for several other mutuals, also challenged the act.[54] The superior court upheld the act and on March 19, 1930, attorneys presented oral arguments before the state supreme court.

The court's opinion, filed on June 12, handed the savings banks a stunning victory. By a 6–3 vote, the justices declared the act void under equal protection grounds. The court interpreted net income as "property" and argued that therefore the act was an attempt to establish a property tax, not an excise franchise tax. Thus, because the tax was not applied equally, it was unconstitutional. Until the constitutional problem could be rectified, none of the banks paid a tax.[55]

The decision struck down the franchise law, but more important, it provided a precedent that would be used successfully five years later to strike down the income tax. The long-term implications, however, were apparent neither to the growing number of income tax proponents nor to the groups that would later challenge the law.

Meanwhile, the blue-ribbon committee began its work by scheduling public hearings in Bellingham, Everett, Seattle, Tacoma, Olympia, Aberdeen, Chehalis, Vancouver, Port Townsend, Port Angeles, Walla Walla, Yakima, Ellensburg, Wenatchee, Waterville, Davenport, Colfax, and Spokane.[56] In accordance with the enabling legislation, the nine members were "drawn from the various sections of the state and widely representative of its agricultural, commercial, and industrial life."[57] Dorsey Hall of Walla Walla was elected chairman. Other members were Wilmot H. Lilly and Arthur G. Cohen, both of Seattle; Thomas S. Galbraith, Eatonville; Fred K. Jones, Spokane; William H. Miller, Ritzville; N. D. Showalter, Olympia; Joseph E. Lease, Centralia; and William D. Butler, Everett. Also included were the three state tax commissioners, who served ex officio.[58]

On such issues as standardizing taxes statewide, the group came to the same conclusions Governor Hart's committee had arrived at a decade earlier. Unlike its predecessor, though, Hartley's committee concluded that a net income tax should be enacted in order to reduce the property tax burden. The basic revenue system of the state should include "(a) a graduated personal income tax without exemptions on net income from all sources; and (b) an excise or net income tax at a uniform rate according to or on the net income of all business conducted for profit in this state by corporations, except that of insurance companies which are now specially taxed."[59] The report described the history of state income taxation and the arguments on both sides of the issue.[60]

After long and careful consideration of alternative revenue systems this Commission has come to the conclusion that the principal revenue system that this state should adopt for the relief of the property tax and to equalize the tax burden among all who have ability-to-pay should be based on the principle of measuring the tax by net income.[61]

The committee then suggested a modestly graduated income tax ranging from .5 percent on the first $2,000 of net income to 5 percent on amounts in excess of $6,000.[62]

The Washington State Grange endorsed the committee's report and, for the second time in as many years, passed a resolution favoring a state

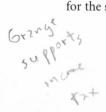

income tax.[63] The state legislature was the logical beginning point. The senate had passed such a bill in 1929, and now, after the governor's own taxation committee endorsed it, the legislature likely would go along. It seemed possible that tax reform would come in 1931 and, with it, an income tax for Washington.

Income Taxation in Oregon: A Parallel Story

Steep increases in real property assessments and a depression in agricultural commodities in the 1920s caused farmer unrest in Oregon and elsewhere. Some believed that relief from high property taxes would be sufficient to allow many marginal farmers to escape foreclosure, while others hoped that income taxation would equalize the burden on everyone, including hard-pressed small-town businesses also caught in the spiral of increasing property taxes. Throughout the country, malapportioned and rural-dominated state legislatures authorized state income taxes. By 1931, there were income taxes in 15 states, including Oregon.[64]

Actually, Oregon had adopted an income tax in 1923, but it was repealed four years later. In 1929 the measure was passed again, and in the general election of November 1930, it was sanctioned by referendum. Just as elsewhere, support for the income tax in Oregon primarily came from farmers, but with a decreasing number of rural residents, eventual success depended on building a coalition with like-minded individuals working in factories and lumber mills throughout the state. The Oregon tax, in fact, owes its beginnings to an informal farmer-labor coalition.

The 1920 Oregon population was almost evenly divided between rural and urban areas. Rural Oregon had a population of 392,370, while urban residents numbered 391,019. Exactly one-third of the population lived in Portland, a city of 258,288 and the only place in Oregon with more than 25,000 people. Salem was the second largest city in the state, with 17,679. After 1920, rural Oregon lost its advantage to the urban centers.[65]

The debate over income taxes had begun in Oregon after World War I with the strongest support coming from the Oregon State Grange. "For state and national purposes we favor an adequate and equitable system of income and inheritance taxes as a source of permanent income," read one of the organization's resolutions in 1921, but the Grange conventions had been on record supporting a graduated income tax annually since 1917. The national convention was held in Portland in November 1921, and the delegates voted to oppose state sales taxes and favor income taxes.[66]

The Grange supporters intended the tax to replace property taxes. "This [reduction] is to be accomplished, if possible, by a graduated income tax to take the place of the state millage taxes, thus relieving the counties of all or a portion of that burden," the legislative committeeman wrote to the members in 1922.[67] As Grangers themselves admitted, the income tax had not been popular when it was first proposed, but in Oregon, as in Washington by 1922, property taxes were rising steadily. "Something must be done to equalize the burden, and not let real estate pay it all, while some hoard up money earned by excessive salaries and securities that are non-taxable," the *Oregon Grange Bulletin* editor wrote in the summer of 1922.[68]

Editors of the major Oregon daily newspapers made no bones about their opposition to the tax. "Income tax is a destructive proposal," one editorial headline read.[69] The *Oregonian* editor labeled it "dangerous and uncertain." The *Oregon Journal* warned tax supporters that they were "sowing the whirlwind."[70]

The 1923 Oregon legislature battled over the income tax throughout the session, while Portland newspapers worried that, somehow, the measure might pass. "Oregon people are not eager for an income tax," wrote one editor, who later urged the proponents to "surrender and save bloodshed."[71] An *Oregonian* editorial was headlined, "Be reasonable."[72]

Even with vocal opposition from the state's major dailies, the legislature passed the tax measure in the waning days of the session. Rural legislators were largely responsible for the victory, although Governor Walter M. Pierce, a Pendleton Democrat, helped gain support from the few urban Democrats. Pierce was an enigmatic character in some respects. Known for his populist stand on the tax and other issues, he had been elected by the largest majority of any governor to that time, supposedly with the help of the powerful Ku Klux Klan in the state.[73]

State government began planning for tax collection, but in June a coalition of tax opponents announced that they had the signatures to force a referendum.[74] The campaign raged throughout the summer with income tax supporters arrayed behind the governor and the Oregon Grange.[75] Organized labor in Oregon, in its annual convention, voted to support the income tax, and the alliance gave supporters hope for success. Meanwhile,

businessmen and other opponents of the income tax did little to fight the measure, preferring to let the influential daily newspapers carry the battle.[76]

Initial reports showed the income tax losing. "The lead against the tax bill in Multnomah, while not as wide as a church door nor as deep as a well, 'tis enough' to overcome the upstate vote," the *Oregonian* election reporter predicted. He was proven wrong, however. When the votes were counted on November 7, 1923, the income tax had won, but by the barest of margins, 58,640 to 58,138 or by just 502 votes statewide.[77]

Support for the tax came from Oregon's rural counties and from working-class areas. In the populous Multnomah County, the state's banking and business center, the majority voted against the income tax 14,569 to 26,507.[78]

The *Oregonian* provided a post-election analysis:

There was organized sentiment in favor of the income tax and this vote went to the polls. Organized labor, in state convention, favored the measure. Opponents of the measure were not organized and they felt so confident of the defeat of the measure by a landslide that they did not think it necessary for them to take the trouble to cast a ballot. The straw votes of civic clubs had shown an adverse vote ranging from 4–1 to 8–1, and thus lulled opponents into lethargy. Analysis of the vote by precincts reveals that in districts where workmen predominate, the support of the tax was substantial.[79]

$ $ $

The support for income taxes evolved slowly in Washington, and the farmers in the state had little success in gaining legislative support for tax reform during the 1920s. Opponents of the income tax were well organized. One house of the legislature passed income tax legislation in 1929 only to have it bottled up in the other chamber. By 1930, income tax proponents believed that they were making progress even though they had learned many lessons in defeat. For example, proponents for income taxes knew that they would have to build coalitions in order to prevail. No longer could they rely solely on rural support for success because the rural population was no longer the majority in Washington. Urban labor was one possible ally, if common interests could be found. Meanwhile, the opposition of businessmen, professionals, and taxpayers' association members would work to keep the two interests apart. In Washington, the stage was set for the battles of the 1930s.

The Oregon population was almost evenly divided between rural and urban areas when the first state income tax law was passed by the legislature in 1923 and sent for voter approval by referendum later that year. Never again would rural Oregon exceed the urban centers in population. By 1930, however, the income tax, proposed and supported primarily by rural interests during the previous decade, had become institutionalized in Oregon. Interest groups in Portland accepted it as a fair and logical means of raising state revenues, and a consensus over the issue developed among business, labor, and agriculture. With the income tax fights only beginning in Washington, to the south in Oregon, the propriety of a state income tax was no longer at issue.

7 The Washington Income Tax of 1931
Veto and Response

Both houses of the legislature, the governor's handpicked Tax Advisory Committee, and the State Tax Commission favored an income tax in 1931. Tax proponents, after years of lobbying, believed that success was close. They did not count on a governor's veto that set them back another year.

Two bills were introduced into the Washington state senate on January 14, 1931, the third day of the 1931 legislative session. Senate Bill 26 provided for a personal income tax, and its companion bill, Senate Bill 27, contained the terms of a corporation income tax. Both were introduced by the Committee on Rules and Joint Rules "by request of the Tax Investigation Committee."[1]

Both bills moved rapidly through the overwhelmingly Republican senate. (John C. Bowen, the 34th District senator from King County, was the sole Democrat in the Washington state senate in 1931.)[2] On February 17, the committee reported out the personal income tax measure with a "do pass" recommendation, but with 21 amendments, one of which changed the exemption from $2,000 to $1,000.[3] The chairman of the committee, Senator E. J. Cleary of Bellingham, and seven of its members signed the majority report. Among them was Senator Wilmer, who had introduced the income tax in the previous session. Only one committee member dissented. He was Senator Daniel Landon of King County, a longtime legislator who had voted for the ratification of the federal income tax amendment in 1911.[4] Senator Charles W. Hall, a Vancouver lawyer, led the measure through the senate on third reading. The senate agreed to four amendments he offered as well as all of the committee amendments. Senate Bill 27 underwent similar amending, but it, too, passed easily following third reading. A crucial feature for both Grange members and the Taxpayers' Association was connection of the income tax to reductions in property tax.[5]

Even after the two bills passed the senate, however, proponents feared that they might become lost in the lower house among other legislative disputes. The senate and the house were locked in a budget battle. The house wanted to pass Governor Hartley's budget as it was submitted, but the senate insisted on cuts amounting to about $2 million. "The bickering in the end may defeat the first real prospect of a serious reduction in state government costs in this commonwealth in many years," wrote the editor of the *Bellingham Evening News*, fearing no tax relief as well.[6]

The Grange leadership, strongly supportive of the initial bill, feared another kind of bickering would destroy the measure. "The advisory tax commission disagreed with the State Tax Commission. The governor wouldn't endorse the former, is seeking to abolish the latter, and not agreeing exactly with either," the editor of the *Grange News* wrote early in the session. He concluded that the executive branch's dispute was a "scheme for a sales tax," as the editorial was titled. A Hartley ally, Senator Harve H. Phipps of Spokane County, introduced a proposal for a 1 percent sales tax, but it died on general file March 9.[7]

Neither the budget dispute nor Hartley's battles with his own appointees slowed down progress on the two income tax bills, however. Following introduction on February 27, both bills were referred to the Committee on Revenue and Taxation. Unlike the 1929 income tax bill, which died in committee, the two bills this session were not held up by the Revenue and Taxation leadership. On March 6, the committee reported the bills out with "do pass" recommendations, although not all the members favored passage. As Representative J. H. Davis, the chairman, pointed out, the members voted "do pass" recommendations "for the simple purpose of getting them before the house." The members did not consider themselves bound by their committee vote.[8] Both bills passed. The personal income tax bill passed by the wide margin of 62 to 32. The corporate income tax measure, taken up minutes after passage of the personal tax, gained the support of four more representatives. It passed 66–28.[9]

In its final form, the personal income tax law provided for a graduated rate, starting at 2 percent for the first $1,000 in income and climbing to a modest 5 percent for income above $5,000. The corporate tax would be a flat 5 percent on net income under that law's terms.[10]

The legislature adjourned. Even though the measures seemed consistent with what proponents had hoped for, neither they nor income tax opponents were happy with the result. The *Grange News* editor groused that the bill had been "drastically changed by amendments," although he hailed the bill as an important step forward. A tax-opposing columnist for the *Willapa Harbor Pilot* warned that the tax "will hit farmers as well as wage earners."[11] He apparently ignored the federal report that the average wage in Washington in 1929 was $749 per year, well below the minimum exemption. Also, the Washington average was far below the national average wage rate of $1,268 per year.[12] The Bellingham editor predicted the governor would veto both tax bills.[13] He guessed correctly.

On March 24, Governor Hartley vetoed the personal income tax and the corporation tax bills.[14] In his veto message on the personal income tax, he wrote that it was "designed to take part of the tax load off real estate, but it would do nothing of the kind." He complained that enforcement would require a "vast army of inspectors, auditors, clerks and other assistants." He concluded his lengthy veto message with a stinging attack against the senate leadership, members of his own party:

A little group of willful men in the state Senate successfully blocked the passage of any legislation designed to reduce the tax burden. It is common knowledge that their entire time was spent in circumventing all efforts to simplify and coordinate functions of government that would have resulted in greatly reduced costs. Practically every bill permitted to pass the Senate was either a special privilege-creating or tax-increasing measure. . . . The disturbing fact is that taxes are increasing much faster than the incomes of our citizens and, when fiscal problems become acute, politicians give no thought to retrenchment, but look wildly around for new sources of revenue. It is this policy, or lack of policy, which is rapidly bringing about confiscation of property by taxation.[15]

He added that his attorney general advised him that the bills were both unconstitutional. He did not provide a detailed analysis, but presumably the attorney general had in mind the supreme court's handling of the Aberdeen case.[16]

The vetoes came as no surprise to Hartley defenders, who endorsed his reasoning. "These two bills did not offer any reduction on real and personal property taxes," the South Bend columnist wrote, applauding the governor.[17] The editor of the *Bellingham Evening News* gave readers a lengthy sermon on the virtues of tax reduction. "Gov. Hartley seems to have the idea that frugality is still a good American virtue, and his rebuff of the income tax law supporters has the wholesome flavor of our good old times," the editor wrote. "Saving, it says in effect, is still a necessity and still according to the best American standard," he concluded.[18]

Republican senators were not surprised at Hartley's vetoes. In 1929 he had vetoed 83 senate bills and two dozen house measures. He vetoed a mere 40 senate bills in 1931, but he turned back 32 from the house.[19]

Hartley's heated disputes with the legislature were not new, but many observers were surprised at the virulence of his attacks in the 1931 veto messages. In actuality, the tax veto was a bit less caustic than his veto message the previous day, in which he called the senate leadership "a bunch of jackasses."[20]

Hartley's opponents struck back. "The governor had no tax program," Republican Lieutenant Governor John Gallatly replied.[21] In his position, Gallatly had presided as president of the senate. Three Republican state senators, W. J. Sutton (Spokane County), Fred W. Hastings (King County), and Ralph Metcalf (Pierce County), defended the senate's record and retorted that Hartley had "spurned the work of his own tax commission."[22]

The deep splits in Republican ranks and the deteriorating condition of Washington's economy convinced some Republicans that Hartley's effectiveness had come to an end. Even though the incumbent governor sought his party's nomination in the 1932 primary election, it was clear by late 1931 that Lieutenant Governor John Gallatly probably would be the party nominee.

During the 1931 session, Hartley failed to eliminate the State Tax Commission, a body with whom he had fought over the role the independent board should play in state budgeting. Hartley wanted no input from the three-man commission even though the three members, Donald McInnes of Clallam County, Fred K. McBroom of Spokane County, and Samuel H. Chase of King County, were all Republicans. In 1931, the commission demonstrated that it did not share his views on taxation. The three men endorsed most of the work of the Tax Investigation Committee, on which they had served as ex officio members. This included the advisory body's endorsement of an income tax, although the tax commission did so with several important provisos: "Income taxes should be imposed at graduated rates, with reasonable exemptions or deductions but without offsets of any kind." The commission further stipulated that the "net income from these taxes should go to the State specifically to reduce or eliminate state levies for property taxes."[23]

To placate income tax opponents and Hartley, the tax commissioners stopped short of endorsing adoption of an income tax without careful study. "Income taxes are eminently sound in theory, but their revenue is most variable and strictly limited," the commission report concluded.[24] The governor continued to make known his displeasure with the board's policies. After failing to gain legislative support for eliminating the board, when Commissioner McInnes died in 1932, Hartley refused to appoint a replacement to complete his term to January 31, 1933.[25]

In the meantime, interest groups tried to line up for and against the income tax. The state's continuing economic woes, along with Governor Hartley's rancorous tax-cutting disputes with the legislature, caused internal strife among the members of the State Federation of Taxpayers' Associations. For example, members of Spokane's influential Taxpayers Economy League found themselves on opposite sides in the 1931 income tax debate. A former vice-president of the organization, Fred K. Jones, served on the Tax Investigation Commission, the group endorsing an income tax. Jones, president of the Central Business Property Company, was a past president of the Spokane Realty Board and the Spokane Insurance Association. Lester Livengood, the Spokane lawyer who managed the league, favored other tax schemes.[26]

The organizations affiliated with the association remained influential on local taxation issues, however, although their public influence declined as the economy weakened. Nonetheless, they provided speakers who discussed broader tax proposals before local clubs. A Seattle real estate man told a Tacoma business audience that high property taxes "discouraged Eastern capital." His solution was not to adopt another form of taxation. "The real estate man suggested the cost of education be lowered in the state and the teachers' salaries cut," a reporter noted.[27]

Some taxpayer organizations merged with local chambers of commerce.

Others disappeared. The Voters' Information League in Seattle reorganized in 1931 as the Tax Reduction League of Washington. The Taxpayers' Economy League continued to be active in Spokane, but it was widely regarded as an instrument of the legal and banking community of the city.[28]

The State Federation reorganized in 1932 as the Washington Taxpayers' Association, "a nonpolitical agency organized to study taxes and government and to aid in keeping the cost of government within the paying ability of the people governed." The statement became a regular part of the masthead for its newsletter, *Washington Taxpayer,* from the first issue. Many of the trustees of the old state federation took similar posts in the Taxpayers' Association.[29] Like the leadership of its predecessor, the Taxpayers' Association trustees consisted mostly of small businessmen and professionals, although the newer organization appears to have had a higher proportion of members from the Puget Sound area.[30]

Organizers formed local chapters of the association. In August 1932, Pierce County, again, had a "taxpayers' association."[31] In the *Tacoma News Tribune* article about the group's formation, no mention of the income tax measure was made, but a few days later a "Direct Taxpayers' Association" supportive of the income tax measure was reportedly formed in Puyallup.[32]

Passage of the income tax bill in 1931 caused widespread anxiety among the mostly Republican taxpayers association members. Governor Hartley's veto of the measure met with predictable hostility from tax proponents, many of whom were farmers who had favored the tax as a means of reducing escalating property taxes.[33]

The farm-business conflicts were not limited to Washington. Businesses, less concerned with taxes on real property than potential taxes on profits and often outnumbered due to malapportionment, tried to hold their own on tax issues in Western legislatures largely dominated by farmers. *Business Week*, in 1931, quoted a farmer who used language less often heard from a farmer than from a *Business Week* reporter: "The narrowing margin of net return to agriculture will not permit us to meet the increasing property tax and the industrialist must help pay for the privilege of living in a state endowed with natural advantages and assume a portion of the expense incurred to enhance them."[34]

In the state of Washington, as the year progressed, Grange leaders took a key role in the controversy. In the month following adjournment of the

1931 legislature, county Grange organizations passed resolutions favoring an income tax and deploring Hartley's veto.[35] Throughout the summer, speakers pumped up interest in—if not enthusiasm for—the income tax by declaring it the "only solution" if property owners wanted any relief from higher real estate taxes.[36]

Legislators who sponsored or spoke in favor of the 1931 income tax bill frequently appeared at Grange meetings, often as the main speakers. State Senator Charles W. Hall's speech to the Clark County Grange was typical. After hearing the senator exhort them to support the legislature's attempts to "broaden" the tax base, the county Grange promptly selected a "tax committee" to help gain signatures for an income tax initiative.[37]

To Grange members, adoption of a sales tax was not a valid alternative. Crandal H. Clark, the managing editor of the *Grange News*, regularly reminded readers that the organization opposed sales taxes down the line. "The [sales] tax is levied against those least able to pay . . . we will never support it," he wrote in one editorial.[38]

Grange officials met with Seattle lawyers in early 1932 and decided to attempt a campaign to gain sufficient signatures to put an income tax initiative before the voters in the general election that fall. The drafters did not consider what might have been a surer step of establishing the income tax through passage of a constitutional amendment. A two-thirds vote by each house of the legislature would have been required to gain a ballot position for the amendment. Even if the 1933 legislature were to give its approval, a constitutional amendment would have needed an electoral majority in the next general election, pushing the date for implementation of the tax back to 1934 at the earliest.[39]

On the other hand, with Grange membership at more than 20,000, the drafters had no doubt that they could obtain the required signatures for an initiative.[40] Further, successful passage would mean that the law could not be amended or repealed for at least two years, theoretically insulating the measure from wealthy, powerful lobbies seeking to water down its provisions. In fact, the income tax seemed to be precisely the type of law envisioned by proponents of the initiative process—individuals from the rural populist tradition in Washington state.[41]

Despite the apparent warnings of the Aberdeen Savings decision, the initiative drafters did not call for a flat-rate tax or one that would be based on a percentage of the taxpayer's federal income tax obligation. The act specifically stated that the tax would be a "graduated income tax" with the resulting brackets, exemptions, deductions, and credits borrowed from the federal system, but not a carbon copy of it.[42] The measure, drafted with an attorney's eye toward avoiding the problems that had befallen the franchise tax law, contained long paragraphs of dense legal verbiage. Apparently, the drafters believed that should it face a court test, the measure's declaration of purpose would hold up by avoiding any connection to judicially defined "property." The statement declared that the purpose was "to tax all annual income within the state as such, and not as property."[43]

Detractors criticized the length of the initiative measure. H. A. Chadwick, conservative editor of the *Seattle Argus*, pointed out that the initiative petition was "26 sections long, fills both sides of two big sheets, four pages in all, of fine print."[44]

The state-produced voters pamphlet for 1932 contained page-length biographies of candidates and several pages each for the ballot initiatives. Initiative 69, however, consumed 22 pages of the publication, more than half of its total bulk.[45] To critics reluctant to confront the income tax on its merits in such harsh economic times, the length argument seemed, if not compelling, at least defensible. As the *Spokane Spokesman-Review* editor put it, "If you had possessed the [voters] pamphlet from the day of its issuance to the day of election, and had given it the study that such measures should have for well-advised action, the time thus taken would have cut deep into your vocation and avocations."[46] The wording on the ballot, however, was far less complex. The measure read:

An act relating to and requiring the payment of a graduated income tax on the incomes of persons, firms, corporations, associations, joint stock companies, and common law trusts, the proceeds therefrom to be placed in the state current school fund and other state funds, as a means of reducing or eliminating the annual tax on general property which now provides revenues for such funds; providing penalties for violation; and making an appropriation from the general fund of the state treasury for paying expenses of administration of the act.[47]

Despite the governor's declared opposition, support for the plan came from most of the members of the State of Washington Tax Investigation Committee, who had recommended the income tax the previous year. More important to the measure's electoral success, however, were the endorsements by the Washington Education Association, the Parent-Teacher Association, and the Seattle Central Labor Council. Additional support came from such depression-era organizations as Seattle's Unemployed Citizens' League and the High School Teachers' League.[48] Although most business groups either opposed the tax or remained neutral in the contest, some organizations favored the initiative's passage. For instance, the Spokane Realty Board endorsed the measure along with the 40-mill limitation initiative as a means of relieving the property tax burden.[49]

The language may not have confused tax experts or the governor, but the Grange knew that the document's bulk would make it necessary to educate signers. Grangers, and members of supporting "liberal organizations," set to work explaining the initiative to voters and gathering signatures. Charles Hodde, who later served in the state legislature, headed a group of Grange members from Eastern Washington who canvassed for signatures in the Seattle area. A Colville area farmer, he had been appointed to the Grange's Taxation Committee earlier that year. "I spent six weeks in Seattle campaigning for the measure," Hodde said. "I'd speak at six or seven meetings every day. So many people were out of work that they'd have meetings and unemployment was a prime topic," he recalled. "Of course, they felt that the tax measure would be all right. 'We won't be paying anything,' they'd say."[50]

Even with bleak economic conditions favoring the signature drive, the initiative sponsors did not have a clear field. Signatures were being secured for another initiative petition drive at the same time. In fact, many political activists as well as editors and readers seemed more interested in the initiative to repeal the state's increasingly unpopular "bone-dry" law than in the complex Grange-sponsored income tax initiative.[51]

Nonetheless, tax advocates addressed numerous farm and labor groups in attempts to gain signatures on the petition. Not all speakers were affiliated with the Grange. For instance, the *Washington State Labor News* reported an address on the income tax bill made to the Seattle Central Labor Council in June 1932 by Andrew Elwick, who represented the High School Teachers' League. "He answered a number of questions put to him by various delegates, who showed interest and support to [*sic*] the bill, which was circulated and received many signers."[52]

The Grange gathered 67,000 signatures on the income tax initiative petitions, 17,000 more than required. The Grange sponsors filed the initiative petition, by then as familiar to Seattle union members as it was to Eastern Washington farmers, on July 7, 1932.[53]

The Grange executive committee member Fred J. Chamberlain of Puyallup appeared before the Washington State Federation of Labor at the organization's 31st annual convention in Yakima soon after the petition was filed. The convention unanimously endorsed the income tax bill.[54] The convention minutes described the action:

In the adoption of the Central Labor Council's and the Unemployed Citizens' League program, the convention endorsed the principle of state income tax legislation, but in order to have a definite program, at the closing session, the convention unanimously endorsed the Initiative Measure Number 69, the State Income Tax Bill, which will be before the voters at the November election and it is urged all unionists and friends cooperate in an effort to make this a law of the state.[55]

Other organizations followed suit. The Washington Education Association directors voted September 23 to throw the organization's financial and political support behind the measure.[56]

Meanwhile, the initiative to repeal Prohibition gained the ballot, as did a state game control law. Both measures were controversial although primary interest in the game law came in Eastern Washington, where it was opposed as "an effort by Seattle to wrest control from local counties" by creating a state department of game.[57] This was a second crucial battleground between urban and rural interests. Another proposed initiative, which would have imposed stiff taxes on chain stores, did not gain the required 50,000 signatures. The measure was sponsored by the Seattle businessman Frank Cannair, who insisted that chain stores were causing high unemployment locally.

The 40-mill property tax limitation initiative, defeated decisively in previous electoral outings, once again had the support of the real estate industry, Washington Taxpayers' Association, and chambers of commerce. Neither the WTA nor the chambers spent money on the initiative drive even though they had long touted the measure as crucial relief from high local property taxes. The entire cost of the campaign was borne by the Seattle Real Estate Board.[58] This fact was not announced prior to the election, however, although opponents correctly guessed the nature of the support. The *Washington State Labor News* columnist Louis Nash wrote:

[Owners of downtown office sites] are the people who are behind the 40-mill tax limit on real estate. The small home-owner is simply being used as a tool to pull the chestnuts out of the fire for those 'big-dough boys' as Homer Bone [Democratic candidate for U.S. Senate] calls them. If they paid taxes on their valuable down town sites in the same proportion as does the small home-owner there would be no reason to limit the taxation to 40 mills.[59]

Opposition to the 40-mill limitation came from the Washington Education Association, organized labor, and most government officers, who feared that without another source of tax revenues local schools would be strangled by such a limit.[60] The Washington Education Association, supportive of the Grange income tax, campaigned fervently against the 40-mill limitation. Its spokesmen pointed out that if the limit passed, even the income tax would not be enough to make up for the shortfall, estimated at a minimum of 5 million dollars.[61]

The Grange took no position on the limitation initiative, but it argued that "with one, we won't have to have the other." Members apparently hoped the organization's neutral stand would encourage the "40-millers" to vote in favor of the income tax.[62] Newspaper editors, generally favorable toward the 40-mill initiative, opposed Initiative 69, the income tax measure. The *Spokane Spokesman-Review* jabbed at the measure editorially throughout the fall but carefully avoided criticizing the merits of the proposal. Instead, the editor argued that length and complexity were the primary problems with the initiative. Two days before the election, he appealed to tradition for its defeat: "Almost from the beginning in this state, people have sensed dangers of initiative measures," he wrote. "In self-defense they have voted 'no', when there is doubt as to the purpose of the small clique that drafted the measure, or fear of hidden jokers and clouded wording."[63] The *Seattle Post-Intelligencer* took no position on the tax, but pointed to the numerous exemptions as a "possible" problem.[64] The *Bremerton Daily News Searchlight*, a paper that called the Democratic congressional candidate Marion Zioncheck a communist (and worse), gave conditional approval to the income tax initiative. "Together, Initiative numbers 64 and 69 could be helpful," the paper's editor wrote the day before the election.[65] The *Seattle Times* recommended that voters oppose it.

There is strong sentiment against a double tax on incomes. The federal income tax is heavy, and by all indications is to be made heavier. . . . This measure is long and very complicated, with many evidences that it has not been carefully prepared. It would provide for collections of as low as a dollar income tax, which is manifestly unsound, since the costs of levy, collection and accounting would far exceed the revenue. At its best, it would merely open a new source of taxes and necessitate the establishment of a new and costly state bureau.[66]

One Seattle daily, the *Star*, opposed the measure but not because it did not want an income tax. The newspaper published a front-page editorial on October 29: "If you vote for the proposed state income tax law—Initiative 69—you will be voting to INCREASE your taxes," the prominently displayed item began. "The principle of the income tax is sound," the editorial continued, but not this particular bill. "Hence, if it is LOWER taxes you want, vote AGAINST Initiative 69."[67] In another front-page editorial, three days later, the *Star* explained its case more carefully: "The *Star* has opposed [the income tax initiative] because it would result in higher taxes, not lower taxes, and because it believed its rates of taxation are wrong: they hit the middle fellow too hard and do not put enough of the load on the big fellows."[68]

Many weekly newspapers came out against the initiative. The editor of the *Snohomish County Tribune* summarized the main points of the opposition:

Initiative 69 would compel every wage earner in Washington earning more than 67 dollars a month, to pay an income tax to the state, unless he owns his home in which case he would receive an exemption. School teachers, state, municipal and federal employees, business agents of unions, secretaries of fraternal orders (including officials of the State Grange) are exempt from paying the tax and hence are the strongest workers for it. It places another big burden on the small wage earner. Its passage would mean the addition of another corps of snoopers and state officials to the state payroll at the expense of the taxpayer. This is no year to increase taxes.[69]

A few observers believed that the tax law was not sufficiently progressive and failed to go far enough in taxing wealthier citizens. A Seattle woman, whose letter to the editor of the *Seattle Star* was published three days before the election, claimed the measure "would make the little fellow tax conscious. . . . Purporting to aid the farmer and the schools, this pernicious bill lets out the power trust, and the big fellow by cleverly inserted exemptions."[70] The *Vanguard*, published by the Citizens Public Education League, editorially supported the initiative but, like the Seattle woman, recognized shortcomings: "The income tax law sponsored by the State Grange is not the kind of income tax measure we should like to see presented, but it is a step in the right direction. It does not bear down heavily enough upon super wealth, but it will make some, who can well afford it, pay more than they are now paying," an October editorial said.[71]

The usually reactionary editor of the *Seattle Argus* favored both measures, grudgingly agreeing with the Grange that adoption of both measures might be desirable if it would "shift tax from property to income."[72]

By election day, the economic conditions in the state were so bad that it was clear to nearly everyone that some form of tax increase would be necessary during the next legislative session. If "no income tax, a sales tax will be passed," the *Argus* editor predicted. He advised the voter to "use your judgment" when voting on the measure.[73]

To the surprise of no one, Initiative 69 passed with an overwhelming margin. More than 70 percent of the voters supported the income tax. In the election of 1932, the Grange was successful in building a coalition with urban labor organizations, schoolteachers, and disgruntled urban property owners and demonstrating that the income tax was beneficial to all interests. The farm organization would not enjoy similar success again.

8 Electoral Success, Judicial Defeat

In the election of 1932 Franklin D. Roosevelt led a Democratic sweep nationally, and in Washington, the Democrats won control of both houses of the legislature for the first time in history.[1] The Democrat C. D. Martin, a former mayor of Cheney, won the race for governor by a substantial margin. Wesley L. Jones, in the U.S. Senate since 1908, lost to Homer T. Bone and then died two weeks after the election. Bone campaigned for himself, Roosevelt, public power, the repeal of Prohibition, and the Grange's income tax.[2]

All of the initiative measures passed comfortably, but the income tax margin surpassed all of the rest—even repeal of the state's "bone-dry" law. Seventy percent of Washington voters cast ballots for the income tax; 62 percent favored bringing back beer; 61 percent approved the 40-mill limitation.

Many income tax proponents failed to realize, however, that the income tax victory did not necessarily ensure the act's implementation. Its constitutionality would be up to the nine elected justices on the Washington State Supreme Court.

The margin for the income tax varied greatly by county. In urban King County, the income tax initiative was not as popular as Prohibition repeal or the new proposal for state game control, which won 53 percent approval statewide but 78.3 percent in King County.

The income tax initiative gained more than 60 percent of the vote in every county except one—Yakima County, where it won 56.8 percent. Counties with high farm populations provided the income tax initiative with its biggest margins of victory. In Douglas County, where two-thirds of the population lived on farms, the initiative had the support of 84.1 percent of the voters. The initiative won more than 80 percent of the vote in five of the nine counties in southeastern Washington. In the other four, the vote was in excess of 70 percent.

The 40-mill limitation initiative (Number 64) did nearly as well, although it failed to gain a majority in eight counties. The results in three can be explained by the peculiar nature of the tax base. Railroads and public utilities paid more than one-third of the tax bill in Kittitas (35.5 percent), Klickitat (34.8 percent), and Skamania (57 percent) counties. Apparently, there was less incentive for tax lids in those counties where the assessed levies in 1931 had been 43.48 mills, 42.96 mills, and 55.65 mills, respectively.[3]

Taxpayers in just seven counties paid less than 40 mills in 1931. Whitman County had the lowest rate in the state with 31.82 mills, and the 40-mill limitation failed to gain a majority there. Voters in rural Adams and Columbia counties enjoyed low tax rates, yet more than two-thirds of the voters in each county favored the limit.

The measure did slightly less well in King County than the income tax initiative, but it did better than the income tax in Chelan and San Juan counties, both places where the levy for state and local government exceeded 50 mills in 1931. Taxpayers in two counties were paying in excess of 70 mills in 1931, and in both—Grays Harbor and Kitsap—the 40-mill limitation barely gained a majority, although in Kitsap County, eight of ten voters favored the income tax.

Grays Harbor County taxpayers paid the highest mill levies in 1931, and it would seem to follow that they would be strongly favorable toward both the 40-mill limitation and the income tax. Railroads and public utilities paid less than 11 percent of the tax bill in Grays Harbor County. Nonetheless, voters there barely gave the limitation initiative a majority, and the 66 percent in favor of the income tax made Grays Harbor one of the few counties that gave the measure less than 70 percent support. One explanation is that the county is distinctly nonagricultural in character (only 11 percent of the population lived on a farm in 1930) and less than 5 percent of the county's population was employed in agricultural pursuits. Only populous King and Pierce counties had a smaller percentage of farmers in their populations.

Counties with large numbers of Grange members generally gave the income tax initiative higher favorable percentages of the vote than counties where the organization was weak. One odd exception, however, is Yakima County, where, in 1932, the Grange had more than 1,640 members, the most of any county in Washington. Yet, the income tax did the worst there of any county in Washington.[4] Part of the explanation may lie in the fact that the farm population was but 41 percent of the county's total. The opposition to the measure voiced by Colonel W. W. Robertson's Yakima newspaper also may have contributed to the result.[5]

The Democratic landslide apparently helped the income tax initiative, although it is difficult to gauge, given the overwhelming nature of the victory. The Democrats registered their greatest gains in Washington history. Some counties went Democratic for the first time ever. For instance, Island County had cast huge majorities for every Republican presidential candidate since 1912. In 1932, Franklin Roosevelt gained 63 percent of the vote there.[6]

Homer Bone, the Democratic senatorial candidate, swept to victory against Wesley Jones, the incumbent. Bone won a plurality against Jones in every county, even in counties where Jones had defeated the Democrat Scott Bullitt by nearly 2–to-1 margins in 1926.[7]

Democrats swept all six congressional seats. Knute Hill, a longtime Grange officer and one of the few Democrats in the 1928 legislature, won in the Fourth Congressional District (southeastern Washington). The youthful, erratic Marion Zioncheck defeated the incumbent in the First District, made up mostly of King County.[8]

Clarence D. Martin soundly beat Lieutenant Governor John A. Gallatly for the governor's chair. Martin won pluralities in all but two counties and lost in Gallatly's home county of Chelan by just 206 votes.[9] The Democratic sweep extended into the state legislature, where the party captured control of both houses for the first time in history. In the house of representatives, just 25 Republicans survived the landslide. Only 8 of the 64 Democrats had any prior experience in the legislature. George Yantis, first elected just two years earlier, was elected house speaker.

In the nonpartisan races for supreme court justice, four candidates emerged from the September primary to receive voter endorsement on November 8. Justices O. R. Holcomb and William Steinert were unopposed, although Holcomb had turned back a strong challenge from Charles A. Reynolds in the September primary. Only Justice Warren W. Tolman faced an opponent in the general election. He failed to win a majority in his

September race against two opponents, the municipal reformer Austin E. Griffiths and Will Beardslee. In the general election, he and Griffiths, the highest finishers in the primary, faced off, and the incumbent justice won with 58.6 percent of the vote.[10]

The incumbent justice Henry E. T. Herman lost in the primary to Bruce Blake, a superior court judge and longtime progressive. After unsuccessful races in 1922, 1924, and 1928, Blake finally realized his lifelong goal by winning election to the supreme court.[11] Herman, a recent Hartley appointee to the bench, had long been a strong supporter of the governor's policies, and his defeat in the same primary in which Hartley lost indicated how closely he had been identified with the governor.[12]

Justice William J. Steinert had been a King County Superior Court judge when Governor Hartley appointed him to a supreme court vacancy in May 1932. Steinert replaced Adam Beeler, a politically ambitious Republican who had resigned to run unsuccessfully for the Republican U.S. Senate nomination in September.

Income tax proponents had no way of knowing how any of the justices might rule if the income tax initiative were challenged nor could they know what grounds the case might take. Steinert had a long record of able service on the superior bench; the other victors in 1932 seemed favorably disposed toward progressive measures. They joined justices with similar judicial temperament. The only certain opponent to the tax had been the defeated Hartley ally, Justice Herman. Income tax proponents could hardly have asked for a better result in 1932.[13]

Justices John F. Main, John R. Mitchell, and William J. Millard had returned to their supreme court positions in 1930. Main was the most senior in years of service. A former University of Washington law professor, he had been appointed by Governor Marion Hay in 1912 and had been reelected in 1918 and 1924. Mitchell, too, had a long record of service. On the court since 1918, he had been appointed initially by Governor Ernest Lister. Neither man faced primary opposition; both were respected jurists.

Millard, however, was a relatively recent addition to the court in 1930. Although he had been appointed by Governor Hartley in 1928, like Main and Mitchell, he had no record of political partisanship. Hartley appointed Millard to avoid political bickering. Millard had been an official of the Washington State Bar Association and, for many years, served as supreme court librarian. According to one historian, Millard was one of the few

Republican lawyers who had not taken sides in the pro- and anti-Hartley disputes in the previous eight years.[14]

In accordance with constitutional rules on initiatives, Initiative 69 became law 30 days after passage. Nonetheless, the law required that the governor sign the proclamation. The lame-duck governor Roland Hartley, who had vetoed the 1931 tax, reluctantly signed the proclamation December 8, 1932.[15]

The state's economy worsened during the winter. Even though a number of politicians believed that the income tax would provide some relief once it took the burden off real and personal property the next year, they knew many people needed immediate help. "Tax collections are working a distress on 45 percent of King County and our citizens who cannot pay their taxes at present are certainly mentally worried," wrote one Seattle Democratic worker.[16]

Quick action was necessary, but so was justice. Another Seattle Democrat urged immediate change to the property tax collecting mechanism. "There is a large amount of evasion under the present system," the Seattle man wrote, giving an example of how a county assessor in a rural county had no leverage when a wealthy, influential man did not allow a legitimate assessment. The man simply estimated his worth, defiantly diminishing its obvious value, and submitted the result to a cowed assessor who was left powerless in the face of audacious evasion. In view of such abuses, the newly elected Democrats wanted immediate tax reform.[17]

In January, following his inauguration, Governor Martin began replacing Hartley appointees in key state positions. Fred McBroom, a tax commissioner since the agency was reconstituted in 1925, resigned to allow Martin to choose a successor. The appointment went to Earle Jenner, a Seattle tax expert who had organized the Washington Title Insurance Company soon after he had graduated from the University of Washington in 1895.[18] To the vacant spot on the State Tax Commission that Hartley had failed to fill following the death of Donald McInnes in 1931, Martin named the Seattle lawyer T. S. Hedges. The state senate confirmed both appointments in the first week of the 1933 session. Samuel Chase, whose term ran until January 1937, became the commission chairman.[19]

Lawyers and legislators were well aware of the possible constitutional flaws in the income tax initiative.[20] Plaintiffs mounted legal challenges to the law in Thurston County Superior Court the day after the governor signed the proclamation. The tax commission had little recourse but to prepare the machinery for tax collection, hoping that such efforts were not wasted by unfavorable court rulings.

Days after the two new tax commissioners were confirmed, Representative John R. Jones, the Democratic chairman of the Taxation and Revenue Committee, asked Jenner to prepare a report on the income tax initiative, particularly those portions that might require adjustment in order to avoid being struck down as unconstitutional. Jenner's report, a nine-page letter, focused on one aspect of the initiative—how the word "property" was construed. The definition was to prove pivotal when the income tax was challenged. Jenner pointed out the flaw to Jones's committee. He described why the crafters of House Joint Resolution 11, the enacting legislation for the income tax, made a change of one word in article 7, section 1 of the state constitution:

The change would have substituted "subjects" for "property": "All taxes shall be uniform upon the same class of subjects."

"Subjects" is a word of wider inclusiveness, which in ordinary speech and also under the weight of authority of judicial interpretation, embraces other than property. The intention is to bring within the rule of uniformity not only property but also occupations, excises, privileges and income taxes, none of which should be considered as property.[21]

Jenner concluded the legal discussion with the warning: "It may be that the graduation of the income tax might be imperiled or destroyed should income be held to be property within the definition in the existing section." Consequently, he recommended that the definition of the word be dropped from the resolution.[22]

While the legislature and the tax commission struggled to ensure that the income tax would pass constitutional muster, the Grange leadership congratulated members for the hard work they had put into the campaign. "Opponents characterized it as the most dangerous measure submitted to the people—long, cumbersome, impractical, destructive of property, anarchistic in principle and used every device to arouse opposition," a Grange official wrote.[23]

Governor Martin sought the advice of tax commissioners on the complex workings of the bill. His secretary, Richard Hamilton, received a detailed reply on February 28, 1933, that did little to resolve the contradictions in the bill. The report pointed out that the funds raised were to be "to the credit of the school fund with whatever surplus to the credit of the institutions of higher learning and the balance to eliminate all other state property tax levies."[24] The funding priorities were necessitated by the passage of the 40-mill limitation, but it appeared to critics that many voters had been misled into supporting the measure, thinking that its passage would lead to property tax cuts. The chairman of the Retail Trade Bureau of the Spokane Chamber of Commerce wrote to Governor Martin reminding him of the property tax reduction goals and urging "proper use be made of the revenue to be derived from the state income tax."[25] Some skeptics believed that victory on Initiative 64, at least, gave taxpayers part of a loaf, mandating cuts in assessments regardless of how the income tax funds were treated. Others found the income tax less innocuous.

Soon after the initiative passed, two groups of Seattle businessmen prepared lawsuits to challenge its constitutionality. Insurance agency operators and auto dealers were heavily represented among the litigants. The suits were brought in the names of William M. Culliton and Earl McHale, prominent principals in the two occupations.

Culliton, twenty-five, a native of Stevens County, operated a small Seattle insurance agency along with his wife, Helen, and one part-time agent who also worked as a salesman for a large printing company. Active in the American Legion, Culliton helped found the Washington Athletic Club and served as an officer in the Seattle Jaycees. He had been reared on a ranch near Thorp in Eastern Washington, where his family still ran cattle.[26]

McHale operated a business of quite a different sort. He ran a downtown Seattle gasoline station that he had started in 1915. During the ensuing seventeen years, he purchased or built nine other stations in the area. An able businessman, McHale built his firm by offering services such as free air and water, previously not done in the area. He was also the first service station operator in Seattle to accept credit cards.[27]

Culliton and McHale, as businessmen, had several common concerns in the winter of 1932–33. One was the newly instituted state income tax. Both men and their respective businesses were subject to the tax, which, even though it was passed in the November election, was retroactive to income earned during 1932. The tax return had to be filed by April 14, 1933. Two months before the deadline, committees of "prominent citizens in Seattle" formed to challenge the tax. One group retained the well-known attorney Harold Preston. In March, in independent actions, Culliton and McHale joined with business friends to bring suit against the state. They sought a permanent injunction restraining the commission from enforcing the income tax act.[28]

Both cases were filed in Thurston County Superior Court against Chase and the rest of the State Tax Commission. Five separate law firms handled the cases for the litigants, including Preston and other attorneys with his prestigious Seattle firm of Preston, Thorgrimson and Turner.[29] Twelve law firms appeared as amici curia, including Charles W. Hall of Vancouver, who had supported the income tax but, as a Republican incumbent in the state senate, lost in the 1932 general election. The firm of house speaker George Yantis also filed an amicus brief in the case. The tax commissioners were represented by the attorney general, G. W. Hamilton, and his assistant, John W. Hanna.

Even before the suit was filed, the tax commission was concerned that court decisions could impede collection efforts already in progress. In its 1932 report, the commission asked for legislative authority to submit tax questions to the supreme court for advance opinions.

No statute involving the possible necessity of constitutional construction can be regarded as stable until such time as the constitutional points involved have been passed upon by the court as litigated issues. Meanwhile, everyone may have been proceeding in error, and, when adverse ruling is forthcoming, more or less chaotic conditions must exist until some solution of the resultant difficulties has been found.[30]

The Thurston County Superior Court Judge D. F. Wright consolidated the two cases for trial in the winter of 1932–33. The legislature was still in session when Wright announced his decision. He entered a decree permanently restraining the commission from enforcing the act. The income tax, in his view, was "wholly unconstitutional."[31]

The State Tax Commission appealed the decision to the Washington State Supreme Court. Oral arguments were scheduled for late spring. Justice Emmett Parker was ill during the winter, but the other eight justices remained hopeful that he would be able to participate in the case.[32]

While the income tax was facing a legal challenge, successful passage of the 40-mill limitation came under fire from some of the Grange's election allies on the income tax measure. The Washington Education Association called an emergency conference the Saturday following the election in order to discuss strategies for dealing with the results of the initiative. Arthur Marsh, the executive secretary of the organization, told reporters, "The educational forces realize that the gravest crisis in the forty-three years of statehood confronts the state's entire system of public education." He reminded the press: "Passage of the measure deprives public education of about one-third of its present revenues from the property tax. The new income tax measure is expected to yield only two or three million, leaving five or six millions of deficiency to be made up by the legislature."[33]

State officials agreed with Marsh on the probable magnitude of the revenue shortfalls. With such prospects in mind, Senator E. B. Palmer of King County introduced a sales tax bill early in the 1933 legislative session.[34] The response from critics was swift and unyielding. A congressional aide to Senator C. C. Dill wrote the freshman legislator Warren Magnuson:

I am very much opposed to a state sales tax myself . . . [;] a sales tax for the purpose of getting away from the fundamental principle of taxation that everyone should pay according to their ability to pay, is all wrong, and has no place in a democracy and I would be compelled to fight the dam [sic] thing regardless whom the sponsor may be.[35]

Magnuson, who sat on the Committee on Taxation and Revenue involved in preparing the income tax law, expressed the overly optimistic view held by most Washington legislators: "If a sales tax is adopted it will be considered only as an emergency measure for a short period and I do not believe will ever become a permanent part of our tax system."[36] Support for "emergency measures" caused one legislator to propose a steep increase in the state cigarette tax, while others introduced legislation to tax business activities of all kinds, including newspapers and radio broadcasting stations.

Predictably, legislators heard from anxious tobacco store owner constituents.[37] They also heard from publishers and broadcasters. "It is unfair to single out newspapers for a higher rate," W. V. Tanner, publisher of the *Seattle Post-Intelligencer*, wrote to Representative Magnuson on February 24, 1933. "If publishers of this state are burdened with unfair taxes they will be unable to carry on in these 'trying times' as they should."[38] O. W. Fisher, president of KOMO radio, wrote Magnuson to protest the proposed 2 percent tax on gross receipts of radio stations. He argued that broadcasters should not have to pay taxes while newspapers were exempt, apparently unaware of the provision to which Tanner objected.[39]

During Franklin Roosevelt's first "Hundred Days" the Washington State Tax Commission was printing income tax forms. The law authorized $15,000 for implementation of the tax.[40] The Culliton-McHale lawsuits loomed ominously on the horizon. On March 14, the tax commissioner Earle Jenner died suddenly in Olympia. According to one obituary, "His work on the newly adopted Income Tax and with the Committees of the recent Legislature proved too great." He had been the spokesman on the tax measure and an influential advisor to Governor Martin.

After his death, the tax commission was, once again, down to two members, but unlike Hartley who left a vacancy, Governor Martin moved quickly to find a replacement. On April 3, he appointed Jenner's brother, T. M. Jenner, a Seattle attorney. Even though he was not a tax expert like his brother, T. M. Jenner shared a similar philosophy. The tax commission remained firmly committed to the income tax and equalization of assessments.[41]

Federal Internal Revenue Bureau figures showed that approximately 50,000 Washingtonians earned sufficient incomes in 1931 to file federal returns. The Washington tax exemptions and brackets varied so significantly from the federal ones that officials found it difficult to estimate how many people would have to file state returns.[42]

As a tax expert advised in the *Seattle Times* in late March 1933, state tax returns "must be filed by a large number of people who have never paid income taxes before."[43] The exemptions were straightforward enough— single people with net incomes of $800 per year or less and married people earning less than $1,750 did not have to file. One problem was with persons owning businesses or practicing professions. Any businessman or professional person with gross income of $2,500 or more had to file even though his net income might be, in fact, lower than the exemption.[44]

As a result of this peculiarity, the tax commission mailed forms to far more than 50,000 households. In fact, the forms went to nearly everyone in the state, including farmers and wage laborers earning less than the minimums. Forms were even sent to persons in occupations exempted from paying the tax.[45] Newspapers statewide printed what apparently had been only an informal response to a reporter's question: "If you received an income tax return form in the mail, you must fill out the return and file it regardless of the amount of your income."[46]

Local newspapers continued to provide tips on the complexities of the tax law. The *Seattle Times* began a special column, "State Income Tax Helps," written by W. D. Rodbury, a certified public accountant. Experts such as Rodbury made no attempt to soothe public fears about the difficulty of filling out the return. (The majority of his readers probably had never seen a federal tax return, much less filled one out.) "Many problems arising from the State Income Tax returns are of such a complex nature that they can be handled only as individual cases by expert accountants or attorneys," Rodbury began his columns. He urged all individuals to seek professional counsel due to the law's complexities.[47] The Seattle accountant Samuel F. Racine rushed into print a tax guide. In it, he printed almost 100 pages of questions and answers on the tax law, many couched in accountant's terminology. It is unlikely that these complex "aids" eased taxpayer anxiety.[48]

Folklore enters the income tax story at this point. According to Charles Hodde, tax forms went into "every mailbox," with some people receiving multiple copies. He speculates that supreme court justices also received the complicated forms, and as a result, some may have changed their views on the tax. The story can be neither proven nor refuted, but as Lawrence M. Friedman observes, "The strongest ingredient in American law, at any given time, is the present: current emotions, real economic interests, concrete political groups."[49] No evidence exists, but almost certainly the justices received mail about the tax forms from worried laymen. The timing of the Culliton case, however, suggests that legal interpretation was a more likely and immutable cause—except for the curious behavior of the mysterious "swing" justice.

Justice Parker never recovered sufficiently from an illness to participate in hearing the Culliton case. Consequently, eight justices heard oral arguments and deliberated in late May and early June of 1933. On June 15, Chief Justice Walter B. Beals told reporters that the supreme court had reached a deadlock on the Culliton case. Four justices believed that the income tax passed constitutional muster; four thought it did not. Consequently, the court agreed to rehear the case in its next term. Justices Mitchell, Millard, and

Steinert dissented, arguing that because the court deadlocked, the lower court's decision should be upheld, striking down the tax as unconstitutional.[50]

By early August, Parker's health had worsened, and he resigned from the bench.[51] Less than a week later, Governor Martin announced that he was appointing a close political ally to the seat—James M. Geraghty, who had served briefly as the governor's director of efficiency. Like Martin, Geraghty came from Eastern Washington, where he had been a longtime political advisor to the governor. Income tax proponents must have been comforted by Geraghty's appointment, because he was known to be supportive of the income tax.[52]

The chief justice scheduled a rehearing on the case in late August. On September 8, 1933, the supreme court announced its decision. Just as the U.S. Supreme Court had decided on the 1894 federal income tax in the Pollock case, the Washington State Supreme Court struck down the state income tax as unconstitutional. As in Pollock forty years earlier, the decision was 5–4.

Geraghty surprised neither the governor nor income tax proponents. Nonetheless, his vote to uphold the tax statute did not turn out to be pivotal. A justice who favored the tax in June changed his position by September. Reporters speculated on who had switched sides. Justices Mitchell, Millard, Steinert, Main, and Holcomb made up the majority. The first three had made it known that they favored allowing the lower court's decision stand; they did not change sides. Chief Justice Beals and Justices Blake, Tolman, and Geraghty dissented. That left only Holcomb, author of the court's majority opinion, and Main. The legal historian Charles Sheldon believes that it was Holcomb: "Holcomb appears to have switched his vote on the income tax measure between the original deadlocked decision of June 15 and this September 8 ruling."[53] Did Holcomb receive the complicated tax form in his mailbox between the two dates?

Holcomb's majority opinion said that the income tax was unconstitutional because it violated the 14th amendment to the state constitution, which required all direct taxes be uniform on all categories of property.[54] Just as the late Earle Jenner had predicted, the peculiar definition of "property" in Washington law allowed the court to declare that net income was "property." Consequently, income taxation fell under the terms of the prohibition; "hence a graduated income tax statute is unconstitutional."[55]

Holcomb wrote that even though the income tax had been an initia-

[handwritten margin notes: ideas Ore. press income tax]

tive, that fact was "of no controlling importance." Also deemed irrelevant were similar phrases in constitutions in the adjoining states of Oregon and Idaho, where income tax statutes had withstood constitutional challenges.

Legal scholars criticized the tortured reasoning in the decision, particularly the portion in which Holcomb distinguished income taxes from inheritance taxes. "The inheritance tax is really not a tax at all," he wrote, arguing that it was "an impost" because it was "laid but one time, and not annually, as is a tax."[56] The distinction confirmed all of the problems that Earle Jenner had pointed out with defining words in statutes and decisions.

Tax opponents were delighted with the court's ruling. "Although the people of Washington voted the income tax law on themselves, they will applaud the decision of the court," a magisterial *Seattle Times* editorial noted. "One glance at the dreadful blanks mailed out by the State Tax Commission was sufficient to convince them they did not want the new system nearly so much as they previously had assumed they did."[57]

Grangers and others who worked for passage of Initiative 69 were outraged at the court's 5–4 decision. "The majority of our Supreme Court is a bunch of juridical clowns," wrote Edgar J. Wright, a contributing editor of the *Grange News*. Wright, however, confirmed the *Times*'s sense of popular opinion on the issue: "[The supreme court justices] make the old Constitution jump through the hoop of what they deem, at the time, to be the present popular sentiment."[58] John M. Reynolds, writing in the same issue of the *Grange News*, urged the people to begin impeachment proceedings against the majority of the justices for "flaunting [sic] democracy." He warned that "nullification of laws by courts must stop."[59]

$ $ $

Income tax supporters, after years of trying, had finally gained a state income tax in Washington in 1932. Voters in all parts of the state supported the tax, but the highest approval came from farm counties. The victory was gained by a coalition of two groups, farmers and urban workers, made nervous by rising property taxes and worsening economic conditions. To both groups in 1932, the income tax represented a means of relief. Declining farm prices placed farm ownership in jeopardy from tax foreclosures. To farmers, the income tax meant lower property taxes and little or no tax on the proceeds from the sale of farm products. To urban workers, an income tax not only provided some relief for home owners from rising property taxes, but it also promised to furnish some badly needed state relief to hard-pressed local governments in areas where unemployment continued to rise.

The coalition was built on shaky ground, however. Put in broad terms, definitions of "relief" varied widely. Urban workers saw the income tax as another source of revenue from which relief activities could be funded. Farmers believed that the income tax would bring lower property taxes.

In fact, the state was increasing its role in helping the mostly urban unemployed, but the income tax seemed unlikely to provide sufficient revenues, by itself, to make much difference. Tax revenues from any source promised to relieve property-owning farmers as long as the new tax would eliminate the need for higher mill levies on farmland. The 40-mill limitation had in it the potential for destroying the income tax coalition by stripping from it farmers' support. The introduction of the sales tax, with potentially higher revenue returns to urban areas, threatened to reduce urban dwellers' support of the income tax.

Temporarily, the fragility of the coalition was masked by the Culliton decision of the Washington State Supreme Court. A 5–4 decision of the court struck down the income tax as unconstitutional. Grange officers and others accepted the challenge of attempting to make the income tax "constitutional," but the question was, Would the 1932 coalition hold together long enough for electoral success in 1934?

Unlike in 1932, when the tax was of central importance to a number of interest groups, in 1934 several issues vied for attention. Organized labor was concerned about issues relating to union organizing and picketing. The Unemployed Citizens' League became increasingly radical, and many of its members worked with the Washington Commonwealth Federation on Initiative 119, a measure touted as a panacea for the average man.

The Grange itself lost some of its enthusiasm for the income tax. For one thing, the 40-mill limitation brought relief to property owners who no longer believed an income tax was essential as an alternative to a high property tax. For another, their numbers were diminishing because of the hard economic times on the farm. Ambitious young organizers like Knute Hill and Charles Hodde were in Congress or the state legislature, occupied with numerous issues of statewide concern. Regardless of the odds, the income tax movement leaders and supporters took a deep breath and prepared to press its case one more time.

9 Attractive Alternatives to an Income Tax, 1933–1940

The spirits of Grange officials and other proponents of the income tax were not dampened by judicial defeat of the income tax in September 1933. The loss only pointed out the need for a more permanent approach to the issue—passage of a constitutional amendment that would overturn the decision and insulate the tax from further judicial interference.

Tax opponents, relieved by the court's decision in the Culliton case, recognized that the electorate could decide the issue a second time in the general election of 1934. Given the huge plurality the measure enjoyed in 1932, the opponents knew that they would have to be better organized in the next round if they hoped to win.

Some state officials were less gloomy about the income tax defeat than they were relieved that the occupational and excise taxes had been upheld. Even the attorney general G. W. Hamilton seemed satisfied with the result. The excise taxes had been passed by the 1933 legislature and amounted to 2 percent of the net sale price of many items. The potential yield far exceeded projections of what the state could have collected with an income tax.

The business excise tax act had wide support when it passed in the 1933 session. The house speaker George Yantis thanked James Taylor of Seattle's Central Labor Council for going along with the bill's passage even though organized labor had previously stood steadfast with the Grange against any sales tax measures. "I very much appreciated your concessions on the sales tax in the last legislature," Yantis wrote, "The sales tax locally was a concession to necessity," he added.[1] Washington industry leaders approved of the tax. "It is the only tax which cannot be evaded by any person, corporation or organization," wrote Clancey M. Lewis, manager of the Manufacturers' Association of Washington, to Governor Martin.[2] By October 1934, 31 suits had been brought involving provisions of this act. Four went to the state supreme court, where all were decided in favor of the act.[3]

Apparently, many state officials agreed that the income tax was unnecessary. "Both the state tax commission and the superintendent of public instruction agreed the loss of the income tax revenue—once estimated at approximately $600,000—would not be of much importance to the new state tax structure," a Seattle-based business newspaper, the *Daily Journal of Commerce*, reported the day the Culliton decision was announced.[4]

The Grange and its supporters, however, persisted, even though other matters occupied voter and press attention. The 1933 legislature authorized the governor to call a special election to choose delegates to a convention during which repeal of the 18th Amendment would be considered. "Wets" won most of the delegate races in the August 29 special election. On October 3, 1933, the convention met in Olympia to ratify the 21st Amendment to the U.S. Constitution.[5] Soon after, the 36th state ratified and national Prohibition was repealed.

Governor C. D. Martin appointed a special commission to develop a state plan for liquor control. When the group failed to agree on whether the system should involve state ownership of liquor outlets or regulated privatization, the governor called a special session of the legislature to resolve the issue. The status quo was not acceptable. Earlier laws controlling licensing of taverns had been expunged from the books during Prohibition, and without a new liquor code, all liquor business would be legalized but unregulated.[6]

Newspaper observers doubted that taxes (except incidental to liquor control) would be an issue during the session, which both political parties and the governor promised would be "short and snappy."[7] Nonetheless, the continuing funding crisis resulting from the effects of the Great Depression and the 40-mill limitation caused local officials to warn of dire consequences unless something was done. "Our present tax system is on the verge of collapse," M. K. Norton, president of the Washington State Assessors' Association, told a *Seattle Times* reporter. Norton said that he asked Governor Martin to instruct the tax commission to prepare "emergency remedies."[8]

The week before the special session was scheduled to convene, the

Washington State Supreme Court issued an opinion on a challenge to the 40-mill limitation. During the summer, a Seattle taxpayer named Robert Denny filed suit in King County Superior Court against the City of Seattle, seeking to enjoin the city from raising the city mill levy by one-half mill for the firemen's relief and pension fund. He also sued King County for levying 4.33 mills on top of the 40-mill limit. The county claimed that the funds were needed to retire emergency warrants issued before December 8, 1932, the date the 40-mill law went into effect. The two cases were consolidated for trial.[9]

A King County Superior Court judge ruled that both the city and the county had to comply with the terms of the 40-mill initiative. When the case was appealed, the majority of justices let stand the portion of the decision denying the City of Seattle the right to raise the levy by one-half mill. The court, however, found in favor of King County in the other portion of the suit. The emergency warrants had been authorized before the effective date of the legislation and, thus, did not violate the limitation.[10] The decision calmed proponents of the 40-mill limitation who had feared the measure would meet the same fate as the income tax initiative.

When the special session opened on December 5, observers noted the discord among the majority Democrats. Many "regulars" who were allies of Governor Martin agreed with the minority Republicans that the legislature should pass the liquor legislation quickly and then adjourn. The so-called left-wing Democrats wanted to use the special session to pass additional legislation. Representatives from rural districts vowed that they would keep promises made to farmer-constituents by seeking a constitutional amendment to allow income taxation.[11]

Besides the administration's plan for liquor control, nearly 200 other unrelated bills and more than a dozen resolutions were introduced into the house during the special session. On December 21, 1933, the eighteenth day of the legislative session, 14 legislators cosponsored House Joint Resolution Number 12 calling for a constitutional amendment to be placed before the voters in November 1934, which, if approved, would allow the legislature to pass a graduated income tax.[12]

Representative John R. Jones, a Waterville farmer and a legislator since 1923, was primary sponsor of the measure. Including Jones, 10 of the 14 cosponsors were farmers; 3 were housewives. One was a "traveling newspaperman." All but two represented districts in Eastern Washington. Even though a dozen of the cosponsors were Democrats, the measure was not strictly partisan. Two cosponsors were Republicans.[13]

The measure was referred to the constitutional revision committee, where it was quickly reported out for floor action. It passed the house by a margin of 84–6, with 9 either absent or not voting. Three of the six opposing the bill were King County representatives. Five other King County legislators, three of whom were Democrats, did not vote on the popular measure. The only "no" vote cast by an Eastern Washington legislator was by Grant Stewart, a Lincoln County Republican whose occupation was listed as "timbering and mining."[14]

Following house passage, the bill went to the senate, where it faced strong opposition, particularly from the King County delegation, one of whose number served as chairman of the constitutional revision committee. On January 11, 1934, the 39th day of the special session, bill supporters managed to bring the measure up for senate vote in the very last hour in which the upper house could consider legislation from the lower chamber. The bill initially failed to gain the necessary two-thirds vote: nine legislators voted against it and seven others were either absent or not voting. Seven of the nine voting against the bill were from King County (five Republicans and two Democrats). The two others voting "nay" were from Spokane and Whatcom counties.[15]

On a motion to reconsider, however, the measure managed to pass by a vote of 32–7, with 7 not voting or absent. The slim one-vote margin was provided by two critical swing votes cast by Senators P. Frank Morrow and Charles H. Todd, both King County Democrats who had voted against the measure earlier. Neither legislator offered an explanation for his change of mind. Todd's switch was particularly interesting. Even though elected as a Democrat, the twenty-six-year-old legislator was spokesman for the ultra-right New Order of Cincinnatus, a supposedly nonpartisan organization formed in Seattle the previous summer as a front for conservative Republicans. The organization's adherents strongly opposed the income tax.[16]

One brief paragraph in the *Seattle Times* described the passage of the income tax resolution and concluded with the sentence: "Initially defeated in the Senate, the resolution was reconsidered and mustered 32 votes, one more than needed."[17] Todd, during the final days of the session, called the "left-wing" of the legislature a "pampered minority." He spoke his mind about other legislators. The same article included his complaints about a committee chairman: "The overstuffed commissioner from King County, the silver-tongued bandit, like a blimp looking for a mooring mast, wasted the time of the house by delaying the vote on the liquor bill."[18]

The daily press paid little attention to the passage of the resolution, but both opponents of the tax and supporters began planning for the fall campaign. Meanwhile, in April 1934, Governor Martin appointed a new chairman of the State Tax Commission to replace Samuel Chase, a Hartley appointee who had resigned. Martin chose Henry H. Henneford of Spokane, a member of the state Democratic party's finance committee. Henneford, a bachelor born in Indiana in 1894, was a graduate of Heidelberg University, Ohio. He taught high school in Spokane and, later, worked in the investment department of a local bank.[19] During the first year of Martin's governorship, Henneford was supervisor of the State Tax Commission's division in charge of administering the state business tax law. Henneford, like his predecessor, strongly favored an income tax.

During the election campaign, the tax commission endorsed the income tax constitutional amendment as well as an amendment to allow for tax equalization. "Should these proposed amendments be rejected," a commission report warned, "any sound and adequate revision of our tax system, in the immediate future, will become impossible." The commission concluded that "these amendments can be defeated only through ignorance on the part of the voters as to their real purpose and effect."[20]

The Grange leadership continued to support the income tax, but farm support for such a measure was clearly ebbing. Two arguments propounded by tax opponents seemed to be turning opinion against the income tax. Property owners (mostly farmers) no longer needed to worry about excessive taxation. The 40-mill limitation, again on the ballot for a two-year extension, eliminated the alarming climbs in property taxes. Besides, income tax opponents argued, the newly instituted business taxes provided far more revenues than an income tax and, if necessary, could be extended as a general sales tax if conditions warranted.[21] The Grange committee members, so successful in waging the 1932 campaign, seemed less able to convince fellow farmers, much less urban workers, of the benefits of the income tax. Even though they campaigned with the blessing of the state tax commissioners and a few union officers, they gained few invitations to address labor forums.[22]

The coalition with labor was evaporating, but even among its own members, the Grange lacked the strong support it had enjoyed in 1932. To try to whip up enthusiasm for the measure among the members, the state Grange master made a last-minute plea for support of the amendment.[23]

It was to no avail. Opponents, silent in 1932, were quick to attack the measure this time. "The constitutional amendment," wrote one critic, "would give the state tax commission, an appointive body, absolute control over all taxes." The Tax Reduction League made similar hysterical claims in press releases.[24]

The voters sided with the opposition. The constitutional amendment that would have allowed for a graduated income tax gained just 43.4 percent of the vote. It went down 134,908 to 176,154.[25]

One member of the Grange's income tax committee blamed the defeat on opponents who were "able to manipulate the metropolitan press." He complained that "30 counties voted right but Seattle alone overwhelmed it with about 20,000 votes against the amendment."[26]

Indeed, only 38.1 percent of King County voters favored the amendment, but the percentage was even lower in nine other counties. Voters in Adams County, a rural county in Eastern Washington, supported the tax in 1932, but in 1934, only 32.4 percent of voters were for it. In Lincoln County, the amendment gained support from only 34.7 percent of the electorate. Barely a third of Spokane County voters cast "yes" votes.[27]

Meanwhile, the 40-mill limitation on property taxes, a measure less popular than the income tax in 1932, scored a second electoral success. This time known as Initiative 94, it further reduced the state levy from five to just two mills and provided for other limits. By a 53.3 percent vote (219,635 to 192,168), Washington voters chose to renew the limit on taxes for another two years. The initiative carried in 20 counties, including King County, where it gained more than 55 percent of the vote. It was even more popular in Pierce County (58.8 percent), a county characterized later the next year by the University of Washington economist Joseph Pratt Harris as one of four in the state "in very unsound financial condition."[28]

Democrats extended their dominance over both houses of the Washington legislature. School district officials and county officers in many parts of the state complained of serious shortfalls in revenue because of the 40-mill limitation and the poor economy. Between the general election and the opening of the legislature in January 1935, many politicians concluded that the tax system would have to be overhauled. Income tax supporters feared a sales tax was in the offing. "The sales tax is a deception and a fraud," wrote one critic. "It is being persistently forced upon us by those seeking to avoid a graduated income tax," he concluded.[29]

Legislators had few alternatives following the success of the 40-mill limitation and defeat of the income tax. "It is thus seen that the state has been unable so far to revise its tax laws so as to secure revenue from the untaxed 65 percent of wealth in the state," wrote Harris.[30]

During the 1935 session, the Washington legislature refashioned the state tax system by passing two important laws. The first, House Bill 237, became known as the Revenue Act of 1935. Among its 17 titles and nearly 200 sections were provisions for business and occupation taxes, public utility taxes, a "radio tax" on the net income of broadcasting stations, a cigarette tax, a corporate net income tax, and a state sales tax.[31] The sales tax provisions, the most controversial in the package, called for a 2 percent retail sales tax, but it did not apply to gasoline (already taxed) or to a few basic food items such as milk and bread. The second bill, the Personal Net Income Tax, calling for a tax of 3 percent on all incomes above $4,000 and up to a 4 percent surtax on additional amounts, was passed separately. Like earlier income tax measures, the bill was prepared by a committee of the Washington State Grange.[32]

Unlike the 1933 tax forms, the 1935 state returns duplicated much of the federal income tax form. Supporters vowed that they did not want a repeat of the mailbox stuffing incident that might have been fatal to the last income tax act, when forms went into everyone's mailboxes. Exemptions also mirrored the federal tax law.[33]

The Revenue Act provided that 58.51 percent of its proceeds were to be credited to the state school fund, 19.05 percent to the general fund, and 17.9 percent to the state emergency relief fund. The University of Washington, weakened by the drastic cuts made necessary the previous biennium by the passage of the 40-mill limitation, was to receive 3.47 percent of the revenues, while Washington State College (now Washington State University) and the three normal schools each would receive less than .5 percent of the monies generated by the tax.[34]

Drafters of the Personal Net Income Tax believed that the measure could survive court challenge because of the careful phrasing in Section 2. Its wording seemed to imply that the state was taxing not income but the privilege of receiving it: "There shall be levied, collected and paid to the state for each income year by every resident of the State of Washington for the privilege of receiving income therein while enjoying the protection of its laws."[35]

The distinction seemed too subtle and the legalese too crafty for some legislators. They introduced Senate Joint Resolution 7, which would again seek to change the constitutional language forbidding a graduated income tax. Even to the sponsors of the Personal Net Income Tax act, the constitutional amendment was "insurance" in case the state supreme court once again struck down the income tax.

The major tax measures passed both houses of the legislature in the waning days of the session. The vote in the house on the Personal Net Income Tax was 88–5, with 6 members not voting. Democrat Martin P. Halleran of Kitsap County joined four of the eight Republicans in the house voting against the bill. Two of the Republicans voting "no" were from King County, but the other two represented mostly rural districts. One of them, Henry J. Copeland, was a Walla Walla farmer. Similar broad support was evident in the senate.[36]

When the bills went to Governor Martin, he exercised his line-item veto on three titles of the Revenue Act and several minor provisions of the income tax measure. Although Martin's own "left-wing," farmers, and such groups as the Unemployed Citizens' League urged him to veto the sales tax provision, he did not do so. Among the provisions he vetoed were taxes on "proprietary medicines and toilet preparations," the gift tax, and taxes on stock issues and transfers.[37]

Opponents of the sales tax were enraged at the legislature's action and Governor Martin's refusal to veto it. "Sales Tax is the Finish for Martin," read a headline in the *Washington Commonwealth Builder*, the official publication of the newly formed, left-leaning Washington Commonwealth Federation. The article listed legislators who had voted for the sales tax, dubbing them "Martin's Marionettes," and concluded: "A man who gives you his word of honor and does not live up to it is Just a Plain Liar. A man who pledges to a party platform and does not live up to it is Just a Plain?"[38]

The Washington Taxpayers' Association officials were no happier with the legislature's products. The editor of the organization's *Bulletin* wrote: "[The legislative session] closed on March 20 was undoubtedly the most incompetent and extravagant legislative body ever assembled in this state.

Without leadership, without a definite program and without an understanding of the problems of government or governmental finance, both houses were easy prey for the army of public employees."[39]

Headlines in the *Commonwealth Builder* read, "Recall Martin! He Gave Us the Tax—Give Him the Axe." On the other side of the political spectrum, the Taxpayers' Association officers were calling the session a "looting" and accusing the governor of being irresponsible.[40] To counter the torrent of newspaper and special interest criticism of the tax plans, Representative George Yantis, chairman of the house Committee on Revenue and Taxation released a statement to the press. "No one needs to apologize for the work of this legislature in the field of taxation," the former house speaker wrote. "Under the imperative necessity of providing revenue, it has not only measurably met the emergency but has gone a long way toward building a just tax system."[41]

To provide for the fractional amounts required by the sales tax statute, the state issued "tax tokens." Because of their shape, they were often called "little metal doughnuts" or, more deprecatingly, "Chinese money." They were to become a familiar feature to shoppers statewide.[42]

While critics on the right and left complained about specific provisions of the new laws, five Seattle men filed three separate suits in Thurston County Superior Court challenging the constitutionality of both the income tax and sales tax provisions. The five plaintiffs in the test case represented a variety of occupations, and the claims alleged several constitutional defects. George A. Jensen was president of a downtown Seattle merchandise brokerage house; he claimed that the law violated equal protection because, unlike many taxpayers, he would have to pay the 4 percent surtax. Herman M. Maples ran a Ballard trucking company. He claimed that he already paid state taxes on his trucks, and the income tax on his business would amount to double taxation. David M. Hoffman operated a cigar store on First Avenue and owned rental properties elsewhere in the city. He contended that he would be liable for taxes on the rents even though he paid city property taxes on the structures. Gail M. Williams was a young attorney associated with a prestigious Seattle law firm. He stated that, because he was unmarried, he would be liable for the tax because he earned more than $2,000 but less than $2,500. Married attorneys, Williams claimed, were liable only if they earned more than $2,500. The plaintiff in a separate action, Philip Bronson, was a partner in an insurance agency.

He, too, argued that the measure was an unequal tax on property, prohibited by the constitution.[43]

Judge D. F. Wright, the same judge who had ruled against the state tax commission in the Culliton case, heard the case after consolidating all of them into one. Wright was first elected to the superior court bench in 1914. Born in Ohio in 1878, he was a professional photographer before he attended law school at Ohio State University. He opened a law practice in Davenport, Washington, about 1906. In 1949 he retired from the bench and his son Charles was elected to his seat. Judge D. F. Wright prided himself on being a crack marksman. Soon after coming to Washington, he "outshot Annie Oakley" in an impromptu match behind his law office. "She would have beat me if she'd been in practice," he told a reporter years later.[44]

Just as he had found in Culliton, Judge Wright ruled that the income tax violated the uniformity provision of the constitution. Further, he agreed with the plaintiffs that the surtax violated the 14th amendment. Again, just as he had in 1933, Wright issued an injunction against state collection of the income tax. The sales tax, however, had no constitutional defect, in Wright's view.[45]

Again, even though the State Tax Commission cooperated with the plaintiffs in bringing the suit, it appealed the case to the state supreme court. Few legal observers were surprised by the result. In a 5–4 decision, the same justices who struck down Initiative 69 as unconstitutional in 1933 also declared the new statute in violation of the constitution.[46] Justice William J. Steinert wrote the majority opinion. "Inasmuch as the majority members of this court, as now constituted, hold the same views as expressed by them in the Culliton Case, it would serve no useful purpose to enter upon a further discussion of the authorities considered in that case," Steinert noted.[47]

The court's majority was not fooled by the legislature's definitions of income. "It is true that the Legislature has so labeled the 1935 act. But the legislative body cannot change the real nature and purpose of an act by declaring its nature and purpose to be otherwise, any more than a man can transform his character by changing his attire or assuming a different name," the majority wrote. The same four justices who dissented in Culliton—Blake, Geraghty, Tolman, and Beals—joined in dissent in Jensen.[48]

Governor Martin, who was first informed of the decision by a *Spokane Chronicle* reporter, told the press, "The decision was not a surprise to me." He claimed that his administration would "balance the budget without revenue from the income tax law."[49]

The editor of the *Grange News* vowed that organization members would "redouble their efforts" to gain an income tax. The words, however, were rhetoric. The Washington State Grange membership no longer seemed willing to go all out for another try at an income tax. Not only were the chances of success diminishing, but the economic conditions were improving. With a sales tax to finance state and local government and a lid still in place on property taxes, why work for an income tax?[50]

Nonetheless, the "insurance policy" was in place—the legislative act placing a constitutional amendment for an income tax on the November 1936 general election ballot. Again, the decision would be left to the voters.

The constitutional amendment in 1936 suffered from some of the infirmities of the 1932 initiative. The language of the amendment caused voter confusion, which played into the hands of tax opponents:

A proposal to repeal section 12, Article XI and amend sections 1 and 5, Article VII of the Constitution of the State of Washington by providing uniform taxation upon the same class of subjects; that the legislature may provide exemptions and graduated income tax; may vest municipalities with power to make local improvements by special assessment or taxation; cannot require counties or municipalities to tax for county or municipal purposes, but may, under legislative restriction, vest them with such authority.[51]

The Grange, weary from more than a decade of tax battles, was turning its attention to other issues affecting farmers, such as price supports for commodities and New Deal mortgage and loan programs. Organized labor endorsed the income tax as a "practical, just and equitable method" of taxation at the Washington State Federation of Labor annual convention in 1936. The organization spent little political capital on it, however, because its attention was drawn to national and state labor issues such as the strike against the *Seattle Post-Intelligencer* in the fall of 1936. The Washington Commonwealth Federation, steadily becoming more radical and purportedly dominated by Communists, showed little interest in the constitutional amendment on the income tax beyond passing a resolution of support at its 1935 convention. The organization's members were pressing for passage of Initiative 119, "Production for Use," modeled after Upton Sinclair's E.P.I.C. programs. When Howard Costigan, editor of the Commonwealth's newspaper, wrote an editorial supporting the tax the week before the election, his endorsement was half-hearted. He advocated that members vote for the tax "because it is the most equitable of all taxes and because big business is opposed to it."[52]

Opponents of the income tax relentlessly attacked the measure. Officers of the Washington Taxpayers' Association, which had started publishing a monthly newsletter in October 1935, blasted it. "The amendment will practically remove every restriction now imposed by the legislature with reference to taxation," an editorial warned, concluding in bold type: "THE QUESTION TO BE DECIDED BY YOUR VOTE ON THIS MEASURE IS WHETHER YOU DESIRE TO GIVE UP THE CONSTITUTIONAL PROTECTION WHICH GUARANTEES YOU UNIFORM TAXATION."[53] A Spokane editor questioned the cost of an income tax. "Even its sponsors don't know," he wrote, suggesting the unfounded view that the tax had some link to the Commonwealth Federation's initiative. Other editors questioned whether the voters should have any direct input into such policies. "[The amendment] would provide for great change in the tax system, involving highly technical problems that the average voter should not be asked to solve," cautioned the editor of a small-town weekly.[54]

While the income tax lost support statewide, the 40-mill limitation, again on the ballot as an initiative measure, received broad endorsement. The initiative was the centerpiece of the Taxpayers' Association ballot drive in 1936. "It is the only initiative whose sole purpose is to protect those who pay for government," the organization's newsletter pointed out, noting that 140,000 people had signed the petition placing the measure on the ballot.

There were a few newspaper editors who offered mild support for the income tax along with the rest of the ballot measures. "There is considerable merit in the amendments," an editor of a central Washington weekly observed.[55] The Spokane newspapers consistently lumped the income tax in with the Production for Use initiative and other ballot measures. On the eve of the election, the chairman of the Spokane Realty Board warned that if any ballot proposal beyond the 40-mill limitation passed, taxes would increase. He pointed to the "viciousness" of the other measures.[56]

Numerous organizations endorsed the 40-mill limitation initiative. They included the Washington State Federation of Women's Clubs, the Washington Savings and Loan League, and the Washington Titlemen's Association. The Washington State Grange also endorsed the limitation measure. Even in earlier elections, farmers noticed the decreases in mill rates in many agricultural counties made necessary by the initiative. Tax relief had come without having an income tax to supplant the property tax assessments. The "certain well-organized minorities" who still worked for passage of the income tax had lost a key campaign point because of the 40-mill measure.[57]

Few voters opposed the 40-mill limitation initiative. Exceptions were schoolteachers and other government workers, whose concerns about the measure were dismissed editorially by the *Washington Taxpayer*: "All tax limiting measures are opposed by those who place their profit from government above their desire for justice in the tax system." Just 3 of the estimated 300 newspapers in Washington in 1936 failed to support the 40-mill limitation.[58] An Aberdeen newspaper was one. "It is our conviction that every initiative should be defeated," wrote an Aberdeen editor. "Initiative legislation is dangerous and wrong in principle."[59]

The income tax constitutional amendment lost in a landslide. The measure gained the approval of just 22.2 percent of the electorate, barely half the support it had received in 1934. In sharp contrast to earlier elections, the income tax lost the most heavily in the eastern, rural counties. In Garfield County, the percentage of "yes" votes was in the single digits—just 7.4 percent; in Walla Walla County, only 8 percent of the voters cast their ballots for the tax. In just two counties in Washington—Whatcom in the northwest and Thurston (site of the state capital)—did the income tax amendment gain even 30 percent of the vote.[60]

At the same time that voters were repudiating the income tax, the 40-mill limitation initiative chalked up a huge victory. Skamania County's 68.4 percent was the lowest percentage of any county. More than 80 percent of the voters favored the initiative in each of 25 counties.[61]

Clearly, voters who favored the 40-mill limitation voted against the income tax amendment. For instance, in Garfield County, where the income tax lost by the largest margin, the 40-mill limitation had its greatest success—91.5 percent support. If the percentage of votes in favor of the income tax and in favor of the initiative were added together, in Mason County the figure nearly equaled 100 percent (23.1 percent for the tax, 77.4 percent for the 40-mill limit).

The income tax was defeated and the initiative passed in urban areas just as in rural counties. The margins in the cities, however, were somewhat less for the 40-mill limitation and a bit more for the income tax. In King

County, the 40-mill limitation passed with 71.9 percent support while the income tax mustered 26.6 percent of the vote. The margin was the second smallest of any county for the initiative, the third largest for the tax.

The 40-mill limitation was the only ballot measure to pass. The Commonwealth Federation's Production for Use initiative did even worse than the income tax amendment. Barely one voter in five voted for it. The editor of the *Spokane Spokesman-Review* congratulated the state's voters for the "perfect score on the ballot measures." He declared that the election results "rang the death knell of the communistic commonwealth federation and other Socialistic plottings."[62]

Except for the ballot measures, the Spokane editor and his allies could find few other electoral successes. The Democratic party increased its dominance in the state legislature, and Governor Martin polled more than 71 percent of the vote to defeat former governor Hartley. The Democrats held on to all six congressional seats. Warren Magnuson, former King County prosecutor, won the First District seat formerly held by Marion Zioncheck, who had committed suicide August 7. The Democratic Congressman Knute Hill, a former Grange officer who had worked for the income tax in earlier years, beat back a strong challenge in his mostly rural Eastern Washington Fourth District. Also elected to Congress for the first time in 1936 was another longtime income tax proponent, John M. Coffee, who won in the Sixth District, made up mostly of Pierce and southern King counties. (Coffee was Senator Homer T. Bone's brother-in-law.) The income tax measure had no impact on any of the election contests. Virtually all of the tax supporters won, many by huge margins, in the same election in which the income tax lost by the largest margin ever. In contrast, the few Republicans who sought to make the income tax a partisan issue went down to defeat.[63]

Even after the 1936 election showed little voter support for it, the income tax continued to be favored by the majority of liberal Democrats in the 1937 legislature. Early in the session, the state senator Fred S. Duggan, a Spokane attorney, introduced Senate Joint Resolution 5, which, again, called for a constitutional amendment to allow implementation of the income tax. Duggan's bill passed the senate by a vote of 38–6, with 2 members absent. Three of the five Republicans in the senate voted against the bill, and they were joined by three Democrats: Joseph Drumheller, a Spokane County chemical engineer; Gordon Klemgard, a Pullman (Whitman County) grain farmer; and David E. McMillan, a farmer from the Stevens-Pend Oreille district. The Republicans against the bill were Henry J. Copeland, the Walla Walla farmer who had voted against the Personal Net Income Tax bill in 1936, and two Puget Sound area senators, Ralph Metcalf of Tacoma and W. C. Dawson, a King County shipping executive. Significantly, four of the six house members opposing the tax were farmers, indicating the shift away from the measure by the group that had once been among its strongest advocates. The bill passed by a vote of 93–1 in the house. Only one Republican, Representative C. N. Eaton, a Walla Walla farmer, voted against the resolution. Five members were absent on final passage.[64]

Resolution 5 provided that the voters in the 1938 general election again be presented with a constitutional amendment to allow for an income tax. The legislative action, however, appeared to be mostly symbolic. Public attention was on other crucial issues before the legislature, such as labor reform, improvements to social services, and education issues. Unemployment remained extremely high in the Puget Sound area in particular, and the public assistance programs were running out of the meager funds they were appropriated. In the opinion of many legislators and Lieutenant Governor Victor Meyers, a special session was needed in the spring of 1938 to address the chronic problems. Governor Martin, out of state when his lieutenant governor attempted to proclaim such a session, returned in time to thwart the effort. The incident highlighted the deep schism within the Democratic party between its right wing (represented by Governor Martin) and its left wing, mostly adherents of the Washington Commonwealth Federation.[65]

The 1938 campaign for the income tax seemed nearly the reverse of the one in 1932, when the opposition to the tax was poorly organized and silent. Six years later, the opponents of the income tax amendment hammered away at the tax in organization newsletters, meetings, and the media. The coalition behind the successful income tax initiative in 1932 tried to unite behind the measure in 1938, but because of disputes on other issues, it seemed to be in irreparable shambles by election day.

The state Grange's sponsorship of a public utility district initiative cost labor support for what was still viewed as the "Grange income tax." Organized labor believed P.U.D.s would cost numerous unionized electricians their jobs, and consequently, it refused to endorse the Grange public utility initiative.[66]

Further, labor organizations in Washington were involved in strikes against the *Seattle Star* and the maritime industry, while at the same time, they were being torn apart by feuding between the American Federation of Labor and the Committee of Industrial Organizations. When a strike-curbing, antilabor initiative, Initiative 130, gained sufficient signatures to appear on the ballot, the labor movement focused much of its energy on defeating it.

The organization responsible for the initiative was the United Farmers of Washington, a group headquartered in Yakima. Even though the United Farmers had no connection to the state Grange (and, in fact, was widely viewed as a front for antilabor business interests), the state Grange failed to quell labor's concerns when it took no position on the initiative.[67] The divisions between the unions and Eastern Washington farmers were illustrated by the story of an electrical union organizer being chased out of a county earlier in the year while "lynching threats were audible."[68] Whatever was left of the coalition in 1936 seemed to be disappearing in the 1938 campaign.

Despite the tensions among them, representatives of organized labor, the Grange, the Washington Commonwealth Federation, and the Washington Education Association met in early October 1938 to develop a campaign strategy for the income tax amendment. The meeting came too late in the campaign to make a difference. The opponents had been campaigning against the income tax for months. They were well organized and ready for battle.[69]

Tax opponents received some unintended help in the primary campaign from the conservative Democratic governor. Martin told reporters that he did not believe that the state needed more revenue, and therefore he believed that an income tax was unnecessary. Nonetheless, Democratic proponents of the tax managed to include it as a plank in the party's 1938 platform. Few party regulars, however, gave it any serious chance for passage, although the lesson of 1936 showed that it did not hurt candidates who endorsed it.[70]

General circulation publications rarely provided readers with interviews of amendment supporters. In fact, the measure was so infrequently mentioned by the press that the anti-income tax columnist Lester Livengood in the *Spokane Spokesman-Review* warned: "The constitutional amendment is probably the most serious because the voters have been given the least information about it."[71] Livengood, a guest columnist, was identified as "manager-counselor of the Taxpayers' Economy League" of Spokane. He also served as a state officer of the Washington Taxpayers' Association.

The income tax gained strong editorial endorsement in one newspaper. Ed Henry's columns in the Washington Commonwealth Federation's newspaper argued forcefully for it. Given the controversial nature of the federation, however, the articles may have been counterproductive, particularly when quoted by newspapers in Eastern Washington, where the WCF was viewed with alarm.[72]

Even though the amendment seemed like a dead letter with little overt support, the income tax opponents did not take its defeat for granted. As early as the winter of 1937, the Washington Taxpayers' Association raised questions about the need for the tax in newsletter editorials. Just before the election, its president wrote that the only supporters of the tax were "left-wing political leaders and radical elements among the educational forces of the state." The *Seattle Times* characterized the contest on the amendment as one not between "the liberal and the reactionary; [but] between madness and moderation."[73]

While some publications resorted to scare tactics, others raised questions about who would be paying an income tax. "Advocates insist only a small percentage will pay," wrote a columnist for the *Seattle Times*, "but opponents point out there are no restrictions." He concluded that the measure sponsors were not motivated by beliefs in equitable taxation, but "influenced largely by the need for more money."[74]

Other newspaper writers raised questions about how much money the income tax would generate and from what sources the revenues might come. "Expert studies in this state have shown that we could not raise more than $6 million a year with such exemptions, yet the promoters of this amendment require not less than $25–$30 million in new taxes," a *Spokane Spokesman-Review* editorial writer noted, adding that to raise such revenue the exemptions would either have to be eliminated entirely or reduced to as low as $300 per year. "It would result in nearly every worker in this state being subject to this tax," the writer concluded.[75]

At the same time, the Taxpayers' Association and many of the newspapers in the state were touting the fourth consecutive appearance of the 40-mill limitation initiative. Because the constitution mandated that the legislature could not overturn successful initiatives before the next general election, the limitation was again offered to keep down property assessments. Property taxes were reduced from $80 million in 1931 to half that amount in 1937, the 40-mill proponents claimed. "Tax delinquencies have been reduced 40 percent and the confiscation of homes and farms has almost stopped entirely," one writer noted. He failed to point out the decreases in population in numerous farm counties during the decade or the improving economy, both factors that affected the number of foreclosures. Official government policy, too, had changed significantly since Governor Hartley's administration in 1931.[76]

Even though election results in 1934 and 1936 pointed out that voters often split their vote on the income tax and the 40-mill limitation ("no" on one, "yes" on the other), the fact was emphasized editorially in the 1938 campaign:

In the later stages of the drive to take the lid off taxation in this state those who have always fought against the 40-mill limit on property taxes have come out into open alliance with advocates of a state income tax. Not only that, but they have also lined up in many districts with left-wing radicals running for the legislature on the Democratic ticket and how the left-wingers feel about taxes is something of which everybody in this state is pretty well aware. In every session since 1933 the radical legislative bloc has labored earnestly for more and higher taxes to yield more tax money for spending on radical projects. That the left-wingers should oppose Initiative 129 [the 40-mill limitation] and favor the constitutional amendment to permit a state income tax is very easy to understand.[77]

The editor of a small weekly in Elma repeated the general theme. He chastised state officials (except for Governor Martin) for wanting an income tax to boost state revenues. "There can be no economy in administration unless the people of the state decline to furnish funds lavishly."[78]

While critics assailed the income tax as an attempt to tax every worker or to bankrupt every taxpayer, editors lavished praise on the 40-mill limitation initiative. A Benton County proponent claimed that it "encourages home ownership which in turn promotes a feeling of security and reduces juvenile delinquency." The same editor characterized the measure as a "Public Godsend."[79]

On both issues, the election results were never in doubt. The income tax amendment lost 2–1 while the 40-mill limitation won by the same margin.[80]

Republicans, hoping to benefit from their opposition to the income tax by making it an issue in many legislative seat contests proved, once again, that support for a popular initiative or opposition to a controversial amendment does not necessarily guarantee a candidate's election. Republicans, reduced to five members in the state senate and to six in the house of representatives in 1936, increased their senate count by one and picked up 20 seats, mostly from Eastern Washington, in the house.[81]

Compared to its showing in 1936, the limitation fared less well in 1938 in most counties. In contrast, and even though it lost badly, the income tax amendment did better in every county than it had in the previous general election. In many of the small Eastern Washington counties, it did twice as well, although in populous Spokane County the increase was a mere 1.1 percent from 1936. Nonetheless, the margin of defeat indicated, even to the strongest proponents, that future attempts to convince Washingtonians to vote for an income tax probably would be fruitless.

The income tax had been popular throughout the state in 1932, but particularly so in rural counties east of the Cascades. Six years later, it was just the reverse. The strongest support in 1938 came from Clark, Kitsap, Island, Mason, Pacific, Skamania, Snohomish, Wahkiakum, and Whatcom counties. All nine are in Western Washington. More significant, the income tax in 1938 polled a higher percentage of the vote in the two most populous counties—King (35.3 percent) and Pierce (35.5 percent)—than it did in any of the "farm" counties of Eastern Washington.

Farmers, once the strongest advocates for the tax, had become opponents by 1938. The electoral history of the 40-mill limitation initiatives during the same period provides one explanation. When farmers were faced with increasing property taxes to sustain state and local government, they turned to the income tax as an alternative source of revenue. Government would be funded, but their property taxes would not continue to climb. The 40-mill limitation eliminated any fear of such property tax increases, and farmers no longer had personal incentives to support income taxation.

Support for the income tax was never very strong in the urban areas of Washington, but the support in those areas remained fairly steady from 1932 to 1938. Self-interest played an important role. Without an income tax, state government resorted to implementation of sales taxes and higher business and occupation taxes. Once those taxes were in place, the public became familiar with their workings. When Charles Hodde was asked why the income tax never passed in Washington after 1932, he observed: "The tax system in place—the sales tax and the business and occupation tax—wasn't so obvious. Paying them was painless. People didn't see that they had to pay a higher price for things because of those taxes."[82]

10 Income Tax Efforts after World War II

The success of the 40-mill limitation encouraged its proponents to try for a constitutional amendment in the general election of 1940. The move was successful and the measure passed, guaranteeing property tax lids of 40 million or less, but allowing voters to pass levies in excess of that amount as long as 60 percent favored the particular issue. The limitation's effect was greater on legislative appropriation than on school district or local government finance. To finance state government operations, the sales tax rapidly took the place of the property tax. Even facing relatively steep levels, the public showed little discontent with the sales tax as a means of raising state revenues. When an income tax initiative was proposed in 1942, it was defeated 69 percent to 31 percent.

Postwar Washington was experiencing a population boom in 1951. Limited revenues, mostly from the business and occupation tax and the sales tax, made it difficult to sustain the level of state services. At the same time, the state faced increasing demands for new schools, colleges were trying to cope with the ballooning enrollments, and highway officials fought to sustain an aging road system with huge increases in traffic volume.

Industries, led by defense contractors, contributed substantially to the economic growth, while the number of farm-related jobs declined. The balance between rural and urban populations was shifting even more heavily toward the cities. Rural counties were losing political influence. The Grange and other farm organizations remained active and powerful in many communities, but they were no longer considered important players in statewide politics. Nonetheless, in alliance with labor unions and urban liberals, the farm groups maintained substantial influence in the Democratic party. Although business remained the bulwark of Republican fortunes, farmers formed a strong bloc in the party. For instance, 11 Republican farmers were serving in the 1951 house of representatives, compared with just seven farmers on the Democratic side.

In 1951, the Democrats held a 54–45 majority in the house. Only eight of the representatives, however, had legislative experience dating back to the 1930s fights over income taxation. Four of them were farmers.

One Democratic farmer was the Colville representative Charles Hodde. A veteran of the income tax fights in the early 1930s, he served as an organizer for the state Grange. He had not been elected to the legislature until 1936. For the 1951 session, Hodde, age forty-four, was elected house speaker.[1]

After near Democratic dominance during the 1930s, Republican fortunes had improved in Washington in 1940 with the election of Arthur Langlie to the governorship. Langlie had a reputation as a progressive. A graduate of the University of Washington College of Law in 1926, he had joined the prominent Seattle firm of Shank, Belt and Fairbrook. His first stint in public office was election to the Seattle City Council in 1936, a year in which Republicans statewide had trouble and Republicans in Seattle were nearly extinct. In 1938, he became mayor of Seattle, and two years later, governor of Washington. Defeated in 1944, he returned to the governor's office in 1949.

In Langlie's 1951 message to the legislature, he proposed a 4 percent corporation income tax. Without such a tax, Langlie warned, the budget could not be balanced.[2] Income tax opponents immediately attacked the measure. "The federal tax burden is bad enough without imposing additional burdens," Daniel Hill, president of the Washington State Taxpayers' Association, responded. As for the looming budget deficit, Hill said that the state officials simply would "have to cinch our belts."[3] Another important business group, the Associated Industries of Washington, also opposed the tax. When a *Seattle Times* reporter asked John Powers of AIW about the effect of such a tax on business, Powers responded, "Business won't leave, but they will reconsider plans to expand."[4]

Commentators noted that the Langlie measure would not tax personal income. Nonetheless, as a *Seattle Times* commentator put it, "The corporation levy may be the entering wedge for an income tax."[5] Pointing to the likelihood of a supreme court test if such a law passed, the writer noted that "liberals believe the court has changed sufficiently in 15 years that the tax would be upheld."[6]

An opening wedge, it might have been. Two Democrats, Representatives David M. Roderick of Seattle and John T. Dootson of Everett, introduced House Bill 549 at the beginning of the session. The Roderick-Dootson bill called for a 3 percent income tax and 4 percent surtax on net income in excess of $4,000. A single person would be given a personal exemption of $1,000; a married couple would be allowed a $2,500 exemption.[7] At the same time, Roderick introduced a bill to remove the 3 percent sales tax from food.[8] The income tax would apply mostly to "upper income" wage earners, the proponents argued, pointing to the median income in the United States of about $3,000 in 1949.[9]

The two measures, Langlie's proposed corporate tax and the Democrats' income tax, began their marches through the legislature. The income tax measure was referred to committee, where it languished. Despite efforts by business lobbyists to stop it, the Langlie measure cleared the House Revenue Committee in early March.[10] Langlie demonstrated his commitment to the bill. In early March, he sent his special assistant, Roger Freeman, to appear before the house, urging passage of the bill.[11] On March 13, the house passed it by a vote of 54–42. Support was not along party lines, even though more Democrats voted for it than Republicans.[12] Urban-rural splits, so apparent in prewar debates on tax questions, were less evident in 1951. Legislators with business connections voted against the bill while representatives from farm districts and labor-oriented urban Seattle voted for it.

The measure was doomed in the business-dominated state senate, however. Despite Governor Langlie's continuing lobbying efforts, the bill went down to defeat.[13] An appropriations bill managed to pass both houses, despite complaints from nearly all quarters. Democrats thought it too parsimonious while Republicans thought it too generous to state agencies. In the clamor late in the session, Governor Langlie vetoed the appropriations bill.

The regular session ended without agreement on either the appropriations or tax measures. Both were essential for continued government operation. Consequently, Langlie was forced to call an extraordinary session that began the day after the regular session ended.

Early in the special session, a 2 percent tax on both corporate and individual income was introduced in the house. The measure apparently rep-

resented a compromise between those wanting a state income tax and representatives not wanting business to have to shoulder the entire burden of
any tax increase.[14] In the spirit of the compromise, the bill was introduced
by two Republicans, A. B. Comfort, a Tacoma real estate agent, and Wesley
R. Eldridge, a Seattle frozen food packer. Because the tax used the same basis
as the U.S. income tax, the proponents proclaimed its progressive nature,
even though the minimum income taxed would be $500, considerably lower
than what the Roderick-Dootson bill, defeated in the regular session, would
have allowed.[15] At the same time, the house considered a bill allowing for
a .5 percent increase in the state sales tax to 3.5 percent.[16] Neither measure
garnered sufficient support for passage.

The corporate income tax lost in the house 44–49, with six members
absent, on March 29. Three days later, the measure was revived on a motion
to reconsider by a vote of 51–43. It went down to defeat again, however,
immediately afterward, when four Republicans defected from the recon-
sideration vote, killing the bill 48–46, with five members absent. (The measure required a "constitutional majority" of members.) Meanwhile, both
the appropriations bill and the tax measure were hitting brick walls in the
senate. Both went down by close margins.[17]

Both houses wrangled over the appropriations bill. The senate's action
met house resistance when the measure came back for approval. After more
than a week in session, it was apparent that the extraordinary session might
last well into the summer unless some compromises were offered.

The president of the senate and the house speaker appointed members
to a "free conference committee," giving them instructions to come up with
a compromise bill, perhaps combining the tax and the appropriations measures. The free conference committee issued its report in the form of a substitute bill, containing both the 4 percent corporate income tax and the
budget bill. Following house passage, the house bill went to the senate, where
the entire bill was struck after the enacting clause, leaving only the appropriations segment intact. The tax measures were gone. The two bodies were
again deadlocked. Nonetheless, in the waning hours of the special session
and after lengthy, heated debate, the new bill passed the house by a vote of
58–41. In the senate, nine Republicans joined fifteen Democrats in passing
the compromise bill.[18] The legislature, exhausted and short-tempered,
adjourned, leaving Governor Langlie to sign the bill on April 16.[19]

Observers quickly predicted that the odd law would be challenged in the courts. Ross Cunningham, a *Seattle Times* columnist, wrote that the "courts would face busy days as a result of the legislators' hasty and confusing actions."[20] Within days of the end of the session, the prediction came true.

Five suits were filed, four by railroad companies, against the 4 percent "excise tax on incomes." The cases were consolidated for trial. The trial court ruled in favor of the plaintiffs. The law, as passed by the legislature, was unconstitutional because, as a tax on property, it was not uniformly applied. On appeal the case went to hearing by the Washington State Supreme Court.[21] John N. Rupp of the Seattle firm of McMicken, Rupp and Schweppe, represented Power, Incorporated. The attorney general Smith Troy and his assistant, Lyle L. Iverson, represented the Washington State Tax Commission. E. W. Anderson, an advisor to the commission since 1933, represented himself.[22]

Again, the Washington State Supreme Court was asked to grapple with the question raised in Culliton and Hannaford in the 1930s as to whether or not income was property. If income was found to be property, following the precedent of the court in the two 1930s cases, the combined tax-appropriations law would have run afoul of the state constitution, article 7, section 1, requiring uniformity of taxation. The companies also questioned the combination of two distinct subjects in one act, alleging that this action, too, violated the state constitution.[23]

Attorneys for the state pointed out that the legislature had called the tax "an excise tax," and it was applied "on incomes of corporations and on certain banks for the privilege of exercising corporate franchises and doing business within the state."[24] The plaintiffs argued that calling it an excise tax was irrelevant. It was an income tax, pure and simple. The court agreed.

Justice Matthew W. Hill wrote the majority opinion. The fifty-seven-year-old jurist was a University of Washington College of Law graduate (1917) who had practiced law in Seattle from 1932 until his election as superior court judge in Seattle in 1945. The next year, the Republican judge was elected to the high court. With five years of supreme court experience, Hill was not the only relative newcomer on the court. Only one of the nine justices, Walter B. Beals, had been on the bench at the time of the Culliton decision.[25]

No matter what the tax is called, Hill wrote, it is still a tax on property and, thus, runs afoul of the uniformity provision of the constitution. He cited the earlier cases. "It is no longer subject to question in this court that income is property."[26] Further, he pointed to the Aberdeen Savings case: "It has been definitely decided in this state that an income tax is a property tax, which should set the question at rest here."[27] He concluded that the tax was not an excise tax but "a mere property tax masquerading as an excise."[28]

Hill's opinion recognized that neither the appropriations bill nor the tax bill could have passed individually. The legislature grouped them under one bill for passage. Hill wrote that such a practice was "precisely why such a provision" was included in the state constitution—so that "log-rolling" would not be practiced in legislating.[29] He concluded that all parts of the statute were unconstitutional and, therefore, voided by the court.

Hill was joined in the opinion by Justices Frederick G. Hamley, Charles T. Donworth, Frank P. Weaver, and Chief Justice E. W. Schwellenbach.[30] Justice Beals, who as chief justice in 1933 had dissented in the Culliton case, wrote an opinion in which he concurred with the majority in part and dissented in part. Contrary to his view in 1933, when he concurred with the dissenting opinion upholding the income tax, he wrote that the taxation portion of the 1951 act indeed was unconstitutional. "Their enactment by the legislature was a mere nullity," he concluded. However, he argued that the appropriations segment should have been left in force because the two acts were "clearly severable."[31] He added, "If any log was rolled, it was [the tax provisions]."[32]

The three dissenting justices, Joseph A. Mallery, Thomas E. Grady, and Robert C. Finley, accepted the argument that the tax was indeed an excise tax and, therefore, not constitutionally defective. As to combining the appropriations act with the tax measure, the dissenters pointed out that "the act in question makes appropriations and imposes taxes to meet them as has been frequently done."[33]

The decision was announced on August 20, 1951. With the $680 million appropriations bill invalidated by the court action, Governor Langlie had no choice but to call the legislature back into another extraordinary session.[34]

Reaction from supporters and opponents of the tax law was predictable. "Solons Ignored Warnings on Joining Bills, Says High Court," read the Seattle Times headline of the story of the court's opinion.[35] The Times associate editor Ross Cunningham, a tax opponent, wrote that the state fund crisis should "compel political factions to forget squabbles."[36] Representative O. H. Olson, a Pasco newspaper publisher and Democrat, expressed the view of most income tax proponents that the result would be an increase in sales tax. "I don't approve of voting a sales tax increase," he told the *Seattle Times*. "The people of the state already have enough of a sales tax burden."[37]

In its editorial the next day, the *Times* took the legislature to task:

The Supreme Court based its decision on considerations of law. But in doing so, it expressed the sentiments of the state's thinking citizens who have become thoroughly dissatisfied with the 1951 legislature's temporizing and repeated refusal to face the most elemental facts of the state's financial problems. . . . It is the duty of the legislature to appropriate funds and levy taxes for the general welfare of the state and its citizenry and not in response to the insistence of high-powered pressure groups and lobbies.[38]

The Grange, various Democrats, and progressive Republicans had succeeded in passing an income tax for the third time in Washington in eighteen years. Like their previous efforts, however, their victory had been undone, not by voters but by the actions of the Washington State Supreme Court. Recognizing the futility of such an action, legislative proponents of the income tax did not reintroduce the bill in the second extraordinary session.

$ $ $

A generation later, Governor Dan Evans supported HJR 42, passed by the 1969 legislature to provide for a constitutional amendment allowing for an income tax. Not only was it supported by one of the most popular governors in the state's history, it also received the editorial endorsement of the largest-circulation daily newspaper in Washington. The *Seattle Times* editorial said of the tax: "If [the income tax measure] is defeated, the additional burden on property and excise taxes will become unbearable."[39]

The 1970 measure would have taxed incomes at 3.5 percent of their adjusted gross with exemptions of $1,000 per family member and numerous deductions. As an added inducement, the sales tax would have been reduced from 4.5 per cent to 3.5 percent and the sales tax on food items rebated up to $15 per person per year. Like the 1942 measure, it lost by a 69–31 margin.[40]

When the income tax was proposed four years later, in 1973, the proposition suffered its worst electoral defeat in state history, a fraction of a percentage point worse than the 1936 landslide loss. Initiative 314, on the ballot in 1975, received the endorsement of fewer than one-third of Washington voters. Evans served as governor from 1965 to 1977 and, despite the unpopularity of the income tax issue, remained one of the state's most popular governors.

A later income tax plan never went beyond the talking stage. In the 1989 legislative session, Governor Booth Gardner recommended a 3.9 percent personal income tax to offset a cut in the sales tax from 6.5 percent to 3.9 percent. Although the tax-reform plan received the lukewarm endorsement of some editorial writers, it got nowhere with the legislature. "Compared to other ways of paying the future costs of state and local government, an income tax doesn't look all that bad," wrote Herb Robinson, editorial writer for the *Seattle Times* in 1989.[41]

Yet, public familiarity with the sales tax, the exemption of food from its provisions (by legislative act in 1978), and the expanding economy of Washington continue to work against any politician proposing an income tax. Besides, the income tax has a poor electoral record in Washington. With only one victory in eight outings since 1932, an income tax in Washington anytime soon appears to be what Robinson calls a "political impossibility."[42]

NOTES

Preface

1. William E. Leuchtenburg, *The Perils of Prosperity, 1914–1932* (Chicago: University of Chicago Press, 1958), p. 227.

2. Robert Alan Goldberg, *Hooded Empire: The Ku Klux Klan in Colorado* (Urbana: University of Illinois Press, 1981).

3. Alan J. Luchtman, *Prejudice and the Old Politics: The Presidential Election of 1928* (Chapel Hill: University of North Carolina Press, 1979).

4. For a discussion of how the urban-rural conflict concept has been used by historians, see Charles W. Eagles, "Urban-Rural Conflict in the 1920s: A Historiographical Assessment," *The Historian* 49 (1986), pp. 26–48. Robert K. Dykstra, among others, has pointed out that the phrase "urban-rural conflict" is "lacking appropriate subtlety." Robert K. Dykstra, "Town-Country Conflict: A Hidden Dimension in American Social History," *Agricultural History* 38 (October 1964), p. 195. For my study, I define "rural" as agricultural, but in quantifying election results I also have included the populations of small communities that are agriculture-based economically.

5. Numerous studies focus on Washington during the depression years. See, for example, William E. Ames and Roger A. Simpson, *Unionism or Hearst: The Seattle Post-Intelligencer Strike of 1936* (Seattle: Pacific Northwest Labor History Association, 1978); Jonathan Dembo, *Unions and Politics in Washington State, 1885–1935* (New York: Garland Publishing, 1983); Robert L. Friedheim, *The Seattle General Strike* (Seattle: University of Washington Press, 1964); William H.

Mullins, *The Depression and the Urban West Coast, 1929–1933* (Bloomington: Indiana University Press, 1991).

6. For the broad issues of American taxation debates, see John Philip Reid, *Constitutional History of the American Revolution: The Authority to Tax,* II (Madison: University of Wisconsin Press, 1986), and Edwin R. A. Seligman and Parker Thomas Moon, *Wealth and Taxation: A Series of Addresses and Papers Presented at the Semi-annual Meeting of the Academy of Political Science, April 15, 1924* (New York: Columbia University Press, 1924). Several scholars considered property taxation aspects in the first third of the century. See, for instance, Charles H. Chomley and R. L. Orthwaite, *The Essential Reform: Land Value Taxation in Theory and Practice* (London: Sedgwick and Jackson, 1909); Benjamin C. Marsh, *Taxation of Land Values in American Cities: The Next Step in Exterminating Poverty* (New York: n.p., 1911).

1 Setting the Stage

1. For a history of the Washington State Supreme Court and efforts to reform it, see Charles H. Sheldon, *A Century of Judging: A Political History of the Washington Supreme Court* (Seattle: University of Washington Press, 1989).

2. For a good overview of the economic conditions in Washington and political responses to them, specifically focusing on Seattle, see Richard C. Berner, *Seattle, 1921–1940: From Boom to Bust* (Seattle: Charles Press, 1992), chap. 19.

3. For the origins of the Grange movement and other aspects of the farmer in politics, see Gilbert Fite, *The Farmer's Frontier, 1865–1900* (New York: Holt, Rinehart and Winston, 1966).

4. *Culliton v. Chase*, 25 P.2d 81 (1933).

5. The other states with no income tax are Alaska, Florida, Nevada, South Dakota, Texas, and Wyoming. Tennessee does not tax income but collects taxes on dividends and interest. Connecticut was the latest state to adopt an income tax. Economic conditions in Alaska in the late 1980s brought calls for taxing income, but proponents were unsuccessful. As of 2000, five states had no sales tax: Oregon, Delaware, Montana, New Hampshire, and Alaska.

6. For instance, in 1990, the Washington legislature considered a wide array of tax measures to fund the so-called Children's Initiative. When Governor Booth Gardner's staff suggested an income tax of 3.9 percent to be offset by a reduction of the sales tax from 6.5 percent to 3.9 percent, commentators on the three

major Seattle television stations were uniformly critical. For an example of lukewarm newspaper treatment of the issue, see Herb Robinson, "Statistical Portrait
of an Unfair Tax System," *Seattle Times*, Jan. 29, 1989, p. A-14.

7. No comprehensive study of the politics of income taxation in the state
of Washington has ever been written, although three works have examined particular aspects of the story. This paucity of materials is understandable, given
that even in states where income taxation has been in place few studies of its
political origins have been made. James V. O'Connor and Robert E. Schillberg,
in "A Study of State Income Taxation in Washington," *Washington Law Review*
(Winter 1958), pp. 398–419, describe the legal issues raised by the state income
tax question. Maurice Wentworth Lee, in *Tax Structure of the State of Washington*,
Economic and Business Studies Bulletin 48 (Pullman: State College of Washington, 1950), provides an economic overview of taxation at the halfway point of
the twentieth century. An informal description of the income tax is presented
in John Fairfield Sly, *Tax Developments in Washington State: How We Got This
Way*, Washington State Research Council Pocket Report Series 1 (Olympia: Washington State Research Council, 1956).

2 Civil War Income Tax

1. The primary sources for this chapter are the assessment record books
of the Department of the Treasury, Bureau of Internal Revenue, Washington
Territory, RG 58, National Archives, Seattle Branch. The records comprise three
large ledgers of about 300 pages each. All newspapers cited are from the microfilmed newspaper collection, University of Washington Libraries. The census
information is from the microfilmed census records, National Archives, Seattle
Branch, unless otherwise stated. An earlier version of this chapter was published
as "Taxing the Few: The First Federal Income Tax in Washington Territory,"
Pacific Northwest Quarterly 79 (April 1988), pp. 56–64. There were but seven
newspapers publishing in the territory, and all were weeklies. They were the
Vancouver Telegraph, the *Washington Standard* (Olympia), the *North-West*
(Port Townsend), the *Statesman* (Walla Walla), the *Puget Sound Herald* (Steilacoom), and the *Overland Press* (Olympia). The seventh paper, the *Golden Age*,
was published in Lewiston in what would soon become Idaho Territory.
Thomas W. Prosch, "Washington 50 Years Ago," *Washington Historical Quarterly*
4 (April 1913), p. 98.

2. The federal government called for troops and set quotas for the states

on May 6, 1861. The Pacific states and the territories were exempt. Washington Territory, however, did furnish 964 volunteers to the Union Army. Fred A. Shannon, *The Organization and Administration of the Union Army, 1861–1865* (Cleveland: Arthur C. Clark and Co., 1928), I, p. 36; II, p. 135. But see Aurora Hunt, *The Army of the Pacific* (Glendale: Arthur C. Clark, 1951), p. 228: "Washington and Oregon did not receive their call for volunteers until three months after California received hers. Oregon promptly recruited six companies of cavalry but Washington found it quite impossible to find more to fill her quota. Therefore, Col. Justus Steinberger, commanding the district of Oregon, secured permission from General Wright to recruit men in California for service in the Washington infantry. . . . Of the ten companies in the first Washington infantry, only two companies were raised in Washington." Hunt probably errs in assuming that the War Department assigned Washington Territory a quota. Official records indicate that Steinberger simply was given permission to raise volunteers for the Union Army. See Thomas A. Scott, acting secretary of war, to Steinberger, Oct. 12, 1861, in *War of the Rebellion: A Compilation of the Official Records of the Union and Confederate Armies* (Washington, D.C.: GPO, 1897), Series I, Vol. L, part 1. For the West as a refuge for draft dodgers, see Shannon, pp. 189–91.

3. The rates and exemptions varied until the tax finally expired in 1872. For a complete summary, see Edwin A. R. Seligman, *The Income Tax* (New York: Macmillan, 1911), pp. 431–35.

4. Seven states, mostly in the Northeast, adopted these "faculty taxes" in the late 18th century. Seligman differentiated faculty taxes from income taxes, stating flatly: "To call [faculty taxes] income taxes is a misnomer." Seligman, p. 386. Regardless of how "faculty taxes" are styled, governments abandoned them early in the 19th century except in Massachusetts and South Carolina, where they lingered on, applied spasmodically, unequally, and with little expectation for raising revenue. In most states, government financed itself from property and poll taxes, and these forms dominated into this century and even beyond in Washington and a handful of other states. Nonetheless, the principle of taxation on nontangibles was present and served as an important precedent for income tax adoption during the 19th century. For detailed analysis of colonial and Revolutionary War tax policy, see Robert A. Becker, *Revolution, Reform and the Politics of American Taxation, 1767–1783* (Baton Rouge: Louisiana State University Press, 1980). Useful studies of Civil War tax policy include Harry Edwin Smith, *The United States Federal Internal Tax History from 1861 to 1871*

(Boston: Houghton Mifflin, 1914); and Sidney Ratner, *American Taxation* (New York: W. W. Norton and Co., 1942), especially chaps. 4–7.

5. In the South, four states already had income taxes by the beginning of the war. Virginia's tax, originally adopted in the 1840s, was raised from 1 percent on yearly salaries and fees in excess of $500 to 1.5 percent in 1862. The next year, the rate went up to 2.5 percent, and although an exemption of $3,000 was allowed, all income received from a trade, business, or occupation was taxed at 10 percent. See Jack P. Maddex, Jr., *The Virginia Conservatives, 1867–1879: A Study in Reconstruction Politics* (Chapel Hill: University of North Carolina Press, 1970), pp. 170–72, for specifics on Virginia in the postwar period. Similar increases were made in North Carolina, South Carolina, and Alabama. In South Carolina, the antebellum system was "light on land and slaves, while mercantile interests bore the brunt." Francis Butler Simkins and Robert Hilliard Woody, *South Carolina during Reconstruction* (Chapel Hill: University of North Carolina Press, 1932), p. 177. Georgia, Texas, and Louisiana adopted income taxes during the Civil War. The Georgia tax, featuring several progressive principles, failed to raise significant revenue. The state's comptroller general complained of the nearly universal tax dodging. *Report of the Comptroller General of Georgia,* 1864, p. 36. The tax was repealed at the close of the war. "The [1863] tax was ineffective in Georgia," according to Kenneth Coleman, ed., *A History of Georgia* (Athens: University of Georgia Press, 1977), p. 192. The Texas tax lasted until 1871. The Louisiana tax, which raised just $2,476 in 1868, .5 percent of all state revenues, lingered inefficiently until 1899. Confederate tax laws are noted in Ralph Louis Andreano, "A Theory of Confederate Finance," *Civil War History* 2 (1956), p. 21. See also Paul L. Van Riper and Harry N. Scheiber, "The Confederate Civil Service," *Journal of Southern History* 25 (1959), p. 450, for a general account of the tax-collecting agencies in the South; for specifics on Confederate war finance, see Robert Cecil Todd, *Confederate Finance* (Athens: University of Georgia Press, 1954), pp. 130–56. For a general overview of early state income taxes, see Clara Penniman, *State Income Taxation* (Baltimore: Johns Hopkins University Press, 1980).

6. Monies gained from the sale of public lands surpassed customs receipts in 1836 ($27 million in land sales to $23 million from customs). Generally, however, public land sales made up less than 20 percent of all federal receipts. *Historical Statistics of the United States: Colonial Times to 1970* (Washington, D.C.: Bureau of the Census, 1975), p. 1106.

7. The total national debt at the end of 1835 amounted to $38,000. The budget surplus that year was $17,857,000, and it rose the next year to $19,959,000.

See E. B. Long, *The Civil War Day by Day* (Garden City, N.J.: Doubleday, 1971), pp. 721–28, for a brief overview of the economics of the war.

8. See, for example, Davis Rich Dewey, *Financial History of the United States* (New York: Longman's, Green and Co., 1934), for a detailed account of this period.

9. *Historical Statistics*, p. 1106.

10. Paul Van Riper and Keith A. Sutherland, "The Northern Civil Service, 1861–1865," *Civil War History* 11 (1965), pp. 351–69. For Chase's views, see Jacob W. Schuckers, *Life and Public Services of Salmon Portland Chase* (New York: D. Appleton and Co., 1874), p. 481, et seq.

11. Albert S. Bolles, *The Financial History of the United States from 1789 to 1860*, 2d ed. (New York: D. Appleton and Co., 1885), pp. 253–59. The discussion of Congressional action on the income tax comes from Seligman, pp. 431–35; and *Congressional Globe*, 37th Cong., 1st Sess., 1861, pp. 313–35, 400, 416.

12. Opponents of the first state income tax in Washington, more than 70 years later, applied similar narrow constitutional interpretations to the tax's application. A majority of the Washington State Supreme Court justices agreed with the arcane interpretation of a section of the Washington State Constitution forbidding taxation on anything "other than property." *Culliton* v. *Chase*, 25 P. 2d 81 (1933). See also chapter 5 of this work.

13. During consideration of the 1862 income tax bill, Senator Justin Morrill of Vermont, the bill's sponsor, argued: "The effect [of current practice] is to require the tax to be put 15 percent higher than would otherwise be called for and the General Government can collect the amount at a much less expense." *Congressional Globe*, 37th Cong., 2d Sess., 1862, p. 1194.

14. Walker to Seward, July 15, 1862. A copy of the letter is included in the U.S. Department of State Territorial Papers, Washington Series, Dec. 5, 1860–Dec. 4, 1872, No. 77, Vol. 2 (microfilm), University of Washington Libraries.

15. See the *Washington Standard*, Jan. 17, 1863, p. 1, c. 2, for details on collection in Washington Territory. According to the territorial treasurer's report to the legislative assembly, Dec. 13, 1862, only three counties—Wahkiakum, Thurston, and Island—had paid anything toward the direct tax assessment. For a list of delinquent states and the amounts each owed, see Smith, p. 38. Colorado had been made a territory on Feb. 28, 1861. For repayment, see also secretary of the treasury's annual report for 1887, in 50th Cong., 1st Sess., 1887, H.E.D. 2 (Serial 2548), p. 338.

16. 12 Stat. 432–489 (1862). For Congressional action, see *Congressional Globe*, 37th Cong., 2d Sess., 1862, pp. 1196, 2574. The 5 percent rate also applied to incomes of all citizens living abroad.

17. John C. Chommie, *The Internal Revenue Service* (New York: Praeger, 1970), p. 11.

18. Van Riper and Sutherland, p. 358, n. 20. The first commissioner of internal revenue, George S. Boutwell of Massachusetts, was hired by the War Department to head the revenue agency in the summer of 1862. He resigned in March of the following year to take a seat in Congress. Following Grant's election to the presidency in 1868, Boutwell was named secretary of the treasury. Four other men served as commissioner during the life of the income tax act. Joseph J. Lewis of Pennsylvania served until the end of the war, resigning effective June 30, 1865. William Orton of New York succeeded Lewis but resigned in October after less than four months as commissioner. E. H. Rollins of New Hampshire was commissioner from November 1, 1865, to March 10, 1869. The final commissioner during this period was Columbus Delano, who served in the Grant administration. The machinations within the agency are described in Herbert Ronald Ferleger, *David A. Wells and the American Revenue System, 1865–1870* (New York: Columbia University, 1942).

19. In the early years, revenue collectors often were paid a percentage of their collections, while revenue inspectors were paid on a fee basis by manufacturers whose property was inspected. The opportunity for abuse is obvious. See Chommie, p. 10, et seq.

20. The earlier tax bill had been printed in Washington newspapers. For instance, see the complete text of the 1861 tax bill printed in the *Vancouver Telegraph*, Feb. 8, 1862, p. 4, microfilm A7251, reel 2, University of Washington Libraries.

21. *Puget Sound Herald*, July 10, 1862, p. 3, c. 1.

22. The first publication of the tax law in Washington Territory appears to have been printed in Olympia. Complete runs of several papers for this period no longer exist, including the *Vancouver Telegraph*, which had published the text of the 1861 law. See *Washington Standard*, Oct. 11, 1862, p. 3, c. 1. The entire act was published in sections in the *Oregonian*, Oct. 8–24, 1862.

23. *Standard*, Aug. 23, 1862, p. 1; *Walla Walla Statesman*, Aug. 30, 1862. In 1863, the Walla Walla paper proposed additional taxable activities, many absent of humor but with a biting political edge: "For lending a newspaper, $5; . . . for declining a government contract, $10,000; Copperheads, $25,000. Other snakes free, including rattlesnakes." *Statesman*, June 27, 1863, p. 4.

24. The act also set death duties. Even with addition of a tax on income, the Lincoln administration never intended for the "internal" taxes to finance the war entirely. Internal revenue receipts simply supplemented customs duties.

In fact, it was the turn of the century before internal revenue sources exceeded duties in generating federal revenues. For a review of available records about the period and a short summary of the provisions of the tax act, see Cynthia G. Fox, "Income Tax Records of the Civil War Years," *Prologue* (Winter 1986), pp. 250–59. For a critical description of the revenue act in economic terms, see Bert W. Rain, *An Analysis and Critique of Union Financing of the Civil War* (Amherst: Amherst College Press, 1962), pp. 20–27.

25. Louis Goldsborough was promoted to rear admiral in 1862 but removed as blockade commander the same year. In 1849–50, he headed an exploring expedition in California and Oregon, which may have influenced his brother to request assignment as a federal official in the Pacific Northwest. For the admiral's biography, see *National Cyclopedia of American Biography* (New York: James T. White, 1892), II, p. 107.

26. Sparks, who remained in the position until President Andrew Johnson replaced him for political reasons in 1866, later became a territorial officer and county official in Thurston County. The appointments were announced in Washington Territory in two newspapers in August 1862. See *Puget Sound Herald*, Aug. 14, 1862, p. 2, c. 1, and *Washington Standard*, Aug. 23, 1862, p. 2, c. 2, both of which incorrectly identified Sparks as "S. G. Parks," and the *Walla Walla States-man*, Aug. 16, 1862, p. 3, c. 1, which identified the new collector as "H. W. Golds-boro." See *Executive Proceedings of the Senate*, Vol. 13 (1887), p. 19, for the Dec. 17, 1862, entry noting confirmation of the nominations of Goldsborough and Sparks; May 2, 1866, for Sparks's removal. An Olympia-based correspondent for a Portland newspaper called Goldsborough "by all odds the best and most popular appointment made for this territory by the present Administration. He is competent to fill any civil position within the gift of the President or people. The major is a very unassuming man. He is not a candidate for Congress, and is about the only officeholder in the territory who is not seeking that position." Letter from "ZED" (an Olympia correspondent whose full name is not given) to the editor, *Oregonian* (Portland), Jan. 22, 1863, p. 2, c. 2.

27. "The Major [Goldsborough] appears hale and robust, and seems to have grown much younger from his trip," the *Washington Standard*, Oct. 11, 1862, p. 3, c. 1, commented on his arrival in the territorial capital. No information exists as to Goldsborough's title. He never served as an officer in the regular army—there is no listing for him in Francis B. Heitman, *Historical Register and Dictionary of the United States Army* (Washington, D.C.: GPO, 1903). The licenses paid for by practitioners various occupations and the stamps required on many important documents brought in considerable revenue nationally.

28. *Walla Walla Statesman,* Oct. 25, 1862, p. 2, c. 1.

29. *Washington Standard,* Nov. 29, 1862, p. 2, c. 4.

30. *North-West* (Port Townsend), Nov. 9, 1862, p. 2, c. 2. See, for example, the debates in Congress of the estimated number of individuals subject to the tax. *Congressional Globe,* 37th Cong., 2d Sess., 1862, pp. 2574–75. In February 1863, Commissioner Boutwell suggested collections in the territories were "barely sufficient to pay expenses and, that exemption would encourage emigration and, thus, increased revenue." *Oregonian,* Feb. 28, 1863, p. 4, c. 1.

31. The Internal Revenue Bureau employed a total work force nationally of 4,031 by 1865. This total did not count the assistant assessors or deputy collectors, who were contract employees of their principals, not government employees. Van Piper and Sutherland, p. 358.

32. The occupations and residences are those listed on the census taken two years earlier. The ages are calculated to the date on which they were appointed assistants. Washington Territory, *Eighth Decennial Census, 1860,* Roll 1398, National Archives, Seattle Branch. The appointments of Ledyard, Bigelow, Dole, and Rector are mentioned in the *Oregon Statesman,* Nov. 17, 1862, p. 2, c. 4. The names of the three deputy collectors were noted in ZED to the editor of the *Oregonian* (Portland), Jan. 22, 1863, p. 2, c. 2.

33. Public Law 97, sections 17, 34. For a complete text of the law, see *Washington Standard,* Oct. 25, 1862, p. 5.

34. Predictably, the Olympia newspaper expressed delight with Sparks's move while its Walla Walla competitor promised that Sparks and the collector would move the entire operation to Walla Walla—within the year. See *Washington Standard,* Dec. 27, 1862, p. 2, c. 1; *Walla Walla Statesman,* Dec. 13, 1862, p. 3, c. 1.

35. *Walla Walla Statesman,* Dec. 6, 1862, p. 3.

36. For example, see the notice from the assistant collector in Walla Walla, D. S. Baker, in the *Statesman,* Feb. 7, 1863, p. 3, c. 2.

37. *Puget Sound Herald,* March 12, 1863, p. 2, c. 1.

38. *Washington Standard,* Feb. 7, 1863, p. 4, c. 1.

39. The story was widely reported and reprinted frequently in late 1862 and early 1863; see, for example, *Washington Standard,* Dec. 6, 1862, p. 2, c. 2. In 1872, the administrator of Lincoln's estate applied for a refund of taxes "improperly assessed." Fox, p. 255.

40. "U.S. Income Tax," *Washington Standard,* April 25, 1863, p. 3, c. 6.

41. Goldsborough became involved in the misadventures of Victor Smith, collector of customs for Puget Sound. The collector delivered a letter to Treasury Secretary Chase on Smith's behalf when Smith was lobbying to move

the customs house to Port Angeles. "Major Goldsborough, brother of the commodore, hands you this and will, in marvelously few words, state why our port of entry should be at Port Angeles," Smith wrote to Chase on Dec. 4, 1861. "Lincoln-Time Letters," *Washington Historical Quarterly* 16 (October 1925), p. 271. Soon after Goldsborough's letter, government officials investigated allegations that Smith was involved in shady dealings, many of them involving port business. The Smith-Chase connection is reviewed in Roland L. DeLorme, "Westward the Bureaucrats: Government Officials on the Washington and Oregon Frontiers," *Arizona and the West* 22 (Autumn 1980), pp. 223–36; and the Smith story is told by Ivan Doig, "Puget Sound's War Within a War," *American West* 8 (May 1971), pp. 22–27.

42. *Washington Standard*, March 19, 1863; Nov. 21, 1863.

43. *Washington Standard*, Oct. 31, 1863, p. 2, c. 6. Goldsborough's activities after he left Olympia are unclear; by 1871, he was a "clerk in the Navy Department in Washington." See "Affidavit of Recommendation for Thornton McElroy from Elwood Evans," Sept. 13, 1871, U.S. State Department Territorial Records, Washington Series, reel 77, microfilm, University of Washington Libraries.

44. For formal announcement of the appointment, see *Executive Journal*, Jan. 21, 1864; for the local announcement, see *Washington Standard*, Oct. 31, 1863, p. 2, c. 6. Nearly a year later, Smith, on his way to Washington, D.C., to defend himself (and Secretary Chase) against corruption charges at the port, drowned off Crescent City, California. The *Oregonian*, Nov. 9, 1863, p. 2, c. 1, announced Goldsborough's resignation and Moore's appointment without comment. Apparently, Moore's appointment was popular locally. The *Oregonian* (Dec. 15, 1863, p. 2, c. 2) hailed his arrival, noting that there had been no opposition to his appointment. "Mr. Moore has brought his family out with him, intending to make Washington Territory his future home," the paper noted. Moore, born in New Jersey in 1826, was editor of the *Newark Morning Star* when he accepted the appointment of deputy collector of customs for Puget Sound in 1862. He served briefly in the Port Townsend customs office, returning to Washington, D.C., in 1863 to accept a post there. In 1870 he was the official census taker for Thurston and Lewis counties. From 1889 to 1894, he was Washington State Librarian. For a biography of Moore, see Edmond S. Meany, "Living Pioneers of Washington," *Seattle Post-Intelligencer*, Dec. 30, 1915.

45. "Removed at Last," *Oregonian*, Dec. 5, 1863, p. 2, c. 1. The Portland newspaper, strongly Republican in its editorials, noted after Smith's recall: "We never had much confidence in any of the charges against Mr. Smith." Jan. 13,

1864, p. 2, c. 2. Later local officials were tainted by scandal. A half-decade after Goldsborough's departure, Edward Salomon, the territorial governor, was removed when a Department of the Treasury auditor discovered a loss of $28,000 in the territorial account. The auditor later found that the governor had "loaned" the money to himself and two cronies for land speculation. See R. H. T. Leipold letter to Treasury Secretary George Boutwell, July 24, 1871, copy in U.S. State Department Territorial Records, Washington Series, Dec. 5, 1860–Dec. 4, 1872, microfilm 77, reel 2, University of Washington Libraries.

 46. *Washington Standard*, Jan. 23, 1864, p. 3, c. 3.

 47. Ibid., June 18, 1864, p. 3, c. 1.

 48. Charles M. Gates, ed., *Messages of the Governors of the Territory of Washington to the Legislative Assembly, 1854–1889* (Seattle: University of Washington Publications in the Social Sciences, 1940), p. 123.

 49. Congress increased the penalties for "willfully failing to render a list" for tax purposes to 25 percent of the tax; for "rendering a false or fraudulent tax list," the tax was doubled. See *Congressional Globe,* 38th Cong., 2d Sess., 1864, p. 480.

 50. Smith, pp. 66–67. There is no evidence that such lists were printed in Washington Territory, at least prior to 1869.

 51. *Washington Standard*, Jan. 21, 1865, p. 3.

 52. Ibid.

 53. Abernethy was and remained prominent in state politics. In 1871, the territorial governor, Edward Salomon, appointed two Washingtonians to the Centennial Commission, charged with attending the national anniversary in Philadelphia more than five years later. Alex Abernethy was one appointee. See Salomon resignation letter to Secretary of State Hamilton Fish, Dec. 7, 1871, in U.S. State Department Territorial Records, Washington Series, microfilm, reel 77, University of Washington Libraries.

 54. *Washington Standard*, Feb. 28, 1865, p. 3.

 55. Ibid., March 17, 1865, p. 3.

 56. For detailed figures, see Smith, appendices. See also C. K. Yearley, *The Money Machines: The Breakdown and Reform of Governmental and Party Finance in the North, 1860–1920* (Albany: State University of New York Press, 1970), pp. 228–29. Yearley concludes that the poorly drawn tax statutes left both officials and taxpayers confused, contributing to rampant evasion.

 57. Message of Governor Pickering to 13th Annual Session, Washington Legislative Assembly, Jan. 10, 1866, quoted in Gates, p. 125.

58. Most tax collection costs were fixed; thus it is apparent that taxes collected in Washington Territory in the first years of the income tax probably barely covered the cost of administration. Political opponents of "internal revenue" taxes apparently argued a valid point, and Pickering may have revealed the costs in an attempt to refute them.

59. Quoted in Gates, p. 126.

60. *Congressional Globe,* 39th Cong., 2d Sess., 1866, p. 1483, lists the Senate vote as 73–26 in favor of removing the progressive tax.

61. Message of Governor Marshall F. Moore to the 1st Biennial Session, Dec. 9, 1867, quoted in Gates, p. 137.

62. H. H. Bancroft, *History of Washington, Idaho and Montana,* Vol. 26 of *History of the Pacific States* (San Francisco: History Company, 1890), p. 275.

63. Seligman, p. 449.

64. Joseph Hill, "The Civil War Income Tax," *Quarterly Journal of Economics* 8 (July 1894), p. 437.

65. *Washington Standard,* May 22, 1869, p. 2, c. 3. The article concluded by giving an example and asking a question: "The idea that production and consumption are regulated by taxation is absurd. For instance, in 1866, when the tax upon distilled spirits was $2 per gallon, the government received less in the aggregate than in 1864, when the tax was only 20–60 cents a gallon. Yet does anyone suppose that ten times less spirits was consumed in 1866 than in 1864?"

66. Only 250,000 people out of the total U.S. population of 39.5 million paid the tax by 1870, less than 1 percent of the population. Ratner, p. 123. See also Jerome R. Hellerstein, *Taxes, Loopholes and Morals* (New York: McGraw-Hill, 1963), p. 8: "The Civil War income tax was distinctly a rich man's tax; it affected only one percent of the population." For Washington Territory, the 254 taxpayers accounted for almost the same ratio, or 1 percent of the total population of 23,955.

67. *Washington Standard,* July 3, 1869, p. 2. Unfortunately, the assessors' lists for Washington Territory before 1868 have been lost. Lists for most other states and territories are available on microfilm from the National Archives. The returns themselves, for the Civil War period and until the tax was ended, were destroyed by Congressional order in 1896. "Following the 1895 Supreme Court decision that declared income taxes unconstitutional, Congress approved a joint resolution requiring that income tax returns be destroyed. The Secretary of the Treasury appointed a committee to carry out the congressional instructions. Because assessors' lists contained information on business licenses and other taxes, they were retained." Fox, pp. 255–57.

68. *Washington Standard*, July 10, 1869, p. 2. The newspaper list, when compared with the official record in the Assessors' Records, held in the National Archives, Seattle Branch, displays numerous inconsistencies in names and amounts of income. All income tax payers, however, are included in the newspaper's two lists.

69. See Yearley, p. 228.

70. Meany biographical file, Special Collections, University of Washington Libraries.

71. Ibid. When plans for the new territorial capitol were being solicited, Giddings submitted a drawing. Apparently, it was not selected. See *Washington Council Journal, 1861–1863* (Olympia, n.p.), Appendix, p. liv.

72. Ibid.

73. O'Brien, born in Ireland in 1846, enlisted for wartime service in New York. Later, from 1876 to 1888, he served as clerk of the Washington Territorial Supreme Court. Meany biographical file, Special Collections, University of Washington Libraries. Singleton W. Beull served in the position in 1870 and also took the census the same year in Cowlitz County. Unfortunately, he did not include himself on his census roll. Another assistant assessor, Henry Winsor, apparently escaped enumeration by the census takers, unless he is the same Henry Winsor listed as a thirty-five-year-old Massachusetts-born farm laborer living in Jefferson County.

74. Statistical computations were made using the Cyber computer, ICE program, University of Washington Computer Center, Seattle, 1988.

75. Rebecca Howard opened her Pacific Restaurant in Olympia in the spring of 1860. *Pioneer-Democrat* (Olympia), May 18, 1860, p. 2, c. 5. She and her husband were coplaintiffs in a real estate lawsuit in 1867. See *Bermeister v. Howard*, 1 Wash. Terr. 208, for the facts in the quiet title action. By 1870, she was operating a "private boarding house." *Daily Pacific Tribune*, Dec. 26, 1870, p. 3, c. 1. Years later, Howard was identified as a business partner of Samuel D. Howe's, the 1870s tax assessor. The two held an exclusive license to sell Plummer Fruit Dryers in a four-county area. *Washington Standard*, April 20, 1878, p. 5, c. 2. Howard died in Olympia in July of 1881. *Washington Standard*, July 15, 1881, p. 2, c. 7.

76. Further, census materials themselves are unreliable. Census takers may miss people entirely or make errors in any of the numerous categories requiring discretion.

77. But see Ratner, p. 138, for farmers' resentments toward "capitalists" who benefited most from the tax changes.

78. The Maine congressional delegation included at least two strong proponents of income taxation. Also, two successive treasury secretaries were Maine born. U.S. Senator William Pitt Fessenden of Maine spoke forcefully for an income tax in 1861. He was the originator of the first proposed tax bill. Lincoln appointed him secretary of the treasury following Chase's resignation in June 1864. When Fessenden resigned to return to the Senate the next year, Lincoln appointed Hugh McCulloch, a native of Maine, to the post. After the war ended, Maine Congressman Frederick A. Pike proposed a 5 percent tax on income over $1,000, 10 percent on income over $5,000. His allies for progressive taxation included a number of Western congressmen, but a strong opponent in 1866 was Congressman James A. Garfield of Ohio, later a U.S. president. For Fessenden's championing of an income tax, see *Congressional Globe,* 37th Cong., 1st Sess., 1861, p. 255; for Pike's proposal, see *Congressional Globe,* 39th Cong., 1st Sess., 1866, p. 2783. Garfield's opposition is apparent from remarks noted in *Congressional Globe,* 39th Cong., 2d Sess., 1867, pp. 1482–83.

79. The ten Southern-born, longtime residents either were included on the 1860 Census of Washington Territory or listed the birthplaces of their children ten years or older as either Oregon or Washington Territory.

3 Civil War Income Tax in Oregon

1. The earthquake was reported in the *Oregonian* (Portland), Oct. 7, 1862, p. 2, c. 3.

2. At the time the Internal Revenue Act passed, Oregon still owed for its share of the direct tax assessed against every state by Congress in August 1861. The Oregon legislature passed a bill to pay the $29,869.09 bill in September 1862. See *Oregonian,* Sept. 24, 1862, p. 2, c. 1, and the *Oregon Statesman* (Salem), Oct. 27, 1862, p. 4, c. 2, for Oregon's payment of the assessment. The bill was introduced in the legislature on the former date. Reports of California's payment were noted in the *Oregon Statesman,* Oct. 13, 1862, p. 3, c. 2.

3. *Oregonian,* Aug. 22, 1862, p. 2, c. 1.

4. For a review of Oregon politics during the period, see Robert W. Johannsen, *Frontier Politics and the Sectional Conflict: The Pacific Northwest on the Eve of the Civil War* (Seattle: University of Washington Press, 1955); for settlement, Malcolm Clark, Jr., *Eden Seekers: The Settlement of Oregon, 1818–1862* (Boston: Houghton Mifflin, 1981); for geographical influences in the state's his-

tory, Samuel N. Dicken and Emily F. Dicken, *The Making of Oregon: A Study in Historical Geography* (Portland: Oregon Historical Society, 1979). For an excellent survey history of Oregon see Gordon B. Dodds, *Oregon: A Bicentennial History* (New York: Norton, 1977).

5. 8th Decennial Census, Oregon (1860).

6. The question of slavery in Oregon was submitted to the people during the vote to ratify the state constitution. Although the constitution was adopted by a vote of 7,195 to 3,215, the voters overwhelmingly repudiated slavery by a vote of 7,727 to 2,645. Oregon opposition to slavery, however, should not be viewed as favorable to blacks. During the same election, Oregonians, by a vote of 8,640 to 1,081, supported adding the following clause to the constitution: "No free Negro or mulatto not residing in this State at the time of the adoption of this Constitution shall come, reside, or be within this State, or hold any real estate, or make any contracts, or maintain any suit therein; and the legislative assembly shall provide by penal laws for the removal of public officers of all such Negroes or mulattos, and for their effectual exclusion from the State and for the punishment of such persons who shall bring them into the State or employ or harbor them." M. P. Deady, comp., *The Organic and Other General Laws of Oregon Together with the National Constitution and Other Public Acts and Statutes of the United States, 1845–1864* (Portland: H. L. Pittock, 1866), n.p.

7. Breckenridge-Lane electors polled 5,074 votes out of more than 14,000 cast. They were edged out by the Lincoln-Hamlin electors, who won the state's electoral votes by polling 5,270 votes. Stephen A. Douglas finished third in Oregon with 3,951. John Bell's Constitutional Union ticket garnered but 185 votes statewide. For the description of Breckenridge-Lane voters in Oregon as proslavery, see T. W. Davenport, "Slavery Question in Oregon," *Oregon Historical Journal* 8 (September 1908), p. 189. Lane, a native of North Carolina, had been appointed Oregon's first territorial governor in 1849. For a complete account of Lane's political machinations during the prewar years, see James E. Hendrickson, *Joe Lane of Oregon: Machine Politics and the Sectional Crisis, 1849–1861* (New Haven: Yale University Press, 1967). The 1860 election spelled the end of Lane's political career. Never again influential in the state's politics, he retired to his farm near Roseburg, where he died in 1881.

8. The four newspapers were the *Albany Inquirer*, the *Democratic Register* (Eugene), the *Evening Advertiser* (Portland), and the *Corvallis Union*. The former three were suppressed in October 1862. "The Traitorous Press in Oregon," *Oregonian*, Oct. 14, 1862, p. 2, c. 1. The Corvallis paper with the ironic name was

closed a month later. *Oregonian,* Nov. 18, 1862, p. 2, c. 1. The order from General Wright suppressing the "treasonous sheets" was printed in the *Oregonian,* Oct. 11, 1862, p. 2, c. 1. The *Democratic Register* is referred to as "Eugene's treasonable sheet" in the *Oregon Statesman,* Nov. 10, 1862, p. 2, c. 6.

9. For an example of a rare violent encounter between Union and Confederate sympathizers in Oregon, see the *Oregonian,* Nov. 13, 1862, report on a "shooting affray" in Marion County. For a general assessment of the strength of opinion on each side in the state, see Robert Treat Platt, "Oregon and Its Share in the Civil War," *Oregon Historical Quarterly* 5 (June 1903); for the military situation in Oregon, see Oregon Adjutant General's Report for 1864, in *Oregon Official State Documents* (various printers and places of publication, 1864–66), pp. 85–160. A copy of the document compilation is in Special Collections, University of Washington Libraries.

10. Gibbs, the first Republican elected governor of Oregon, represented Umpqua County in the 1852 legislature, moved to Multnomah County, and won election there to the legislature in 1860. Following his term as governor, Gibbs tried unsuccessfully for a U.S. Senate seat. In 1872 and 1873, he served as the U.S. Attorney for Oregon. He died in London in January 1887. The state's first Republican senator, Edward D. Baker, served as a colonel in the Union Army during the early days of the war. Baker's close friend, Abraham Lincoln, named a son for him (Edward Baker "Tad" Lincoln). Baker was killed in the Battle of Ball's Bluff in 1861.

11. The arguments were made by editors in several newspapers. The best examples are from the *Oregonian* and the *Oregon Statesman* (Salem) in almost every issue throughout the summer of the gubernatorial campaign.

12. *Oregon Statesman,* Sept. 15, 1862, p. 2, c. 4.

13. Ibid., p. 3, c. 3–4.

14. *Oregon Statesman,* Sept. 29, 1862, p. 1, c. 6.

15. *Oregonian,* Feb. 3, 1863, p. 2, c. 2.

16. *Oregonian,* Jan. 23, 1864, p. 2, c. 1, quoting the *Kittaning* (Pa.) *Monitor,* which had blamed high taxes on Lincoln and the Republicans. The Oregon paper refuted the charge as "political opportunism" on the part of "secessionist-minded" Lincoln opponents. McClellan did not run well in Oregon in 1864. Lincoln's electors piled up huge margins in Multnomah, Marion, Clackamas, and the smaller northwestern counties. McClellan won expected victories in Jackson and Josephine counties in the southern part of the state and in the two lightly populated eastern counties. *Oregonian,* Dec. 7, 1864, p. 2, c. 4. Democrats continued to use the increasingly unpopular tax as a campaign issue, but the

Republican response in Oregon seemed to nullify much of its effect. See, for example, the plank in the 1868 Democratic party platform calling for taxation "upon property instead of the industries." William D. Fenton, "Political History of Oregon," *Oregon Historical Quarterly* 3 (March 1902), p. 50.

17. *Oregonian*, Oct. 8, 1862, p. 3, c. 1.

18. The Confederate tax plan was reported in the *Oregonian* (Oct. 17, 1862, p. 3, c. 1), but not without editorial comparisons between the relatively light taxes of the Union and the harsh duties set by the Confederacy. Throughout the war, the *Oregonian* continued to call attention to the Confederacy's tax woes. For instance, see "The Rebel Tax," Sept. 24, 1863, p. 2, c. 3, in which the writer claimed, "No officers can be found who are willing to execute [the Southern tax]."

19. The "silver plate" decision (that the tax need not be paid only in gold) was published in the *Oregonian*, Nov. 18, 1862, p. 4. Other tax decisions appeared on the pages of the *Oregonian* throughout the Civil War period. For examples, see Nov. 15, 1862, p. 1; Feb. 2, 1863, p. 1; Feb. 17, 1863, p. 1, c. 6; Feb. 28, 1863, p. 4; June 10, 1863, p. 4, c. 2.

20. *Oregonian*, Oct. 29, 1862, p. 2. For an excellent overview of Deady's years as a federal judge, see Ralph James Mooney, "The Deady Years, 1859–1893," in Carolyn M. Buan, ed., *The First Duty: A History of the U.S. District Court for Oregon* (Portland: U.S. District Court of Oregon Historical Society, 1993).

21. *Oregon Statesman*, Sept. 8, 1862, p. 2, c. 3.

22. *Oregonian*, Aug. 22, 1862, p. 2, c. 1. Later in the war, the *Oregonian* reported on the New York millionaire A. T. Stewart's problems with the tax code. "[Stewart] is said to be so entirely in the dark as to the amount on which his income tax should be based that he has the credit for telling the Assessor his trouble, and adding that he couldn't tell whether his income for 1863 was more or less than two million, but he was willing to pay tax on that amount, as being in his opinion nearly enough correct for all practical purposes. So saying, he handed over his check for the neat little sum of $60,000! There is little room to doubt whether any other individual in the country will go into the income tax business this year with such a looseness as the New York Merchant Prince." *Oregonian*, Aug. 6, 1863, p. 2, c. 2.

23. The Internal Revenue force nationwide numbered 3,882 employees by March 1863. *Oregonian*, March 19, 1863, p. 4, c. 1. The two Oregon appointees were not named in initial reports. For instance, when the law was first announced, one Oregon editor simply noted: "We suppose Oregon will comprise one Collection District, for which a Collector and Assessor have already been

appealed by the President." "The National Tax Bill Law—Its Collecting Provisions," *Oregonian*, Aug. 22, 1862, p. 2, c. 1.

24. Frazar's biography is from *Portrait and Biographical Record of Portland and Vicinity* (Chicago: Chapman Publishers, 1903), pp. 856–58.

25. Ibid., p. 857.

26. His name appears in a listing of Republican delegates printed in *Republican League Register* (Portland: Register Publishing Co., 1896).

27. For Coe's military commission, see Report of the Adjutant General, 1864, in *Oregon State Documents* (Salem: H. L. Pittock, 1864), p. 150. The identities of the collector and assessor were not publicly reported in Oregon until September 10. "We learn that Thomas Frazar, Esq., has received a commission as assessor and will immediately enter upon his duties. L. W. Coe, Esq., Collector of Taxes we are informed gave bonds in the States." *Oregonian*, Sept. 10, 1862, p. 2, c. 2.

28. "United States Assessor's Notice," *Oregonian*, Oct. 7, 1862, p. 4. The notice ran virtually unchanged in successive issues until November 13.

29. *Oregonian*, Oct. 7, 1862, p. 4.

30. Word of the suspension was carried in the *Oregonian*, Feb. 18, 1863. The long-awaited arrival of $250,000 in stamps from San Francisco is mentioned in the *Oregonian*, March 10, 1863, p. 2, c. 3. The legal requirements apparently were not affected by the commissioner's suspension order. A newspaper article in mid-March reminded Oregon taxpayers that stamps had to be added to "all documents executed since Oct. 1 in order for them to be valid in court even though they had not been required to have stamps until March 1." *Oregonian*, March 13, 1863, p. 2, c. 2. The continuing shortage of stamps remained a problem for months.

31. *Oregonian*, April 25, 1863, p. 3, c. 1.

32. *Oregonian*, April 8, 1863, p. 2, c. 4. Frazar also released revenue rulings on lottery ticket proceeds and "other games of hazard," *Oregonian*, Dec. 15, 1863, p. 2, c. 3; perfumes, Dec. 7, 1863, p. 2, c. 2; and in a notice earlier in the year he clarified some confusion over the definition of what constituted a repair: "The manure purchased by farmers to maintain their lands in present productive condition will be allowed as repairs in estimating the income of farmers," June 6, 1863, p. 2, c. 1.

33. "To the Public," *Oregonian*, Nov. 13, 1862, p. 2, c. 4.

34. "Delinquents," *Oregonian*, Jan. 14, 1863, p. 3.

35. *Oregonian*, Oct. 7, 1862, p. 4.

36. The assessment records are in the Department of the Treasury, Bureau

of Internal Revenue, State of Oregon, RG 58, National Archives, Seattle Branch. Records for Oregon exist for the years 1867 through 1873.

37. *Oregonian*, Sept. 23, 1863, p. 2, c. 1. The totals by district were:

District 1 (Clatsop, Columbia, Tillamook)	1,718.80
District 2 (Yamhill and Washington)	5,365.22
District 3 (Multnomah)	45,644.73
District 4 (Clackamas and Marion)	14,367.19
District 5 (Polk and Benton)	3,976.15
District 6 (Lane and Linn)	6,557.60
District 7 (Douglas and Umpqua)	4,262.11
District 8 (Coos and Curry)	550.00
District 9 (Josephine and Jackson)	9,180.55
District 10 (Wasco, Umatilla, Baker)	17,220.58
Total	$108,842.93

38. In 1867, the total for Oregon was $133,402.69. Multnomah's contribution was up to 55 percent of the total ($73,463.25). The 1868 figure of $108,823.75 included $62,596.95 from Multnomah County, 58 percent of the total. In 1869, the total was $108,540.01 with 63 percent of that amount, $68,710.36, coming from Multnomah County. The figures were calculated using the totals listed in the Assessment Records for Oregon, RG 58, National Archives, Seattle Branch.

39. 9th Decennial Census, Oregon (1870). The population of Washington Territory was one-third of Oregon's, but the tax revenues raised there were significantly lower per capita.

40. All calculations for this section are derived from the 1870 census for the state of Oregon, microfilm, and the Assessment Records for the State of Oregon, 1867–1873, Department of the Treasury, Bureau of Internal Revenue, RG 58, both in National Archives, Seattle Branch.

41. The Department of State administered the territories until the 1850s, when the job went to the Department of the Interior.

42. Some authors now dispute this commonly held view of presidential appointments to territorial posts. See, for example, Kermit L. Hall, *Politics of Justice: Lower Federal Judicial Selection and the Second Party System, 1829–1861* (Lincoln: University of Nebraska Press, 1979); Gordon M. Bakken, *The Development of Law on the Rocky Mountain Frontier: Civil Law and Society, 1850–1912* (Westport, Conn.: Greenwood Press, 1983); and John D. W. Guice, *The Rocky Mountain Bench* (New Haven: Yale University Press, 1972).

4 Consensus I: Federal Income Tax and Washington's Reaction, 1894

1. One of the best sources of information on the condition of Washington agriculture and the shape of Populist policies is the *People's Advocate*, a weekly, four-page newspaper published in Chehalis in the early and mid 1890s. The first issue was published October 7, 1892, as the "official paper of the Farmers' Alliance and Industrial Union of Lewis County," according to the masthead. Microfilmed copies are held in the collections of the University of Washington Libraries. For some insights into Populism in Washington, see chapter 3 of David B. Griffiths, *Populism in the Western United States, 1890–1900* (Lewiston, N.Y.: Edwin Mellen, 1992); and Thomas W. Riddle, *The Old Radicalism: John R. Rogers and the Populist Movement in Washington* (New York: Garland, 1991).

2. In 1890, the state and its subdivisions collected a total of $6,007,000 in taxes. Of that amount, $4,802,166 was raised from property taxes. The next highest amount, $416,093, came from bridge and road assessments. See *Compendium of the Census for Washington* (Washington, D.C.: GPO, 1890), pt. 3, pp. 972–73; and pt. 2, p. 448.

3. For territorial conditions in Washington Territory, few recent works match the color of H. H. Bancroft, *Washington, Idaho and Montana*, Vol. 26 of *History of the Pacific States* (San Francisco: History Company, 1890). Comprehensive histories exclusively about Washington for adult readers are scarce, but see Norman H. Clark, *Washington: A Bicentennial History* (New York: W. W. Norton, 1976). Regional rivalries, mostly between the areas east and west of the Cascades, remained politically divisive. See Keith A. Murray, "The Movement for Statehood in Washington," *Pacific Northwest Quarterly* 32 (October 1941), pp. 349–84, for an account of the continuing attempts to incorporate northern Idaho into Washington or join Eastern Washington to northern Idaho, creating a separate state. One motive of the proponents was to provide a greater population base from which Walla Walla could draw in electoral contests against the Puget Sound area.

4. *Tacoma Daily Ledger*, Aug. 2, 1889, p. 3.

5. For a description of the constitutional debates, see John D. Hicks, *The Constitutions of the Northwest States* (Lincoln: University of Nebraska Studies, 23 [January–April 1923]), pp. 5–152.

6. Harriet Ann Crawford, *The Washington State Grange, 1889–1924: A*

Romance of Democracy (Portland: Binfords and Mort, 1940), p. 13. See also Gus Norwood, *Washington Grangers Celebrate a Century* (Seattle: Washington State Grange, 1988).

7. For examples of the tone of their rhetoric in the early 1890s, see the Farmers' Alliance newspaper in Lewis County, the *People's Advocate* (Chehalis); for opinion on the organization's militancy, see Gordon B. Ridgeway, "Populism in Washington," *Pacific Northwest Quarterly* 39 (October 1948), pp. 292–93. For the influence of the Southern Farmers' Alliance in the West, see Robert C. McMath, Jr., *Populist Vanguard: A History of the Southern Farmers' Alliance* (Chapel Hill: University of North Carolina Press, 1975), pp. 110–57. The Farmers' Alliance should not be confused with the Farmers' Union, an organization that organized for the first time in Washington at Waitsburg in 1907. See "The Farmers' Union: Washington-Idaho Division—History, Aims and Purposes" (undated pamphlet), Special Collections, University of Washington Libraries. For the Grange movement nationally, see Dennis Sven Norden, *Rich Harvest: A History of the Grange, 1867–1900* (Jackson: University Press of Mississippi, 1974); and Thomas A. Woods, *Knights of the Plow: Oliver H. Kelley and the Origins of the Grange in Republican Ideology* (Ames: Iowa State University Press, 1991).

8. Ridgeway, p. 285. Ridgeway asserts that farmers' complaints "were based on experience and opinions acquired prior to their residence in Washington." Such a view merely points out that less-established farmers may have faced greater economic difficulties in Washington because land prices and costs of agricultural implements, already owned by established farmers, continued to increase while the prices of agricultural products stayed relatively flat or declined in real terms. See also Thomas W. Riddle, "Populism in the Palouse: Old Ideals and New Realities," *Pacific Northwest Quarterly* 65 (1974), pp. 97–109.

9. An "obsession with the money question" was one of five dominant concepts in Populism, according to the historian Richard Hofstadter in *Age of Reform* (New York: Knopf, 1954).

10. For a comprehensive discussion of the complicated issue of tariffs, from which much of the previous two paragraphs were drawn, see Tom E. Terrill, *The Tariff, Politics, and American Foreign Policy, 1874–1901* (Westport, Conn.: Greenwood Press, 1973), pp. 159–83 on the McKinley tariff.

11. Norman H. Clark, *Mill Town: A Social History of Everett, Washington* (Seattle: University of Washington Press, 1970), for the bank closures, p. 29; for the wage decline, p. 34. The panic was particularly devastating to Everett's fortunes because the new town was closely linked with Eastern capital and dominated by one company. The same bad fortunes befell towns established near

railroads when those particular companies, weakened by the economic distress, laid off workers or fell into receivership.

12. Ridgeway, p. 286. For Coxey's army, see Carlos A. Schwantes, *Coxey's Army: An American Odyssey* (Lincoln: University of Nebraska Press, 1985), and Donald L. McMurray, *Coxey's Army: A Study of the Industrial Army Movement of 1894* (New York: AMS Press, 1970); for the Pullman strike, see William H. Carwardine, *The Pullman Strike* (Chicago: Illinois Labor History Society, 1970), and Almont Lindsey, *The Pullman Strike: The Story of a Unique Experiment and a Great Labor Upheavel* (Chicago: University of Chicago Press, 1964.)

13. *Biographical Directory of the American Congress, 1774–1971* (Washington: GPO, 1971); Washington Biographical File, Special Collections, University of Washington Libraries; Dumas Malone, ed., *Dictionary of American Biography*, Vol. 10 (New York: Scribner's, 1936), pp. 338–39; *Seattle Post-Intelligencer*, Nov. 11, 1912 (obituary). Wilson served a term in the U.S. Senate and remained a power in Washington state and Republican party politics. In 1899, with a loan from his close friend, the railroad magnate James J. Hill, Wilson bought controlling interest of the *Seattle Post-Intelligencer*. He was publisher at the time of his death in 1912.

14. *Biographical Directory of the American Congress*, p. 873; Washington Biographical File, Special Collections, University of Washington Libraries.

15. C. B. Bagley, *History of Seattle from Earliest Settlement to the Present Time*, Vol. 3 (Seattle, 1916); Washington Biographical File; *Dictionary of American Biography*, Vol. 9, pp. 491–92; *Biographical Directory of the American Congress*, p. 1740.

16. Allen would have voted with the Stalwarts, too, if his prior record is any indication. An Indiana native and Civil War veteran, Allen graduated from the University of Michigan Law School. He moved to Washington in 1870 to accept the presidential appointment as U.S. Attorney for the Territory. He moved to Walla Walla in 1881. Washington Biographical File; *Biographical Directory of the American Congress*, p. 506.

17. "The People's Party Platform of 1892," in George B. Tindall, ed., *A Populist Reader* (New York: Harper and Row, 1966), p. 91.

18. Allan Nevins, *Grover Cleveland: A Study in Courage* (New York: Dodd, Mead, 1944), p. 667.

19. William Jennings Bryan, a young congressman from Nebraska, gained his first national acclaim from service on the committee during the tariff and income tax debates. Louis W. Koenig, *Bryan: A Political Biography of William Jennings Bryan* (New York: G. P. Putnam's Sons, 1971), p. 93. For one Washington

editor's attitudes about regional conflict during the period, see the *Pullman Tribune*, April 20, 1895, p. 2: "The West is anxious to see the East and the South prosper, as it is to see itself prosper. The West is not selfish or sectional; but it does feel that its interests would be a great deal safer with a Western man at the head of the government, and its purpose now, judging from the 'sign of the times' is to have such a man after the next general election. New York has dominated the parties (and the country, too, for that matter) quite long enough."

20. For details about the tariff, see Festus P. Summers, *William L. Wilson and Tariff Reform* (New Brunswick: Rutgers University Press, 1953).

21. For the roll call vote on the entire tariff bill, see *Congressional Record*, 53rd Cong., 2d Sess., 26 (part 7), Feb. 1, 1894, pp. 1796–97. For a description of the political intrigues surrounding the tariff bill, see Nevins, pp. 572–83.

22. *Congressional Record*, 53rd Cong., 2d Sess., 26 (part 7), Feb. 1, 1894, p. 1795. For Senate passage, *Congressional Record*, 53rd Cong., 2d Sess., 26 (part 7), July 3, 1894, p. 7136. The first conference committee failed to agree on the bill and it went back and forth to both houses until the House finally yielded in August. See Summers for the bill's circuitous journey through Congress.

23. Ibid., p. 7135. Hill won election as lieutenant governor of New York in 1885 and succeeded to the governor's chair when Grover Cleveland became president. He was elected to the Senate in 1892. *Biographical Directory of the American Congress*, p. 1117. Hill made one more attempt to eliminate the income tax provision on August 14, but his amendment failed and the bill finally went to the president. Cleveland, badly bruised by the long Congressional deadlock, let the bill become law without his signature. See Nevins, p. 586.

24. "The Tariff Bill," *Seattle Times*, Aug. 14, 1894, p. 2, c. 1; *Tacoma Daily Ledger*, Aug. 14, 1894, p. 1.

25. Amasa J. Parker, "Income Tax of 1894—Its Provisions and Constitutionality," *Albany Law Journal* 50 (Dec. 29, 1894), p. 416.

26. Robert Sewell, "The Income Tax: Is It Constitutional?" *American Law Review* 28 (November–December 1894), p. 808.

27. *People's Advocate* (Chehalis), Dec. 22, 1893, p. 4.

28. *Springer v. United States*, 102 U.S. 586 (1881). The case began in June 1866, in Springfield, Illinois, when William M. Springer refused to pay an income tax of $4,799 assessed on his income of $50,798. The government seized some property he owned to pay the claim, and he sued for restitution, claiming that the tax was unconstitutional because it violated Article I, Section 9 of the Constitution. The decision gained little notice nationally at the time it was

decided because the Civil War tax on which the court was ruling had been repealed nearly a decade earlier.

29. Ibid., p. 599.

30. "The Income Tax: Returns Received Surpass Expectations of the Revenue Department," *Tacoma Weekly News*, April 5, 1895, p. 2.

31. "Returns All In: Income Tax Collector Will Now Have a Breathing Spell," *Seattle Times*, April 16, 1895, p. 1.

32. *Compendium, 1890*, part 1, p. 3.

33. *People's Advocate*, March 29, 1895, p. 2.

34. The three are noted but not named in *Tacoma Weekly News*, April 5, 1895, p. 2. No tax returns for 1895 survive. The only evidence of compliance, numbers of returns, and their contents comes from contemporary newspaper reports. Congress passed a joint resolution in 1896 ordering destruction of all income tax returns in the aftermath of the Pollock decision. Cynthia G. Fox, "Income Tax Records of the Civil War Years," *Prologue* (Winter 1986), pp. 255–57.

35. *Seattle Times*, April 16, 1895, p. 1.

36. Lawrence M. Friedman, *A History of American Law* (New York: Simon and Schuster, 1985), p. 567. Friedman's comment related to the decision by the United States Supreme Court in the Pollock case. Regardless of the decision's weak history and logic, he notes that its "instincts were rather shrewd."

37. *People's Advocate*, Feb. 2, 1894, p. 4.

38. Robert T. Swaine, *The Cravath Firm and Its Predecessors*, Vol. 1 (New York: privately printed, 1946), pp. 518–36, describes in detail how the case was litigated.

39. Article I, Sec. 9.

40. Also listed in the U.S. Supreme Court decision as counsel arguing the case were Clarence A. Seward, Benjamin H. Bristow, David Willcox, and Charles Steele. *Pollock* v. *Farmers' Loan and Trust Co.* (rehearing), 158 U.S. 601 (1895), at 602.

41. See the front-page stories during March of 1895 in the *Seattle Times* for the dates of the oral arguments and for an example of how even newspapers distant from the capital played the story.

42. *People's Advocate*, April 5, 1895, p. 2.

43. In the original case, Fuller's opinion is pp. 553–86; Field's concurring opinion, pp. 586–608; White's dissenting opinion (in which Harlan concurred), pp. 608–52; Harlan's further dissenting opinion, pp. 652–54. In the rehearing decision, Harlan's dissent, pp. 638–86; Brown's dissent, pp. 686–95; Jackson's dissent, pp. 696–706; and White's dissent, pp. 706–15.

44. Pollock, p. 671. Ironically, former Treasury Secretary Hugh McCulloch, who headed the department during the collection of the Civil War income tax, died on May 24, 1895, four days after the Pollock decision was announced.

45. *People's Advocate*, May 31, 1895, p. 2.

46. Sylvester Pennoyer, "The Income Tax Decision and the Power of the Supreme Court to Nullify Acts of Congress," *American Law Review* 29 (July-August 1895), p. 558.

5 Consensus II: Washington Ratifies the Federal Income Tax, 1911

1. William T. Kerr, Jr., "The Progressives of Washington, 1910–1912," *Pacific Northwest Quarterly* 55 (January 1964), pp. 16–27. See also Robert D. Saltvig, "The Progressive Movement in Washington," Ph.D. dissertation, University of Washington, 1966, for a thorough review of Progressive legislation and politics.

2. For an overview of the ratification process in each state, see John D. Buenker, *The Income Tax and the Progressive Era* (New York: Garland Publishing, 1985). See p. 181 for his brief description of the Washington legislature's ratification.

3. There were but four Democrats in the Washington state senate: D. S. Troy, a Jefferson County farmer; Henry M. White, a Bellingham lawyer; Peder Jensen, a Tacoma pharmacist; and J. E. Chappell, a Goldendale merchant. *Senate Journal of the 12th Legislature* (Olympia: E. L. Boardman, Public Printer, 1911), pp. 1096–97. Of the 97 house members, just 12 were Democrats. Close examinations of voting records divide the Republicans between conservatives ("standpatters") and progressives ("insurgents").

4. Nationally, the Democratic party included a call for the tax in its 1908 party platform. To some extent it was a remnant of earlier Bryan-Populist crusades. By most measures, the issue was losing its partisan cachet. Two successive Republican presidents, Theodore Roosevelt and William Howard Taft, endorsed federal income taxation. Except for a few conservative holdouts, a national consensus on the issue was clear after the 1908 election. For a discussion of the evolving support nationally, even in much of the Northeast, see Buenker, pp. 47–56; and C. K. Yearley, *The Money Machines: The Breakdown and Reform of Governmental and Party Finance, 1860–1920* (Albany: State University of New York Press, 1970), pp. 193–225.

5. *Senate Journal* (1911), pp. 52–53.

6. Bryan's biography is from Ryan's *Washington Legislative Manual*, 1911, p. 70; the *Senate Journal* (1911), p. 1096; Washington Biography File, Special Collections, University of Washington Libraries. His ownership of the Bremerton paper is noted in an article about its sale in "Pro Bono Publico," *Bremerton Searchlight*, Jan. 27, 1911, p. 4, and "Unified Press Has Many Benefits," same date, p. 1. There is no evidence that he was related to the "Boy Orator of the Platte," William Jennings Bryan.

7. *Senate Journal* (1911), pp. 52–53, for first reading; second reading, p. 126. For the exact wording of the ratification measure, see SJR No. 1, *Washington Session Laws* (1911), p. 653.

8. *Senate Journal*, p. 229. The absent members were Senators Allen, Bowen, Hall, Huxtable, and Metcalf. Hall and Huxtable were members of the committee that had reported out the bill.

9. For the characterization of the five as "standpatters," see "State Senate Wants No Halt to Alaska Land Grab," *Spokane Spokesman-Review*, Jan. 26, 1911, p. 2; and their recorded votes on "progressive" measures introduced during the session.

10.. Personal data on the five was obtained from the brief biographies in *Washington Legislative Manual*, the *Senate Journal* listing, and various newspaper clippings held in the Washington Biographies, Special Collections, University of Washington Libraries.

11. *Washington Legislative Manual*, p. 79.

12. Ibid., p. 74.

13. Ibid., p. 64.

14. Ibid., p. 74.

15. Ibid., p. 78.

16. *Seattle Times*, Jan. 11, 1911, p. 1. For an example of other activities deemed more interesting than the tax ratification, see, "Piper for Suffragists Turned Down in Senate," *Seattle Times*, Jan. 11, 1911, p. 1.

17. For receipt from senate, see *House Journal of the 12th Legislature* (Olympia: E. L. Boardman, Public Printer, 1911), p. 154; first reading, p. 158; committee action, p. 158; second reading, p. 160; third reading, p. 160; signed by speaker, p. 221. Daniel Landon was the only representative still serving in the 1930s when the legislature passed state income tax legislation.

18. *House Journal* (1911), p. 160. House members listed as "absent or not voting" were: William M. Beach (Mason), W. P. Christensen (Skamania), George E. Dickson and J. C. Hubbell (Kittitas), E. L. Farnsworth (Lincoln), Edward W. French (Clark), J. A. Ghent, Fred W. Hastings, and George B. Webster

(King), W. J. Kelly (Garfield), J. E. Leonard (Lewis), L. D. McArdle (Jefferson), D. N. McMillan (Whatcom), J. G. Megler (Wahkiakum), and J. O. Rudene (Skagit). Farnsworth, Megler, Rudene, and Ghent were listed as absent on earlier and subsequent votes. Ghent was a progressive who was on record supporting the income tax ratification. In fact, he was a cosponsor of the ratification resolution. The positions of the others were not revealed in the record and can be only assumed by reference to key votes dividing the "standpatters" from the "progressives."

19. *Seattle Times*, Jan. 21, 1911, p. 6.

20. For instance, see *Seattle Times*, Jan. 22, 1911, p. 6: "Oregon and Ohio are the latest of the states to fall in line for the income tax amendment to the Constitution of the United States. President Taft should begin to feel better about it, especially since Gov. Robert H. Bass of New Hampshire, has sent a message to the Legislature advising ratification." The *Times* noted in a small story: "Montana Senate Favors Income Tax Amendment" (Jan. 28, 1911, p. 3).

21. Four Seattle papers were especially involved in the contest. Two of the dailies took strong positions on the recall. The *Seattle Times* printed glowing editorials favorable to Gill, while the *Seattle Star* vehemently opposed him. The *Seattle Argus* and *Post-Intelligencer* were a bit less hysterical in their coverage. See also the Joe Smith Papers and the Erastus Brainerd Papers, University of Washington Libraries. Smith was an editorial writer for the *Seattle Star* who took a leading role in pursuing the Gill case.

22. Examination of issues of five urban dailies shows that no stories appeared that focused exclusively on the income tax amendment. There were infrequent mentions in general legislative reports. No editorial that took a position on the issue was found for the two-month period. The papers examined were the *Seattle Times, Seattle Post-Intelligencer, Seattle Star, Tacoma News Tribune,* and *Spokane Spokesman-Review*. Outside Seattle, the editorial pages commented on what news observers viewed as the biggest battle in the legislature— the fight between "wets" and "drys" over whether to prohibit local-option liquor legislation during the session. The wets prevailed. News ink flowed reporting the story almost as readily as liquor poured in certain locales. For examples of the attention given the liquor question, see "State Capital News," a weekly column in the *Bremerton Searchlight*, Jan. 6–Feb. 9, 1911; and "News of the State Capitol," a weekly report in the *Anacortes American* for the same period.

23. *Spokane Spokesman-Review*, Jan. 12, 1911, p. 2.

24. *Spokesman-Review*, Jan. 25, 1911, p. 2.

25. *Bremerton Searchlight*, "Legislature Makes Progress," Jan. 20, 1911, p. 1.

26. *Searchlight*, Feb. 10, 1911, p. 3.

27. *Anacortes American*, "News of the State Capitol," Jan. 26, 1911, p. 7.

28. For the characterization, see Buenker, p. 181. *Searchlight*, March 17, 1911, p. 1. Incidentally, in the middle of the legislative session, Bryan sold his interest in the *Navy Yard American* newspaper to the publisher of the *Searchlight*. The senator had started the competing weekly Sept. 30, 1909, after a dispute with the former *Searchlight* owner editor. See "Pro Bono Publico," p. 4, and "Unified Press Has Many Big Benefits," *Searchlight*, Jan. 27, 1911, p. 1.

29. The wording is cited in *Anacortes American*, "Anacortes-La Connor High Schools Will Debate," Jan. 12, 1911, p. 1.

30. *Anacortes American*, "Anacortes Loses to Kirkland in Debate," March 2, 1911, p. 1.

31. *Anacortes American*, "Preparedness—A Matter of Duty," Jan. 5, 1911, p. 4.

6 The Background for Tax Reform, 1914–1931

1. Manuscript, "Your Income," Folder 1/18, Roy J. Kinnear Papers, University of Washington Libraries.

2. For a description of the debates over tax policy as a method of controlling economic concentration and the Roosevelt administration, see Ellis Hawley, *The New Deal and the Problem of Monopoly* (Princeton: Princeton University Press, 1966), pp. 344–59.

3. State Board of Tax Commissioners, *Second Biennial Report*, p. 15. The board was created in 1905. A copy of the pamphlet, published in Tacoma by the State Federation of Taxpayers' Associations in 1916, is held in Special Collections, University of Washington Libraries.

4. Vanderveer Custis, *The State Tax System of Washington* (Seattle: privately printed, 1916), pp. 17, 129. The University of Washington sponsored a State Tax Conference in May 1914. Following three days of papers and discussions, conference participants considered formal endorsement of a taxation program. Custis demurred. "This is a conference and not a convention," he said, "and for that reason anything in the way of formal resolutions would hardly be in order." See *Taxation in Washington: Papers and Discussions of the State Tax Conference at the University of Washington, May 27, 28, 29, 1914* (Seattle: University of Washington, 1914), p. 7.

5. Bureau of Internal Revenue, *Statistics of Income* (Washington, D.C.: GPO, 1918), p. 77.

6. Bureau of Internal Revenue, *Statistics of Income* (Washington, D.C.: GPO. 1919), p. 97.

7. Ibid. (1920), p. 111; *14th Decennial Census* (Washington, D.C.: GPO, 1920).

8. Several papers presented at the 1914 tax conference on the University of Washington campus predicted future problems along these lines. See, for instance, J. E. Frost, "Separation of Sources of State and Local Taxation," in *Taxation in Washington: Papers and Discussions,* pp. 240–45.

9. See C. R. Jackson, "The State Board of Tax Commissioners," in *Taxation in Washington: Papers and Discussions,* pp. 246–52. The assessors, in some counties, were subjected to strong pressures and according to some observers, there was "a large amount of evasion under the . . . system." See M. M. Anderson to Warren Magnuson, Jan. 25, 1933, Incoming Letters, AB, Folder 1/3 (1933), Warren Magnuson Papers, University of Washington Libraries.

10. For the strengthening of the commission's powers, see *Washington Session Laws, 1917,* chap. 54, pp. 210–11; for abolition of the commission, see *Session Laws, 1922,* chap. 7, sec. 135; sec. 53 for creation of the new director's post.

11. *Report of the State of Washington Tax Investigation Committee* (Olympia: Lamborn, Public Printer, 1922), pp. 3–4. Eckstein was a prominent civic leader who served as president of the Schwabacher Brothers and Company wholesale grocery in downtown Seattle. *Seattle City Directory* (Seattle: R. L. Polk, 1922), pp. 615, 1449. Harlin was listed in the 1922 city directory as a miner, but his position was clarified in the next edition as a manager of Bucoda Coal Sales Company in downtown Seattle. *Seattle City Directory, 1922,* p. 793; 1923, pp. 428, 734. Elliott owned a Tacoma real estate firm. *Tacoma City Directory* (Tacoma: R. L. Polk, 1931), pp. 117, 249. Oakley was a Tacoma lawyer. *Tacoma City Directory, 1931,* p. 565. Twohy was board chairman of Old National Bank and Union Trust Company of Spokane. *Spokane City Directory* (Spokane: R. L. Polk, 1928), p. 796. Robertson published a daily newspaper in Yakima; Polson was a lumberman; and Penrose was a college president. McGregor's occupation is not known.

12. *Report of the State of Washington Tax Investigation Committee,* p. 4; for recommendations, "Summary of Recommendations and Suggestions," pp. 6–7; "Tax on Fuel Oils," pp. 60–61.

13. Ibid., "The State Income Tax," pp. 63–67.

14. Ibid., p. 67.

15. Ibid., pp. 65, 66–67.

16. Ibid., "General Sales Tax," p. 67.

17. "Average Rates of Levies in Mills," Table 21, *First Biennial Report of the Tax Commission of the State of Washington* (Olympia: Jay Thomas, Public Printer, 1926), pp. 53–54. See "State Tax System Will Be Changed," in Scrapbook, Box 1, Kinnear Papers, University of Washington Libraries.

18. Voters' Information League (Seattle), *Bulletin* 24, Dec. 1, 1922, in scrapbook, Box 1, Kinnear Papers, University of Washington Libraries. Kinnear was an outspoken foe of labor unions who served as president of the Associated Industries of Seattle in 1924. Included in his collection are reports to the Associated Industries made by undercover agents who had infiltrated labor organizations in 1920.

19. John F. Sly, *Tax Developments in Washington State—How We Got There* (Olympia: Washington State Research Council Pocket Report Series 1, 1956). See also Alfred Harsch, "The Washington Tax System—How it Grew," *Washington Law Review* 39 (January 1965), pp. 944–75.

20. *Tax Facts* 1 (January 1924), p. 1. The organization claimed the major credit for the defeat of the bond initiative, but numerous other groups also opposed the measure. For the organization's growth, see "Annual Meeting of the Board of Trustees of the State Federation of Taxpayers' Associations," *Tax Facts* 1 (December 1924), p. 2. Other officers were N. C. Richards of Yakima, second vice-president; and C. E. Arney, Jr., of Seattle, secretary-treasurer. *Tax Facts* 1 (January 1924), p. 1. Gose, born in 1860, was appointed to the court in 1909 and gained election to the post the next year. *Ryan's Washington Legislative Manual* (Tacoma: Commercial Bindery, 1911), p. 31. Livengood, a Spokane attorney and merchant, presented a paper at the 1914 tax conference at the University of Washington on "A Budget System for the State of Washington." *Taxation in Washington: Papers and Discussions*, pp. 253–61. He appeared at that meeting as a representative of the Spokane Chamber of Commerce.

21. *Tax Facts* 1 (April 1924), p. 4.

22. *Tax Facts* 1 (September 1924), p. 1. Claudius O. Johnson claims farmers supported the 40-mill limitation after the "legislature was unsuccessful in adopting an income tax in 1924." Claudius O. Johnson, "Adoption of the Initiative and Referendum in Washington," *Pacific Northwest Quarterly* 36 (January 1945), p. 43. For support of Johnson's view, see remarks by the Grange Master in *Grange Proceedings* 36 (1924), p. 51.

23. Goss, born in Rochester, N.Y., in 1882, served in the top Grange post until 1933, when he was appointed by President Franklin Roosevelt to the Federal

Credit Administration, where he became known as the "Federal Land Bank commissioner." For a short biography of Goss, see Gus Norwood, *Washington Grangers Celebrate a Century* (Seattle: Washington State Grange, 1988), pp. 95–96.

24. Lewis remained Grange secretary until his death in March 1937. Also important in Grange activities was Fred J. Chamberlain of Puyallup. Born in New York in 1857, Chamberlain once owned and edited an Iowa newspaper before coming to Puyallup in 1900 to operate a berry and fruit farm. He organized the Puyallup Grange in 1910 and took an active role in the state organization's legislative lobbying during the 1920s and 1930s. See Norwood, p. 106.

25. For a description of Hartley's troubled administration, see Albert Francis Gunns, "Roland Hill Hartley and the Politics of Washington State," M.A. thesis, University of Washington, 1963. For an example of the changing alliances of "anti-Hartley" and "pro-Hartley" legislators, see "Senate Downs Hartley to Carry Pension Bill," *Olympic Tribune* (Port Angeles), Jan. 28, 1927, p. 1.

26. The story is told in Charles M. Gates, *The First Century at the University of Washington* (Seattle: University of Washington Press, 1961), pp. 166–70. Also of interest are the newspaper articles collected in nine scrapbooks in 1936 and held in Special Collections, University of Washington Libraries. The scrapbooks are titled "Roland Hill Hartley Recall, 1926," but they contain other articles, including numerous news stories about the tax issues of the day.

27. *Session Laws,* 1925, chap. 130.

28. For confirmation of the three new commissioners, see *Senate Journal,* Special Session, 1925, p. 48.

29. "McInnes is Named on Tax Commission," *Olympic Tribune,* April 3, 1925, p. 1.

30. Gates, p. 170. See "Hartley Recall Will Probably Be Dropped," *Olympic Tribune,* Feb. 11, 1927, p. 2.

31. For the depiction of the spoils system, see "Suzzallo's Removal Calamity," *Wenatchee Daily World,* Nov. 8, 1926, p. 1. For the story about Hartley misappropriating funds, see clippings from various newspapers in "Roland Hartley Recall" scrapbooks.

32. For a complete list of increases by county, see *Camas Post,* Nov. 26, 1926, p. 1. The same issue contains a cartoon showing a taxpayer confused by "Hartley's tax increase" on the one hand and, on the other, a sign telling about President Calvin Coolidge's plan to decrease the income tax by 10–12 percent.

33. "Increase in Taxes Arouses Protests," *Centralia Chronicle,* Dec. 14, 1926.

34. "Recall Costs Could Be $300,000," *Everett News,* Nov. 5, 1926, p. 1.

35. "Chamber Warned Tax Gains Are Too Great," *Seattle Times,* Dec. 8,

1925, p. 14. Other guest speakers included William Bailey, former president of the National Tax Association, and Dr. Henry Suzzallo, recently ousted president of the University of Washington.

36. For the bill's introduction, see *Senate Journal*, Special Session, 1925, p. 191; committee report, p. 318. For a short description of the bill, see *Seattle Times*, Dec. 8, 1925, p. 18.

37. *House Journal*, Feb. 3, 1927; *Senate Journal*, Feb. 18, 1927.

38. "Arguments for the Constitutional Amendment," *Grange News*, Aug. 20, 1928, p. 1.

39. See, for example, the pre-election issues of the *Washington Farmer* published in October 1928. Attention to the relationship between the Cowles papers and the "interests" was raised by the *Grange News*, Dec. 20, 1928. It called the *Washington Farmer* a "so-called farm paper" that was a "wolf in sheep's clothing."

40. For an example, see the editorial page of the *Seattle Times*, Nov. 4, 1928.

41. *Grange News*, June 5, 1928, p. 1.

42. "The Business Chronicle," *Grange News*, Nov. 5, 1928, p. 4; and March 5, 1929, p. 1. The newspaper attacked the Cowles publications and Robertson's Yakima newspapers in an article on Nov. 20, 1928, p. 10, and repeated the charges in the issue of March 5, 1929.

43. *Grange News*, March 5, 1929, p. 1.

44. "Tax Dodgers Defeat Tax Amendment," *Grange News*, Nov. 20, 1928, p. 10.

45. "Senate Roster" in *Senate Journal*, 1931, p. 671. For Whitman County's Grange population, see *Roster of the Washington State Grange*, various years, Special Collections, University of Washington Libraries

46. For a review of the house maneuvers, see A. S. Goss in "Hasty Review of Work of 1929 Legislature," *Grange News,* April 5, 1929, p. 3.

47. "Rep. Lindsay Claims Tax Relief Measure Ignored," *Olympic Tribune,* March 29, 1929, p. 1.

48. *Grange News*, Dec. 5, 1928, p. 13.

49. Heifner introduced Senate Bill 66 on Jan. 17, 1929. *Senate Journal,* 1929, p. 61. For the committee report to the full senate, see p. 283.

50. Raymond R. Frazier, "The Washington State Excise Tax of 1929," pamphlet (Seattle: Washington Mutual Savings Bank, 1930), p. 2. Frazier had been president of the mutually owned bank for 22 years.

51. *Session Laws,* 1929, chap. 151, pp. 380–98. For introduction of House Bill 217, see *House Journal,* 1929, p. 225. See *Senate Journal,* 1929, p. 622, for the roll call vote.

52. *Session Laws,* 1929, chap. 151.

53. *Session Laws,* 1929, chap. 127, pp. 316–17. The bill to authorize the committee was introduced by Representative Ed Davis "by executive request" on Feb. 7, 1929. *House Journal,* 1929, p. 225. The Democratic party had been weaker. In the 1921 session, there was but one Democrat in the entire legislature!

54. Frazier, pp. 2–3.

55. *Aberdeen Savings and Loan Association* v. *Chase,* 157 Wash. 351, 289 P. 536 (1930), consolidated with *Burr, Conrad and Broom* v. *Chase,* 157 Wash. 393, 289 P. 551 (1930).

56. *Report of the Washington Tax Investigation Committee* (Olympia: State Printing Office, 1930), p. 7.

57. *Session Laws,* 1929, chap. 127, p. 316.

58. Butler resigned before the hearings began and was replaced by Robert Moody, also from Everett. Lease died before the committee completed its final report. *Report of the Washington Tax Investigation Committee,* p. 6.

59. Ibid., p. 12.

60. Ibid., pp. 40–46.

61. Ibid., p. 46.

62. Ibid., p. 47. The committee amended the figures following the adoption of the tax amendment in 1930. The new recommendation was for a 1 percent tax on the first $1,000 in income and a top rate of 5 percent on income over $4,000. See ibid., "Revised Plan for a Personal Income Tax," p. 72.

63. The State Grange convention in June 1929 passed resolutions favoring an income tax and opposing a sales tax. *Washington State Grange Proceedings* 41 (1929). Such resolutions were reprinted in *Grange News* throughout the summer of 1931.

64. The following states had income tax laws in place by the end of 1931: Arkansas, Delaware, Georgia, Massachusetts, Mississippi, Missouri, New Hampshire, New York, North Carolina, North Dakota, Oklahoma, Oregon, South Carolina, Virginia, and Wisconsin.

65. *14th Decennial Census of Population,* Oregon, 1920. Portland's metropolitan area numbered close to 300,000 people of a total state population of 783,389. By contrast, Seattle, the largest city in Washington, had just 22.9 percent of its state's population.

66. *Oregon Grange Bulletin* (November 1921), p. 45; for the reference to earlier Grange support, see M.M. Burtner, "A Letter to Lane Pomona Grange," *Oregon Grange Bulletin* (January 1922), p. 4. The report of the national meeting is in *Oregon Grange Bulletin* (January 1922), p. 2. The 10-day convention,

November 16–26, ended with resolutions on other matters such as "favoring stricter censorship of motion pictures; . . . [and] opposing laxity in prohibition enforcement." The National Grange's taxation committee consisted of members from New Jersey, West Virginia, Wisconsin, Illinois, Connecticut, and Idaho.

67. M. M. Burtner, "A Letter to Lane Pomona Grange," *Oregon Grange Bulletin* (January 1922), p. 4.

68. "The Grange Income Tax Bill," *Oregon Grange Bulletin* (August 1922), p. 8, c. 2.

69. *Portland Telegram,* July 27, 1922, p. 8; *Oregonian,* July 29, 1922, p. 8.

70. *Oregon Journal,* March 27, 1923, p. 16.

71. *Telegram,* Feb. 19, 1923, p. 1; Feb. 20, 1923, p. 6.

72. *Oregonian,* Feb. 13, 1923, p. 8.

73. For Pierce's memoirs, see Arthur H. Bone, ed., *Oregon Cattleman/ Governor, Congressman: Memoirs and Times of Walter M. Pierce* (Portland: Oregon Historical Society, 1981); for Klan activity in Oregon, see Eckard V. Toy, "The Ku Klux Klan in Oregon," in G. Thomas Edwards and Carlos A. Schwantes, eds., *Experiences in a Promised Land: Essays in Pacific Northwest History* (Seattle: University of Washington Press, 1986).

74. The organization was the Oregon Just Tax League, apparently organized to fight the tax. See *Oregon Journal,* April 8, 1923, p. 3.

75. "Governor Pleads for Income Tax," *Oregon Journal,* Oct. 18, 1923, p. 1.

76. "Opponents of Income Tax Claim Law Will Penalize State, Check Investments," *Telegram,* Oct. 19, 1923, p. 8; "State Income Tax Bill Void, Lawyers Told," *Telegram,* Sept. 19, 1923, p. 1. But see "Roseburg Banker Strongly Favors Income Tax," *Oregon Journal,* Nov. 4, 1923, p. 8.

77. "Tax on Incomes Wins by Margin of 502 Votes Statewide," *Oregonian,* Nov. 10, 1923, p. 1.

78. "County Downs Tax by 11,938 Majority," *Oregonian,* Nov. 8, 1923, p. 1.

79. Ibid.

7 The Washington Income Tax of 1931: Veto and Response

1. *Journal of the Senate of the 22nd Legislature* (Olympia: Jay Thomas, Public Printer, 1931), p. 44.

2. "Senate Roster," *Senate Journal,* 1931, pp. 669–71.

3. Ibid., pp. 267–68.

4. Ibid., pp. 268, 670.

5. Ibid., pp. 268–69, 271–73.

6. "Budget Bickerings," *Bellingham Evening News*, Feb. 25, 1931, p. 4.

7. "Scheme for a Sales Tax," *Grange News*, Jan. 20, 1931, p. 4; *Senate Journal*, 1931, p. 299, for introduction of Phipps bill; p. 433, for majority and minority reports on the measure from the Committee on Revenue and Taxation.

8. *Journal of the House of the 22nd Session* (Olympia: Jay Thomas, State Printer, 1931). For introduction, p. 353; for first reading and referral to the committee, pp. 354–55; for committee's "do pass" recommendation, p. 451; for Davis's statement about members not being bound, p. 564.

9. *House Journal*, 1931, pp. 564–65. Three members were absent for both votes.

10. Ibid.

11. "Income Tax Law Passed," *Grange News*, March 20, 1931, p. 1; Jimmie Kay Browne, "Political Gossip," *Willapa Harbor Pilot* (South Bend), March 26, 1931, p. 3.

12. U.S. Bureau of Economic Analysis, *Report on State Per Capita Income* (Washington, D.C.: GPO, 1929).

13. *Bellingham Evening News*, March 20, 1931, p. 2.

14. Albert Francis Gunns, "Roland Hill Hartley and the Politics of Washington State," M.A. thesis, University of Washington, 1963. Gunns provides no details on Hartley's role in the income tax debates. The governor's official papers, held in the State Archives, provide few clues. With the exception of a letter from the American Taxpayers' League, Jan. 19, 1932, opposing all tax increases, and a published pamphlet written by William Randolph Hearst on taxation, the files contain no substantive evidence on the nature or volume of mail Hartley may have received on the issue. Hartley Papers, Subject Files, Box 39, Washington State Archives, Olympia. The bulk of Hartley's personal papers, if they still exist, are not held in collections open to public inspection.

15. "Governor's Veto Messages," *Senate Journal*, Appendix, pp. 615–17. "Everything said in vetoing Senate Bill 26 applies with equal force" to his veto of the personal income tax. He added one additional objection: "The approval of this bill would have a disastrous effect upon pay rolls and wages" (p. 617).

16. Ibid., pp. 616, 617.

17. Jimmie Kay Browne, "Political Gossip," *Willapa Harbor Pilot*, April 2, 1931, p. 3. The writers in the South Bend newspaper did not always agree. For instance, a column published in the March 19, 1931, issue sounds more like an item in a radical leftist pamphlet than an opinion column in a small-town weekly paper: "You rich men and women . . . haven't you any sense at all? Can't you

see you are heading right into a cyclone that will blow you into Kingdom-come if you don't let up on some of your selfishness and give these men and women, the farming and the toiling masses, a fairer chance for their share of the country's profits?" The editor, Edwin M. Connor, who included both views in his paper, was a longtime friend of Franklin D. Roosevelt. In a fascinating column published in the *Harbor Pilot* (Sept. 22, 1931, p. 8), Connor described Roosevelt's physical condition in great detail, but added that his mental powers made up for his physical condition. He concluded with a call for Roosevelt's nomination to the presidency in 1932.

18. "Test Income Tax Veto," *Bellingham Evening News*, March 24, 1931, p. 2.

19. For 1931, see *Senate Journal*, 1931, pp. 613–36, and *House Journal*, 1931, pp. 717–35. For the comparison with 1929, see "Hartley Vetoes Income Tax Bill," *Bellingham Evening News*, March 24, 1931, pp. 1, 8. The *Seattle Post-Intelligencer* downplayed Hartley's vetoes of the tax measures. See "Hartley Signs Three Major Supply Bills," March 25, 1931, p. 1. The vetoes are mentioned several paragraphs into the story.

20. See veto message of Senate Bill 137, March 23, 1931, *Senate Journal*, pp. 611–13; "Hartley Vetoes Abandoned Horse Act and Takes Occasion to Call Some Members Senate Jackasses," *Bellingham Evening News*, March 23, 1931, p. 1.

21. "Governor Had No Tax Program—Gallatly," *Seattle Post-Intelligencer*, March 27, 1931, p. 16.

22. "Senators Say Hartley Bills Fairly Treated," *Seattle Post-Intelligencer*, March 27, 1931, p. 16.

23. Washington State Tax Commission, *4th Biennial Report* (1932), p. 27.

24. Ibid.

25. Before the controversies arose, however, he had reappointed McBroom and Chase. See *Senate Journal*, 1931, p. 45, 385–86.

26. George L. Fuller, *The Inland Empire: Who's Who* (Spokane: H. G. Linderman, 1928), pp. 129–30. Lester Livengood, the manager, was a veteran Spokane lawyer. *Spokane City Directory* (Spokane: R. W. Polk, 1928), p. 509.

27. "Declares Taxes Retard Growth," *Tacoma News Tribune*, July 28, 1932, p. 4, c. 1. The editor of the *Weekly Vanguard*, published by the Citizens Public Education League, countered with an editorial titled "Tax Dodgers Want to Cut Teachers' Pay." Weekly *Vanguard*, Sept. 2, 1932, p. 4, microfilm A4817, University of Washington Libraries.

28. See, for example, "Articles of Incorporation for Tax Reduction League," in Roy J. Kinnear Papers, box 1–17, University of Washington Libraries. No mention is made of the organization's position on the income tax in its statement of

purpose, which begins: "The purpose of the organization shall be to support such legislation and measures, local, state and national, that will minimize governmental waste and extravagance." For an example of the group's proselytizing efforts, see *Tacoma News Tribune*, Aug. 3, 1932, p. 11.

29. *Washington Taxpayer* 1 (October 1935), p. 1. A brief history of the association was published in the first issue. Old federation officers in the new organization included the *Tax Facts* editor, L. M. Livengood, who represented Spokane County and, later, wrote articles for the *Washington Taxpayer,* and E. D. Cowen, a regular writer for *Tax Facts* who also submitted articles to the newer publication.

30. Initial membership rolls do not exist, but the impression of a higher percentage of Puget Sound members comes from the pages of the *Washington Taxpayer*, like the earlier *Tax Facts*, published in Seattle. The earlier organization contained numerous articles about members from southeastern Washington, but few mentions were made of members from west of the Cascades.

31. *Tacoma News Tribune*, Aug. 10, 1932, p. 2, c. 3.

32. Ibid., Aug. 22, 1932, p. 10.

33. Hartley had admirers, however, even among Democrats. As Edwin M. Connor, South Bend editor, wrote: "There has been nothing that his opponents could hang on him or his administration to sully the lustre of an honest accounting to the people of his stewardship." *Willapa Harbor Pilot*, March 12, 1931, p. 4.

34. "Tax Laws of Farm Legislatures Threaten Industry in the West," *Business Week*, April 15, 1931, p. 30.

35. *Grange News*, July 5, 1931, p. 1; *Washington State Grange Proceedings* 41 (1929). The Grange's "legislative agenda" continued to list the income tax as a prime goal throughout the early 1930s. For a later example of such a call, see *Grange News*, Jan. 4, 1936, p. 1.

36. The "only solution" is quoted in "Definite Tax Program Promised," *Grange News*, June 20, 1931, p. 1.

37. The Hall speech is reported in *Grange News*, June 20, 1931.

38. For earlier opposition to sales taxes, see *Proceedings* for 1929 and 1930, in which resolutions were passed supporting income taxes but condemning sales taxes. Opposition to the sales tax remained a part of the Grange's program throughout the decade. "Grange Remains Dyed-in-the-Wool Opponent of the Sales Tax," *Grange News*, Dec. 5, 1934, p. 4.

39. John F. Sly, *Tax Developments in Washington State—How We Got There* (Olympia: Washington State Research Council Pocket Report Series 1, 1956).

40. Membership stood at 22,009 in 1932, down from 23,438 the previous year. There were 416 Granges in Washington in 1932. Also, there were 37 Pomona (women's auxiliary) organizations with a combined membership of 6,763. *Grange Roster* (1933), pp. 85, 86.

41. For operation of the initiative process in Washington, see Claudius O. Johnson, "Adoption of the Initiative and Referendum in Washington," *Pacific Northwest Quarterly* 35 (October 1944), pp. 291–303; and 36 (January 1945), pp. 29–48. Johnson asserts that initiative proposals always gained strong support from rural areas. See pp. 301–2.

42. Initiative 69, *Laws 1933*, c. 5, sec. 1, p. 50.

43. The intention is clear on the face of the document, although few prudent lawyers could hope that this definition would avoid the "equal protection" attack that proved fatal in Aberdeen Savings. Initiative 69, *Laws 1933*, c. 5, sec. 1, p. 49.

44. *Seattle Argus*, July 16, 1932, p. 8. The petition was printed in full on four complete tabloid-sized pages of the *Argus* on July 16.

45. "Election Pamphlet for the General Election on Nov. 8, 1932" (Olympia: Jay Thomas, Public Printer), a copy of which is held in the 1932 Election Folder, Washington State Archives, Olympia.

46. "If in Doubt, Vote No," *Spokane Spokesman-Review*, Nov. 2, 1932, p. 4.

47. "Ballot Initiatives: Wording for Initiative 69," Secretary of State's Office, memorandum to all newspapers of general circulation in Washington, October 1932, copy in Taxation file, Box 66, Martin Papers, Washington State Archives.

48. The WEA had a membership of almost 11,000 in 1932. See *Washington State Labor News*, Sept. 30, 1932, p. 3. The WEA, PTA, and Central Labor Council each published regular newsletters. The Citizens Public Education League newsletter, the *Weekly Vanguard*, began publishing weekly on August 12, 1932. Started in January 1930 as a monthly, the newsletter was mailed from the league headquarters, listed as 567 Empire Building, the office of the Seattle attorney Donald R. McDonald. Microfilm A4817, University of Washington Libraries. Pamphlets and irregularly published newsletters from the Unemployed Citizens' League are held in Special Collections, University of Washington Libraries. The league's primary goal was full employment. For a thorough treatment of the league's activities, see Terry Willis, "The Unemployed Citizens of Seattle, 1900–1939: Hulet Wells, Seattle Labor, and the Struggle for Economic Security," Ph.D. dissertation, University of Washington, 1997. For the Grange's attempts to ally with local chambers of commerce in the early 1920s, see "Director to Speak for Farmers," *Washington State Chamber News*, November 1923, p. 10.

49. W. R. Orndorff letter to C. D. Martin, Jan. 28, 1933: "We also helped to enact Number 69 . . . ," Box 66, Taxation file, Martin Papers, Washington State Archives, Olympia.

50. Charles Hodde interview, Jan. 12, 1987. Among the many presentations he made for the initiative were several speeches to the Seattle Central Labor Council and allied organizations. His address to the Labor Council is noted in *Washington State Labor News*, Sept. 30, 1932, p. 1. The organization gave him credentials to appear before their affiliated groups. See *Washington State Labor News*, Oct. 7, 1932, p. 1, c. 6.

51. For example, see *Seattle Times*, July 8, 1932, p. 1. The income tax initiative gained little more than a paragraph in a "jumped" story, and even there the proponents were not identified by name or organization. Nonetheless, Hodde said that the *Seattle Times's* attitude toward the measure "wasn't too bad" compared to bitter opposition encountered from the Spokane newspapers.

52. "Income Tax Advocate Heard," *Washington State Labor News*, July 1, 1932, p. 1, c. 1.

53. *Seattle Star*, July 8, 1932, p. 1; "Grange Income Tax Initiative Filed," *Seattle Argus*, July 16, 1932, p. 8.

54. Chamberlain's appearance was noted in *Washington State Labor News*, July 22, 1932, p. 1, c. 5. The unanimous endorsement was reported on the same page under the headline "Convention Backs Grange Initiative." The labor organization had a membership of 24,805 in 1931, dropping to 19,172 the next year because of the depression. By 1933, the membership had fallen to 13,796. *Washington State Federation of Labor Proceedings*, 1933, p. 27.

55. Charles W. Doyle and James A. Duncan, "Convention Report," *Washington State Labor News*, July 29, 1932, p. 4.

56. *Washington State Labor News*, Sept. 30, 1932, p. 3.

57. *Chronicle-Dispatch* (Dayton), July 7, 1932, p. 4.

58. *Seattle Times*, Nov. 13, 1932, p. 3, c.1. See also *Voters' Information League Bulletin* 24 (Dec. 1, 1922), p. 1, announcing the establishment of the "40 Mill Tax Limit League." The *Bulletin* article noted: "Real estate and personal property is paying 87 percent of the entire tax burden of this state." A chief backer of the bulletin was Roy J. Kinnear, president of the Associated Industries of Seattle and a prominent real estate developer. See Scrapbook in Roy J. Kinnear Papers, University of Washington Libraries.

59. "Taxation—Why a Burden?" *Washington State Labor News*, Aug. 12, 1932, p. 2. Nash had extensive experience in government. Born in Minnesota, he graduated from the University of Minnesota Law School in 1903 and was admitted

to practice there. After serving a three-year term as parks commissioner for St. Paul and 13 years on the Ramsay, Minnesota, city commission, he moved to Seattle to take a job as advertising manager for a local clothier. He was elected president of the Retail Clerks' Union local, and by 1932, he had been appointed to the city's Civil Service Commission. A regular newspaper columnist for four years, he was fired from the Civil Service Commission by the mayor in 1932 during the 1932 campaign. He ran successfully for county commission in the fall election as the labor candidate.

60. Only five mills could go to the state general fund, with an additional mill levied for debt amortization. Robert E. Berney, *Tax Structure of Washington* (Pullman: Washington State University Press, 1970). All three Seattle dailies favored the 40-mill initiative (Initiative 64). For an example of positive press reviews, see *Seattle Times*, Oct. 29, 1932, p. 3. Unlike the tax measure, which enjoyed relatively little opposition in 1932, the 40-mill limit was well enough debated in the 1920s that strong opposition had organized to defeat it each time it was proposed. A similar "awakening" of opposition would doom future income tax measures in Washington.

61. Arthur L. Marsh, WEA executive secretary, repeated the claim after the election. He contended that the income tax would bring in "just two or three million dollars, leaving five or six millions of deficiency." *Seattle Times*, Nov. 11, 1932, p. 5.

62. Hodde interview.

63. *Spokane Spokesman-Review*, Nov. 6, 1932, p. 4, c. 2.

64. *Seattle Post-Intelligencer*, Nov. 7, 1932, p. 8.

65. *Bremerton Daily News Searchlight*, Nov. 7, 1932, p. 4.

66. "How the Times Would Vote on Propositions," *Seattle Times*, Nov. 6, 1932, p. 10.

67. "The Income Tax," *Seattle Star*, Oct. 29, 1932, p. 1.

68. "Income Tax: Measure Long and Complicated but Backers Sincerely Believe It Right Step," *Seattle Star*, Nov. 1, 1932, p. 1. In another article on the same page, the newspaper noted that the price of wheat on the Chicago Board of Trade had fallen to a new low of 42 7/8 cents per bushel.

69. Thomas E. Dobbs, editorial, *Snohomish County Tribune*, Nov. 3, 1932, p. 6.

70. "State Income Tax Bill Attacked by Mary Blair, Says Measure Would Make Little Fellow Tax Conscious if Passed," *Seattle Star*, Nov. 5, 1932, p. 8.

71. "Vote for the Income Tax Law," *Weekly Vanguard* (Seattle), Oct. 7, 1932, p. 4.

72. *Seattle Argus*, Oct. 1, 1932, p. 3.

73. *Seattle Argus*, Oct. 29, 1932, p. 3.

8 Electoral Success, Judicial Defeat

1. The 1932 election results for Washington are from *Abstract of Votes Polled in the General Election, 1932* (Olympia: Secretary of State, 1933).

2. For a general description of the Washington political scene during the period, see Richard Lowitt, *The New Deal and the West* (Bloomington: Indiana University Press, 1984).

3. *Fourth Biennial Report of the Tax Commission of the State of Washington* (Olympia: Jay Thomas, Public Printer, 1932), pp. 50–51.

4. *Washington State Grange Roster*, 1933, p. 85.

5. As noted in the previous chapter, Robertson served on Governor Hart's Tax Investigation Committee. In the early 1920s, he was chairman of the taxation committee for the Washington State Chambers of Commerce. See *Washington State Chamber News*, April 1924, p. 2.

6. *Island County Farm Bureau News* (Oak Harbor), Nov. 10, 1932, p. 1. In the previous week's issue, the editor noted that the income tax initiative faced "no organized opposition."

7. *Abstract of Votes Polled in the General Election, 1928* (Olympia: Secretary of State, 1929), p. 4.

8. Hill was Grange lecturer 1921–23 and 1931–33. See *Grange Roster* for the specific years.

9. Ironically, Chelan County was one of only three counties that Martin carried when he failed in a bid to gain the Democratic nomination for governor in 1940. See *Wenatchee World*, Sept. 14, 1940; *Abstract of Votes Polled in the Primary Election, 1940* (Olympia: Secretary of State, 1940), p. 16. Gallatly returned to Chelan County, where he became county Republican chairman in 1938. *Wenatchee World*, Sept. 19, 1938, p 5.

10. For biographies of all justices, see Washington Biography File, Special Collections, University of Washington Libraries. For an important study of supreme court judicial recruitment, see Charles H. Sheldon, *A Century of Judging: A Political History of the Washington Supreme Court* (Seattle: University of Washington Press, 1989).

11. Sheldon, p. 87.

12. Sheldon, p. 92.

13. The characterization is my own, drawn from court decisions, extensive reading of state newspapers during the period, and general items found in each man's biography.

14. Sheldon, p. 90.

15. *Journal of the House of the 22nd Session* (Olympia: Jay Thomas, State Printer, 1931), pp. 920–23. The Unemployed Citizens' League spokesman told a reporter that several state legislators-elect might be forced to walk to Olympia because they were without funds. See "New State Legislators; Broke, May Have to Walk to Olympia," *Seattle Times*, Nov. 16, 1932, p. 1.

16. Jack Best to Warren Magnuson, Jan. 19, 1933, Box 1/3, Magnuson Papers, University of Washington Libraries.

17. M. M. Anderson to Magnuson, Jan. 25, 1933, Box 1/3, Magnuson Papers.

18. For Jenner's confirmation, see *Senate Journal,* 1933, p. 124.

19. Hedges remained on the tax commission until 1950. For Hedges's career, see his obituary, *Wenatchee Daily World*, May 26, 1957, p. 1. Soon after McBroom's, Chase also resigned. For Hedges's confirmation, see *Senate Journal*, 1933, p. 124.

20. Earle R. Jenner to John R. Jones, Feb. 25, 1933, Box 1/10, Magnuson Papers.

21. Ibid., p. 3.

22. Ibid., p. 6.

23. *Grange Proceedings, 1933,* p. 89.

24. George L. Harrigan, Tax Commission Secretary, to Richard Hamilton, Secretary of Governor Martin, Feb. 28, 1933, Box 66, Martin Papers, Washington State Archives, Olympia.

25. P. H. Pugsley to Martin, Feb. 18, 1933, Box 66, Martin Papers.

26. Edgar I. Stewart, *Washington: Northwest Frontier* (New York: Lewis Publishing Co., 1957), III, p. 93; *Seattle City Directory* (Seattle: R. L. Polk, 1932), p. 370.

27. Stewart, p. 207; *Seattle Times*, Nov. 24, 1953; *Seattle City Directory,* 1932.

28. Initiative 69, *Session Laws, 1933,* chap. 5, p. 49.

29. *Seattle Argus*, March 4, 1933, p. 3, for formation of the committee and retention of Preston. For the legal theories, see *Culliton* v. *Chase,* 25 P.2d 81 (1933).

30. *Fourth Biennial Report of the Tax Commission of the State of Washington* (Olympia: Jay Thomas, Public Printer, 1932), p. 33

31. *Culliton* v. *Chase,* at 81.

32. Sheldon, p. 96.

33. "WEA Holds Emergency Meeting," *Seattle Times*, Nov. 11, 1932, p. 5.

34. Senate Bill 16, introduced Jan. 11, 1933, *Senate Journal,* 1933, p. 96.

35. Frank T. Bell to Magnuson, Jan. 31, 1933, Box 1/9, Magnuson Papers.

36. Magnuson to Bell, Feb. 7, 1933, Box 1/15, Magnuson Papers.

37. For example, see Fred W. White to Magnuson, Jan. 31, 1933, Box 1/10, Magnuson Papers.

38. W. V. Tanner to Magnuson, Feb. 24, 1933, Box 1/9, Magnuson Papers.

39. O. W. Fisher to Magnuson, March 3, 1933, Box 1/6, Magnuson Papers.

40. See Harrigan to Hamilton, Feb. 28, 1933, Martin Papers, Washington State Archives.

41. "Death of Earle Jenner," *Washington Historical Quarterly* 24 (April 1933), p. 158. For T. M. Jenner's confirmation, see *Journal of the Senate,* Extraordinary Session, Dec. 4, 1933—Jan. 12, 1934, pp. 80–81.

42. U.S. Treasury Department, Bureau of Internal Revenue, *Statistics of Income* (1932), p. 127. The figures listed are cited in *Washington State Taxpayers' Association Bulletin,* Aug. 5, 1935, p. 1. The federal figures after 1922, unfortunately, include Alaska in the Washington total. The *Taxpayers' Bulletin* uses the same figures, thus not eliminating the Alaska taxpayers from Washington's total. The figures show 56,434 Washingtonians (and Alaskans) had sufficient incomes to file a federal return in 1932. Of that number, 454 reported incomes of $10,000 per year or more. Three earned in excess of $100,000 during the year.

43. W. D. Rodbury, "Helpful Hints on Your State Income Tax," *Seattle Times,* March 26, 1933, p. 3.

44. Ibid.

45. For the attorney general's decision that federal employees were exempt, see E. P. Donnelly, assistant attorney general, "Opinion—March 31, 1933," *22nd Biennial Report of the Attorney General* (Olympia: State Printing Plant, 1935), pp. 26–28. The opinion was in response to inquiries from C. P. Nelson, Oscar W. Dam, and J. Speed Smith, all of Seattle. "In giving this opinion," Donnelly cautioned, "we have assumed the act to be constitutional," indicating the uncertainty still attending the constitutionality of the act less than two weeks before the returns were due.

46. "Helpful Hints," *Seattle Times,* March 26, 1933.

47. See, for example, "State Income Tax Helps," *Seattle Times,* March 27, 1933, in which Rodbury answers questions about taxation of rent receipts.

48. Samuel F. Racine, *Income Tax Guide Applicable to the State of Washington* (Seattle: Western Institute Press, 1933). The cover indicates that the first

edition was published December 10, 1932, barely a month after the initiative passed. For "questions and answers," see pages 67–163.

49. Lawrence M. Friedman, *A History of American Law* (New York: Simon and Schuster, 1985), p. 19.

50. *Seattle Times*, June 16, 1933, p. 1.

51. See Parker's biography and obituary, Washington Biography Files, Special Collections, University of Washington Libraries.

52. *Seattle Times*, Aug. 15, 1933, p. 1.

53. Sheldon, pp. 97 fn.

54. *Culliton* v. *Chase,* at 82. Justice Blake wrote a six-page dissenting opinion. Although it lacked the eloquence and depth of legal reasoning that U.S. Supreme Court Justice John Harlan exhibited in the Pollock dissent 40 years earlier, Blake's piece did exhibit similar passion.

55. Ibid.

56. See, for example, Harold Hestnes, "Constitutionality of State Income Taxes," *Washington Law Review* 8 (May 1933), pp. 81–84. It was widely believed that the court would uphold the tax because earlier, in a 5–3 decision before Geraghty's appointment, the court upheld the Emergency Relief Organization, a state agency funded by a $10 million bond proposal that clearly exceeded the debt limitation clause of the state constitution. The court sidestepped the problem in order to uphold the statute. See Stewart, II, p. 300.

57. "Income Tax Invalid: Court OKs Classified Levy Put on Businesses," *Seattle Times*, Sept. 9, 1933, p. 1. The *Times* story concluded that there was "no way of knowing who switched as no record is announced on ties."

58. "Coop Comment," *Grange News*, Sept. 20, 1933, p. 2.

59. "The People v. the Supreme Court," *Grange News*, Sept. 20, 1933, p. 6.

9 Attractive Alternatives to an Income Tax, 1933–1940

1. See George Yantis to James Taylor, June 2, 1933, in Box 6/11, Magnuson Papers, University of Washington Libraries.

2. Clancey M. Lewis to Governor Martin, Aug. 21, 1933, Box 66, Martin Papers, Washington State Archives, Olympia.

3. For details about the act, see "Law Providing for a Tax Upon Business Activities" (Olympia: State Printing Plant, 1933). The 28-page pamphlet described the workings of the business tax laws passed as Chap. 191, *Laws*, 1933. For a

description of the administration of the tax, see Tax Commission of Washington, *Fifth Biennial Report* (Olympia: State Printing Plant, 1935), pp. 5–10. The court sustained the business excise tax in the case of *State ex rel Stiner* v. *Yelle*, 25 P.2d 91, 174 Wash. 402 (1933).

4. "State Officials Pleased Over Ruling on Sales Tax—See $5 Million Revenue," *Daily Journal of Commerce* (Seattle), Sept. 9, 1933, p. 1.

5. The convention proposal passed the house by a vote of 76–11 and had strong support in the senate. See *Seattle Argus*, March 4, 1933, p. 4, for comments on the legislative passage; *Argus*, March 25, 1933, p. 4, for Governor Martin's decision to set the date. See also Martin's address to the legislature, the entire text of which was published in the *Seattle Times*, Dec. 5, 1933, p. 11. See also Box 1, Martin Papers, Washington State Archives. Prohibition supporters won in only three counties (Whitman, Columbia, and Garfield), and repeal passed 490,088 to 208,206. See Edgar I. Stewart, *Washington: Northwest Frontier* (New York: Lewis Publishing Co., 1957), II, p. 302.

6. The "repeal convention" received extensive press coverage. For example, see "Historic Session Tomorrow Will Draw Throngs," *Seattle Times*, Oct. 2, 1933, p. 8. Warren Magnuson was an officer of the convention. For brief mention of his role and some correspondence about it, see Box 6/14, Magnuson Papers, University of Washington Libraries.

7. "Few Changes in Legislature," *Seattle Times*, Dec. 3, 1933, p. 1.

8. "Assessors Urge State Emergency Tax Legislation," *Seattle Times*, Dec. 2, 1933, p. 3. The article contained no mention of any specific proposal that Norton might have offered.

9. For a clear description of the decision and the issues involved, see "Decisions Upheld by High Court in Olympia," *Seattle Times*, Dec. 1, 1933, p. 1; and *Fifth Biennial Report*, p. 12.

10. *Denny* v. *Wooster*, 27 P.2d 328, 175 Wash. 272 (1933).

11. For the disputes between "regulars" and "left-wing" Democrats, see, for example, *Seattle Times*, Dec. 5, 1933, p. 10. Several "regulars" resigned house seats to accept positions in the Martin administration. For a list, see *Seattle Times*, Dec. 4, 1933, p. 3.

12. *House Journal*, Special Session (1933), p. 149.

13. Occupations of the cosponsors were determined from the "House Roster," *House Journal*, Extraordinary Session (1933), pp. 438–41. The "traveling newspaperman" was 61-year-old H. H. Brown of Pierce County, serving his first term. The other cosponsor from west of the Cascades was Island County representative Pearl Wanamaker, who had been one of the five Democrats in the 1929 session.

14. *House Journal*, Extraordinary Session (1933), p. 149, for introduction; p. 194, for committee report; p. 257, for second reading; p. 354, for final passage.

15. *Senate Journal*, Extraordinary Session (1933), p. 252, for initial introduction; p. 249, for first and second reading; p. 298, for third reading. The roll call votes are on pp. 298–99.

16. *Senate Journal*, p. 299.

17. "Conference Plan on Liquor Bill is Passed by House," *Seattle Times*, Jan. 12, 1934, p. 7.

18. "Liquor Control Bill to Conferees," *Spokane Spokesman-Review*, Jan. 11, 1934, p. 2. For Todd's associations with the New Order of Cincinnatus, see "Youth in the Saddles," *Spokane Spokesman-Review*, April 15, 1936, p. 4. For a history of the organization, see George William Scott, "New Order of Cincinnatus," M.A. thesis, University of Washington, 1966.

19. For a brief biography, see "H. H. Henneford State Tax Head," *Spokane Spokesman-Review*, April 15, 1934, p. 6. For Henneford's position with the state Democratic party, see Henneford to Magnuson, Sept. 9, 1932, Box 6/8, Magnuson Papers, University of Washington Libraries. For senate confirmation of Henneford's appointment, see *Senate Journal* (1935), p. 81.

20. *Fifth Biennial Report*, pp. 14–15.

21. These arguments were to become the mainstays of opposition to the income tax in future elections. See, for instance, *Washington Taxpayer* 2 (October 1936), pp. 5–6.

22. Hodde interview by author, Jan. 12, 1987. Committee members were A. S. Goss, Fred J. Chamberlain, Charles Hodde, and Ira Shea.

23. "Two Constitutional Amendments Pave Way for Redistribution and Equalization of the Tax Burden," *Grange News*, Nov. 5, 1934, p. 5; "State Master Favors Tax," *Grange News*, Oct. 20, 1934, p. 4.

24. J. H. Brown, "Under the Capitol Dome," *Seattle Argus*, Nov. 3, 1934, p. 10. A Tax Reduction League broadside is in Box 1/17, Roy J. Kinnear Papers, University of Washington Libraries.

25. *Abstract of Votes Polled at the General Election, November 3, 1934* (Olympia: State Printing Plant, 1934), p. 3.

26. "Tax Tangles," *Grange News*, Dec. 20, 1934, p. 5.

27. *Abstract of Votes Polled, 1934*, p. 3.

28. Joseph Pratt Harris, *County Finances in the State of Washington* (Seattle: University of Washington Publications in the Social Sciences, 1935), p. 275. The other three counties in serious condition were Grays Harbor, Pacific, and

Thurston. Pratt listed 18 counties as "materially affected" by the tax limitations: Chelan, Clallam, Clark, Douglas, Ferry, Jefferson, King, Kitsap, Klickitat, Lewis, Okanogan, Mason, San Juan, Skamania, Snohomish, Stevens, Whatcom, and Yakima. He listed eight with relatively few problems: Benton, Cowlitz, Island, Kittitas, Skagit, Spokane, Wahkiakum, and Walla Walla. Nine, in Pratt's view, were in "excellent financial condition." All nine were east of the Cascades: Adams, Asotin, Columbia, Franklin, Garfield, Grant, Lincoln, Pend Oreille, and Whitman.

29. Fred J. Chamberlain, "Tax Tangles," *Grange News*, Dec. 10, 1934, p. 5. See also the thorough discussion of taxation by Paul Hacker on p. 6 of the same issue. "The Grange remains a dyed-in-the-wool opponent of the sales tax," wrote the editor, C. H. Clark. "Grange Opposed to Sales Tax," *Grange News*, Dec. 5, 1934, p. 4.

30. Joseph Pratt Harris, "Washington Tax Limitation Measures," in *Property Tax Limitation Laws*, Public Administration Bulletin 36 (February 1934), p. 76.

31. *Session Laws*, 1935, chap. 180. The business and occupation tax is in title II, sec. 4–15; public utility tax, title V, sec. 36–43; radio tax, title X, sec. 74–77; cigarette tax, title XII, sec. 82–95; corporate net income tax, title XVII, sec. 159–84; sales tax, title III, sec. 16–30.

32. "Grange Sponsors Net Income Tax Bill at State Legislature," *Grange News*, Feb. 23, 1935, p. 1. Late in 1934, Tax Commissioner Henneford wrote Governor Martin proposing that an income tax bill be prepared for legislative action but recommending that it be called an "excise tax to be measured by the amount of net income received." Henneford to Martin, Dec. 29, 1934, Box 66, Martin Papers, Washington State Archives.

33. *Session Laws*, 1935, chap. 178. The description of the tax form is in *Grange News*, March 16, 1935, p. 1.

34. *Session Laws*, 1935, chap. 180, title XIX, p. 847. Operating funds for the University of Washington, before 1933, had been fairly consistently about $1.7 million. The regents were forced to cut back to $824,000 following passage of the first 40-mill limitation initiative in the November 1932 election. See Harris, "Washington Tax Limitation Laws," p. 73. For an example of the press coverage of the university's funding problems, see "Regents Slash Pay to $620,000," *Seattle Times*, April 3, 1933, p. 1. In the 1935 bill, the exact amounts for the colleges were .46 percent for Washington State; .265 percent for the "Bellingham Normal School"; .045 percent for the "Cheney Normal School"; and .28 percent for the "Ellensburg Normal School."

35. *Session Laws, 1935,* chap. 178, sec. 2, pp. 661–62.

36. The Personal Net Income Tax was H. B. 513. For the bill's introduction on Feb. 20 and the list of 53 cosponsors, see *House Journal* (1935), p. 303; "do pass" recommendation from committee, p. 395; second reading, p. 444; third reading and final vote, p. 447. The others voting against the bill were: Dr. D. F. Bice, Yakima County; John W. Eddy, a King County lumberman; and DeWolfe Emory, a King County lawyer. The conference committee of house and senate members reached agreement on the bills early on March 14. Both houses passed the measures by the end of the day. See Charles Hodde, "One Man's Opinion," *Grange News,* March 23, 1935, for a complaint that "just six of 145 legislators met in secret to decide" on the final wording of both bills.

37. See *Session Laws, 1935,* chap. 180, for specific portions vetoed, but see also his veto message, *Senate Journal* (1935).

38. *Washington Commonwealth Builder,* April 19, 1935, p. 1. The organization formed in 1933 and began publication of the newspaper the next year. Throughout 1934, the monthly paper carried laudatory articles about Upton Sinclair's E.P.I.C. campaign for the California governorship. Before the 1934 general election, the newspaper printed endorsements for Marion Zioncheck for Congress and Lewis R. Schwellenbach for the Senate. It also endorsed, as a candidate for King County prosecutor, the legislator Warren Magnuson, who resigned his state house seat to serve as the first Democrat ever elected to that office in King County. *Washington Commonwealth Builder,* Nov. 2, 1934, p. 3. For a history of the organization, see Albert Anthony Acena, "The Washington Commonwealth Federation: Reform Politics and the Popular Front," Ph.D. dissertation, University of Washington, 1975.

39. *Washington Taxpayers' Association Bulletin* 61 (March 25, 1935). The editor was particularly angered by public employee lobbying: "Delegations from the public payroll brigade constantly swarmed in the lobbies and legislative chambers." He called it little more than "an organized looting of the taxpayers."

40. *Commonwealth Builder,* March 29, 1935, p. 1; March 25, 1935, p. 1.

41. Parts of the nine-page statement were printed in *Washington Taxpayers' Association Bulletin* 64 (April 15, 1935).

42. Stan Smith of Seattle called my attention to the tokens. See also "Tax Tokens Will Be Issued Soon," *Seattle Business,* April 11, 1935, p. 3.

43. Names of four of the five men appear in the *Seattle City Directory,* 1936. The occupations are from the listing in that source. The exception is Hoffman, whose name and occupation are listed in the 1934 *Seattle City Directory,* p. 1612. A short biography of Williams is in Stewart, IV, pp. 93–94. The characteriza-

tions of the tax's potential impact on each individual are taken from the initial paragraphs of the court decision.

44. "At 90 He Nurtures Rare Wit," *Tacoma News Tribune*, Jan. 21, 1968, pp. 1, 3. In the same article, he described then-Chief Justice Earl Warren: "Warren is not really a judge. He's more a legislator in judicial robes."

45. "1935 State Income Tax Law Fails to Get by First Test," *Evening Record* (Ellensburg), Aug. 21, 1935, p. 1; "New Levies on Personal Earnings Hit by Decision," *Seattle Times*, Aug. 21, 1935, p. 1; Stewart, II, p. 307.

46. *Jensen v. Henneford*, 53 P.2d 607, 185 Wash. 209 (1936); "State Income Tax Voided by High Court," *Seattle Times*, Jan. 14, 1936, p. 1.

47. *Jensen v. Henneford*, at 610.

48. Ibid. The corporate net income tax was voided by the court in *Petroleum Navigation Co. v. Henneford*, 85 Wash. 442 (1936). As in Jensen, the court said it violated the uniformity clause of the state constitution.

49. For Martin's first reaction to the news and the fact that he learned it from a *Chronicle* reporter, see "Court Crushes Net Income Tax," *Spokane Spokesman-Review*, Jan. 15, 1936, p. 1. See also "Decision Won't Upset Budget, Says Martin," *Seattle Times*, Jan. 15, 1936, p. 1. The lead story in the *Times* was not about taxation. It concerned the erratic Congressman Marion Zioncheck, who, referring to a New Year's Eve incident in the nation's capital in which he blew smoke in the eyes of an arresting officer, said, "Of 450,000 drunks, I was the only one in jail."

50. "1935 Income Tax Nullified," *Grange News*, Jan. 18, 1936, p. 1. The statement of improving economic conditions is from Hodde interview.

51. Notice of General Election, Voters and Candidates Pamphlet (1936), copy in Box 66, Martin Papers, Washington State Archives.

52. "I was back in Colville trying to grow potatoes," Charles Hodde remembered about the 1936 campaign. He was also running for a legislative seat in District 2 (Stevens-Pend Oreille counties). Hodde interview. For the Washington State Federation of Labor endorsement, see *Proceedings*, 35th Annual Convention (1936), p. 88. The resolution was presented by the Central Labor Council of Bremerton. The Commonwealth Federation's campaign for their own initiative dominated the pages of their newspaper throughout the summer and fall of 1936. For an example of the campaign claims made in favor of the initiative, see "Production for Use Means Full Recovery," *Washington Commonwealth Builder* (hereafter cited as *WCB*), July 4, 1936, p. 2. For the organization's resolution of support in 1935, see "Platform Plank No. 7," *WCB*, Oct. 19, 1935, p. 3. The plank was included in a second platform passed in April 1936. See Acena, p. 140. For

Costigan's endorsement, see "The People Initiate," *WCB*, Nov. 1, 1936, p. 4. For the assertion that the organization was increasingly dominated by Communists, see Acena, pp. 135–37. The Communist party's unofficial Northwest organ turned over its membership list to the *WCB* in October 1936, and Costigan officially joined the party. Acena, pp. 136, 137. Few farmers were active in the Commonwealth Federation. One exception was the former state Grange master William Bouck of Sedro-Woolley, who organized for the WCF in 1936. See Acena, p. 131. Few of the organization's members lived east of the Cascades. Acena, p. 109.

53. "SJR #7 (Taxation Amendment)," *Washington Taxpayer* 2 (October 1936), p. 5. The capital letters are in the original. As an indication of the organization's growing membership and influence, and in contrast to the mimeographed *Bulletin* released irregularly in previous years, the new publication was printed on high-quality paper and issued monthly.

54. "If in Doubt About Measures on Ballot Tuesday, Vote 'No,'" *Spokane Spokesman-Review*, Nov. 1, 1936, p. 3. The newspaper amended its view the next day: "Voters Should Back Initiative 114 and Ballot Against All Others," *Spokesman-Review*, Nov. 2, 1936, p. 2. The cautionary note is from the *Elma Chronicle*, Oct. 29, 1936, p. 4.

55. *Okanogan Independent*, Nov. 7, 1936, p. 2.

56. "Taxes to Jump if Bills Carry," *Spokane Spokesman-Review*, Nov. 1, 1936, p. A-9.

57. The list of organizations endorsing the measure was widely published. See, for example, *Washington Taxpayer* 2 (October 1936), p. 3; "Voters Should Back Initiative 114 and Ballot Against All Others," *Spokane Spokesman-Review*, Nov. 2, 1936, p. 2. The characterization of the opponents as "certain well-organized minorities" is from *Washington Taxpayer* 2 (October 1936), p. 3.

58. "Initiative No. 114—40-Mill Limit," *Washington Taxpayer* 2 (October 1936), p. 1.

59. "Endorsements," *Grays Harbor Pilot* (Aberdeen), Oct. 31, 1936, p. 2. The paper endorsed the Landon-Knox ticket and Roland Hartley in his unsuccessful bid to return to the governor's chair. The estimate of newspaper support for the 40-mill limitation is from an article in the *Washington Taxpayer* 2 (September 1937), p. 2, advocating another renewal for the measure by initiative in the 1938 general election.

60. Secretary of State, *Abstract of Votes Polled at the General Election, 1936* (Olympia: State Printing Plant, 1936), p. 41.

61. Ibid., p. 40.

62. Editorial, "Perfect Score on Ballot Measures," *Spokane Spokesman-Review*, Nov. 5, 1936, p. 4. Governor Martin held similar views about the Commonwealth Federation. In the primary campaign, he warned voters of the "left-wing danger." *Wenatchee World*, Aug. 12, 1936, p. 1. Later, he told a radio audience that his WCF-endorsed opponent represented "the combined forces of communism and political spoils." *Daily Olympian*, Sept. 2, 1936, p. 1.

63. For evidence of Magnuson's support for the income tax, see his condemnation of the Washington State Supreme Court decision in the Jensen case. "Speech Condemning the Court Decision on the Income Tax," Box 10/1, Magnuson Papers, University of Washington Libraries. The separation of support for a candidate and rejection of his endorsement of the income tax was evident in 1970 when the popular Governor Dan Evans campaigned for an income tax but only 31 percent of the voters agreed. In 1970 it went down 282,040 to 616,314. For comments on the 1970 result and the contrast with the Oregon income tax, see "Strange Tax Contrast," *Oregonian* (Portland), Nov. 27, 1970, p. 42. For a summary of Oregon's income tax, see Willis C. Warren, "A Brief History of Oregon's Income Tax," *Oregon Historical Quarterly* 38 (June 1937), pp. 193–205.

64. For introduction of SJR No. 5, *Senate Journal* (1937), p. 40; for third reading and final passage, p. 401. Occupations of the senators are from the "Senate Roster," *Senate Journal* (1937), pp. 792–94. For house passage, *House Journal* (1937), p. 100. The two versions differed in language, and a conference committee of three members from each chamber hammered out a compromise resolution. Charles Hodde was chairman of the conference committee. See *Senate Journal*, p. 771, for senate action on the final conference committee report.

65. Total sales tax receipts in 1937 were in excess of $12 million. See *Seventh Biennial Report* (Olympia: State Tax Commission, 1938); M. J. Ludy, "Save Property by Tax Limits," *Spokane Spokesman-Review*, Nov. 6, 1938, p. A-11. The slapstick antics of Lieutenant Governor Meyers in attempting to call a special session while he was acting governor in Governor Martin's absence from the state are recounted in Richard L. Neuberger, *Our Promised Land* (New York: Macmillan, 1939), pp. 272–75.

66. Washington State Federation of Labor, *Proceedings* (1938), p. 18.

67. For articles denouncing the antistrike measure and the United Farmers, see the *Washington State Labor News*, July 29, 1938, p. 1; July 15, 1938, p. 1; Sept. 30, 1938, p. 1; and all four issues published in October 1938.

68. For the story and the analysis of the break-up of the coalition, see

"Farmer-Labor Split Widens," *Seattle Times*, Nov. 6, 1938, p. 14. But for a different view, see "Grange, Labor, WCF, School Groups to Push Tax Measure," *Washington New Dealer*, Oct. 8, 1938, p. 1, in which the writer tried to paper over the deep divisions on other issues by pointing to their mutual support of the income tax. (The name of the Commonwealth Federation's publication was changed September 17, 1938, to the *Washington New Dealer*.)

69. A report on the meeting appeared in the *Washington New Dealer*, Oct. 8, 1938, p. 1. Evidence of the well-organized opposition includes frequent mentions of new county chapters of the Taxpayers' Association as well as the focus of the organization's newsletter on two key issues—the income tax amendment and the 40-mill limitation initiative. See *Washington Taxpayer*, monthly issues from October 1937 through November 1938.

70. For the adoption of the party plank on the graduated income tax, see *Seattle Star*, July 14, 1938, p. 2; *Tacoma News Tribune*, July 14, 1938, pp. 1, 13. For Martin's views on the financial condition of Washington, see *Spokane Spokesman-Review*, Nov. 6, 1938, p. A-11. For evidence of candidates endorsing the tax without necessarily working for passage of the amendment, see the campaign advertisements of candidates in the *Grange News* for the weeks leading up to the general election.

71. Lester M. Livengood, "No Vote Best on Amendment," *Spokane Spokesman-Review*, Nov. 6, 1938, p. A-7.

72. For an example of the rhetoric, see Edward E. Henry, "Legal Snapshots," *Washington New Dealer*, Sept. 24, 1938, p. 2.

73. For examples of the pre-election year editorializing against the income tax, see John Ledgerwood, "Organized Special Interests; Organized Bureaucracy; Unorganized Taxpayers," *Washington Taxpayer* 3 (November 1937), p. 1. For Ledgerwood's characterization of tax supporters, see "Vote Against Constitutional Amendment," *Washington Taxpayer* 4 (November 1938), p. 1. The "madness and moderation" statement is in an editorial titled "Find Out," *Seattle Times*, Oct. 2, 1938, p. 6.

74. "Tax Grabbers Unite," *Seattle Times*, Nov. 7, 1938, p. 6.

75. "No Vote Best on Amendment," *Spokane Spokesman-Review*, Nov. 6, 1938, p. A-7.

76. "Amendment and Three Initiatives Up," *Seattle Times*, Nov. 6, 1938, p. 14. The writer of the lead story a week earlier in the *Washington New Dealer* estimated that no more than 2 percent of the population would be liable to pay the tax. "Income Tax Would Hit Less Than 2 Per Cent of State Population," *Washington New Dealer*, Oct. 22, 1938, p. 1.

77. "Tax Grabbers Unite," *Seattle Times*, Nov. 7, 1938, p. 6.

78. "Taxes are High Enough," *Elma Chronicle*, Oct. 27, 1938, p. 4.

79. "40-Mill Limit Bill Supported by Women," *Benton County Independent*, Oct. 14, 1938, p. 5; "Why Initiative 129 Serves as Public Godsend," *Independent*, Oct. 28, 1938, p. 1.

80. Organized labor managed to defeat the antistrike initiative, but the measure won the majority in most farm counties of Eastern Washington. See Secretary of State, *Abstract of Votes Polled at the General Election, 1938* (Olympia: State Printing Plant, 1938), p. 23, for the county vote totals for the ballot measures.

81. Conservative Democrats, successful in primary races against "left-leaning" Democrats, tried similar strategies against the Republicans in the general election, with mixed results. See "Voters Approve 40-Mill, School Election Bills," *Seattle Times*, Nov. 9, 1938, pp. 1, 15.

82. Charles Hodde interview, Jan. 12, 1987.

10 Income Tax Efforts after World War II

1. "House Roster," *Journal of the House*, Extraordinary Session (1951), pp. 89–94.

2. "State Income Tax Law Proposed," *Seattle Times*, Feb. 16, 1951, p. 9.

3. *Seattle Times*, Feb. 23, 1951, p. 8.

4. Ibid.

5. "Cunningham Comments," *Seattle Times*, Feb. 18, 1951, p. 11.

6. Ibid.

7. "State Income Tax Law Proposed," *Seattle Times*, Feb. 16, 1951, p. 9.

8. House Bill 544 (1951). Roderick was a 29–year-old "waterfront arbitrator" from Seattle. Dootson, age 36, had an interesting dual occupation: lawyer and Great Northern Railway engineman. "House Roster," *Journal of the House*, Extraordinary Session (1951), pp. 90, 93.

9. *Seattle Times*, Feb. 18, 1951, p. 34.

10. "Langlie Tax Bill Cleared House Committee," *Seattle Times*, March 2, 1951, p. 15.

11. "Langlie Aide Asks House to Pass Tax Bill," *Seattle Times*, March 11, 1951, p. 8.

12. "Solons Not Agreed on Number of New Taxes," *Seattle Times*, March 14, 1951, p. 1.

13. "Senate Killed Langlie 4% Tax," *Seattle Times*, March 18, 1951, p. 8.

14. "New Income Tax Proposal Offered," *Seattle Times*, March 30, 1951, p. 8.

15. Ibid.

16. *Seattle Times*, April 3, 1951, p. 1.

17. "Senate, in Test Vote, Beats Sales Tax Boost to 3 1/2%," *Seattle Times*, April 3, 1951, p. 1.

18. "Sub. H. B. #1," *Legislative Record*, Extraordinary Session of the 32nd Legislature, Washington Legislature (1951).

19. Governor Langlie vetoed certain items, but the gist of the bill remained intact. *Legislative Record*, p. 7.

20. "Cunningham Comments," *Seattle Times*, April 5, 1951, p. 4.

21. The four companies were all represented by Seattle law firms. The companies were the Union Pacific, represented by Skeel, McKelvey, Henke, Evenson and Uhlmann; the Northern Pacific Railway, represented by Dean Eastman and Harold G. Boggs; the Chicago, Milwaukee, St. Paul and Pacific Railroad, represented by B. E. Lutterman and Charles F. Hanson; and the Great Northern Railway, represented by Thomas Balmer and R. Paul Tjossem.

22. Smith Troy (born 1906) was a University of Washington College of Law graduate who had served as attorney general since 1940. He was a Democrat. E. W. Anderson (born 1892), legal advisor to the tax commission since 1933, was a Republican.

23. *Washington Constitution*, article II, sec. 19: "No bill shall embrace more than one subject, and that shall be expressed in the title."

24. *Power, Inc.*, v. *Huntley*, 235 P.2d 173, 175.

25. Biographical files, Special Collections, University of Washington Libraries.

26. *Power, Inc.*, v. *Huntley*, at 175.

27. Ibid., at 176, citing to *Aberdeen Savings and Loan Association* v. *Chase*, 157 Wash. 351, 289 P. 697 (1930).

28. *Power, Inc.*, v. *Huntley*, at 177. Here, Hill acknowledged that the lawyers for the state conceded that just because the legislature called it an "excise tax" didn't necessarily mean the tax was one. Hill's "masquerade" comment comes from the state's argument.

29. Ibid., at 178.

30. Schwellenbach issued a curiously worded concurrence: "I have signed the majority opinion, but in fairness to all concerned it should be stated that after this case had been assigned to one of the judges, and his opinion did not meet with the approval of the majority, the case was then reassigned to Judge Hill for opinion." Ibid., at 181.

31. *Power, Inc., v. Huntley*, at 182.

32. Ibid., at 186.

33. Ibid.

34. Virtually all state appropriations were included in the bill except for funds for the Department of Highways, which had been included in another bill. *Seattle Times*, Aug. 21, 1951, p. 1.

35. *Seattle Times*, Aug. 21, 1951, p. 5.

36. Ibid.

37. "Expenses Must Be Cut or Taxes Boosted," *Seattle Times*, Aug. 21, 1951, p. 5.

38. "Legislators, By Now, Should Have Learned" (editorial), *Seattle Times*, Aug. 22, 1951, p. 6.

39. *Seattle Times*, Nov. 1, 1970, p. A-12.

40. *Seattle Times*, Nov. 2, 1970, p. A-16.

41. "Statistical Portrait of an Unfair Tax System," *Seattle Times*, Jan. 29, 1989, p. A-14.

42. On the other hand, other commentators have pointed out that the laws authorizing an income tax are still in place, even though they were found unconstitutional by the courts. For an enlightening discussion of the question, see Hugh D. Spitzer, "A Washington State Income Tax—Again?" *Puget Sound Law Review* 16 (1993), pp. 515–70.

COMMENT ON SOURCES

Secondary Literature

Although policy analysts and political scientists have written on the topic of state taxation, political histories of state taxation are scarce. One exception is a work on the Wisconsin taxation experience. Elliot Brownlee, Jr., effectively ties the income tax issue in that state to the Progressive movement in *Progressivism and Economic Growth: Wisconsin Income Tax, 1911–1929* (1974). Another effective treatment is Manuael M. Stockwell's work on California taxation titled *Studies in California State Taxation, 1910–1935*, published in 1939. Rebecca Brownlee's 1942 doctoral dissertation from the University of Pennsylvania focused on "The Income Tax in Delaware." Several early efforts at describing the interaction of taxation policy and politics include Roy G. Blakey's 1932 study titled simply *The State Income Tax*. At the time the book was written, however, western states had not adopted such a tax. Clara Penniman's study, *State Income Taxation*, published in 1980, focuses on contemporary tax issues with little discussion of their histories.

The history of federal taxation, however, has received greater attention. Colonial taxation methods are discussed in Robert A. Becker, *Revolution, Reform and the Politics of American Taxation, 1767–1783* (1980). Useful studies of taxation during the Civil War period have included a 1942 biography by Herbert Ronald Ferleger titled *David A. Wells and the American Revenue System, 1865–1870*. A. B. Hart's 1899 biography *Salmon Portland Chase* also refers to the Civil War taxation question. Bert W. Rain, in *An Analysis and Critique of Union Financing of the Civil War* (1962), provides arguments used by tax proponents and opponents. Also still useful, particularly for the Civil War period, is the 1942 work by Sidney Ratner titled *American Taxation*.

Although taxation is not their central subject, many works note income tax debates as an important segment of the political discourse. One such work is *The Winning of the Midwest: Social and Political Conflict, 1888–1896*, in which Richard Jensen describes the Populist income tax proposals. Gabriel Kolko's provocative *Railroads and Regulation, 1877–1916* (1965) contains similar references to the importance of taxation debates on Populist and Progressive policies. Lawrence Goodwyn describes Populist aspirations for an income tax in *Democratic Promise: The Populist Movement in America* (1976). Particularly valuable for this study was John D. Buecker, *The Income Tax and the Progressive Era* (1985).

Studies of various farm organizations include references to their advocacy of income taxation. Examples include Robert C. McMath, Jr., *Populist Vanguard: A History of the Southern Farmers' Alliance* (1975). The Washington Grange was central to the taxation question in the 1930s. Two general works on the organization were useful for this study: Harriet Ann Crawford, *The Washington State Grange, 1889–1924: A Romance of Democracy* (1940); and Gus Norwood, *Washington Grangers Celebrate a Century* (1988). Organized labor's role in the tax controversies was significant, too. An excellent treatment of organized labor in Washington is Jonathan Dembo, *Unions and Politics in Washington State, 1885–1935* (1983).

A number of tax studies, most written for contemporary policy makers, were examined for this book. These include the pioneering analysis by Vanderveer Curtis, *The State Tax System of Washington* (1916); Joseph Pratt Harris, *County Finances in the State of Washington* (1935); Maurice Wentworth Lee, *Tax Structure of the State of Washington* (1950); and Robert E. Berney, *Tax Structure of Washington* (1970).

The political context in Washington has been examined in a number of works. Particularly useful for this study were: Howard Allen, *Poindexter of Washington: A Study in Progressive Politics* (1981); William E. Ames and Roger A. Simpson, *Unionism or Hearst: The Seattle Post-Intelligencer Strike of 1936* (1978); Mary W. Avery, *Washington: A History of the Evergreen State* (1965); Paul L. Beckett, *From Wilderness to Enabling Act: The Evolution of the State of Washington* (1968); Norman H. Clark, *Washington: A Bicentennial History* (1976) and *Mill Town: A Social History of Everett, Washington* (1970); Gordon B. Dodds, *The American Northwest: A History of Oregon and Washington* (1986); and Earl Pomeroy, *The Pacific Slope* (1965).

Useful for understanding the early period were Robert W. Johannsen, *Frontier Politics and the Sectional Conflict: The Pacific Northwest on the Eve of the Civil War* (1955); Aurora Hunt, *The Army of the Pacific* (1917); Malcolm Clark, Jr., *Eden Seekers: The Settlement of Oregon, 1818–1862* (1981); and James E. Hendrickson, *Joe Lane of Oregon: Machine Politics and the Sectional Crisis, 1849–1861* (1967). Two studies focusing on legal development were helpful: John D. Hicks, *The Constitutions of the Northwest States* (1923); and Charles H. Sheldon, *A Century of Judging: A Political History of the Washington Supreme Court* (1988).

Also useful were studies of particular areas of the state of Washington, including Roger Sale, *Seattle: Past to Present* (1976); Murray Morgan's two anecdotal histories of the Puget Sound area, *Skid Road: An Informal Portrait of Seattle* (1982) and *Puget's Sound: A Narrative of Early Tacoma and the Southern Sound* (1979); Herbert Hunt, *Washington West of the Cascades* (1917); Dorothy O. Johanson, *Empire of the Columbia* (1967); George L. Fuller, *The Inland Empire* (1928); and C. B. Bagley's highly biographical *History of Seattle from Earliest Settlement to the Present Time* (1916).

Several biographies provided insights into attitudes toward tax policy. These included: Howard Allen, *Poindexter of Washington: A Study in Progressive Politics* (1981); Arthur H. Bone, *Oregon Cattleman/Governor, Congressman: Memoirs and Times of Walter M. Pierce* (1981); James B. Hedges, *Henry Villard and the Railways of the Northwest* (1930); Albro Martin, *James J. Hill and the Opening of the Northwest* (1976); and the 1903 collective biography of Oregonians titled *Portrait and Biographical Record of Portland and Vicinity* (1903).

Primary Sources

Essential to this study were a number of manuscript collections held by the University of Washington Libraries and the Washington State Archives. For the Progressive era tax debates, the papers of Erastus Brainerd, Joe Smith, and Austin Griffiths, all in the Manuscripts Division, University of Washington Libraries, were particularly important. For the 1930s income tax debate, the papers of Warren Magnuson, University of Washington Libraries, were essential. Also of value were the papers of George Yantis and Roy J. Kinnear, University of Washington Libraries. Heavy reliance was placed on the papers of Washington governors. Two collections, both in the Washington State Archives, were particularly important: the Roland Hartley and C. D. Martin papers.

The study of how Civil War taxation affected Washington would not have been possible without examining the Assessment Roles, Territory of Washington, 1868–1872, and Assessment Roles, State of Oregon, both in Record Group 58, National Archives, Seattle Branch. Cross-checking the names on the Assessment Roles with the 1860 and 1870 censuses, also held in National Archives, Seattle Branch, provided a demographic picture of the taxpayers. The Washington Biographies manuscript collection held in the Special Collections, University of Washington, were valuable for details about many principals in tax debates, including legislators and government officials.

State documents such as reports by legislative committees and various Senate and House *Journals,* were useful. Of particular value were the Biennial Reports of the Tax Commission of Washington and the two reports of the Washington Tax Investigation Committee (1922 and 1930).

Court decisions, several of which struck down tax laws as unconstitutional, are central to the study of Washington taxation. Particularly significant were: *Culliton* v. *Chase,* 25 P.2d 81 (1933); and *Jensen* v. *Henneford,* 53 P.2d 607 (1936); both struck down income tax statutes.

Tax debates were aired in a number of organizational newsletters and magazines. Essential to this study were the *Grange News, Washington Commonwealth Builder, Washington State Chamber News, Washington State Labor News,* and the variously named publications of the Washington Taxpayers' Association.

Extensive reliance was placed on editorial and news columns in some 40 Washington newspapers, ranging from the pioneering *Washington Standard* (Olympia) to various local weeklies. Three Seattle dailies, the *Post-Intelligencer,* the *Times,* and the *Star,* were important for the 1930s story. The weekly *Seattle Argus* contained comments about taxation in most editions during the 1930s debates. The Oregon story could not be as well understood without reference to the *Oregonian,* the *Oregon Journal* (both published in Portland) and the *Oregon Statesman* (Salem).

Unfortunately, many of the principals involved in the taxation debates were no longer living in the 1980s when this study was begun. Nonetheless, I had the good fortune of interviewing Charles Hodde, who served not only as a legislator during the 1930s but also as a Grange organizer earlier. He graciously supplied many answers that could not have been found in any printed source.

INDEX

Aberdeen Savings case, 79, 124
Abernethy, Alex S., 16, 137n53
Ainsworth, J. C., 32
Allen, Sen. John B., 41, 148n16
American Federation of Labor (AFL):
   feud with CIO, 115
Anderson, E. W., 123
Antietam, battle of, 7
Arthur, President Chester A., 40
Assessed valuations, increases in, 58
Assessment districts, Oregon, 30
Assessment rolls: compared with
   census records, 20
Assessors: lists, 138n67; payments
   made to, 13; in Oregon, 31
Associated Grange Warehouse
   Company (Seattle), 62
Associated Industries of Washington
   (AIW), 120

Baker, D. S., 12
Baker, Edward D., 142n10
Bankers: oppose 1928 tax, 64

Banks: failures, 40; tax laws for,
   66–67
Beals, Walter B., 96, 123, 124;
   and Jensen case, 109
Beardslee, Will, 89
Beeler, Adam, 89
Beer: initiative legalizing sale of, 86
Bellingham Evening News: on tax
   reduction, 76
Bigelow, D. R., 12
Blake, Bruce, 89, 97; and Jensen case,
   109
Board of Regents, University of
   Washington, 63
Bonds: proposed by WEA, 60, 61;
   tax proposed on, 64
Bone, Homer T., 83, 113; election
   to Senate, 86, 88
Bone-dry law, 81; repealed, 3, 86
Boutwell, George S., 28, 133n18
Bowen, John C., 73
Breckenridge, John C., 26
Bremerton Navy Yard, 54

Broadcast stations: taxation of, 94
Bronson, Philip, 108–9
Brown, Dr. E. J., 52
Brown, Edward, 51
Brown, H. H., 171n13
Bryan, Sen. James W., 48, 53
Bull Run, battle of, 8
Burbank, A. R., 12
Bureau of Internal Revenue, 10
Bushwiler, Aaron, 28
Business Chronicle: opposes 1928
    tax, 65
Business excise tax act, 100, 101
Business Week: on Washington
    income tax, 78
Butler, William D., 68

Cannair, Frank, 82
Census, Oregon: consistency with
    tax rolls, 33
Central Business Property Company,
    77
Chadwick, H. A., 80
Chain store tax initiative, 82
Chamber of Commerce, 64; merged
    with taxpayer organizations, 77;
    favors 40–mill limitation, 82
Chamberlin, Fred J., 82, 157n24
Chase, Salmon P., 8
Chase, Samuel, 76; as tax commis-
    sioner, 62, 90, 104
Children's Initiative, 128n6
Chinese workers, in Oregon, 33
Choate, Joseph, 45
Cigarette tax, 94
Civil War, 8–25 passim; income tax
    during, 7
Clallam County, Washington, 21

Clark, Crandal H., 79
Clark County Grange, 79
Clatsop County, Oregon, 32–33
Cleary, E. J., 64, 73
Cleveland, President Grover, 39, 41
Coastal defenses, 54
Coe, Lawrence W., 30
Coffee, John M., 113
Cohen, Arthur G., 68
Colfax, Schuyler, 8
Colfax, Washington, 40
Collection districts: establishment
    of, 10
Collector of revenue, 11, 13
Columbia County, Oregon, 32–33
Comfort, A. B., 122
Commerce: in Oregon and
    Washington, 35
Commissioner of public lands, 58
Committee on Revenue and Taxa-
    tion, Washington legislative, 74
Communist party, 176n52
Confederacy, 28
Confederate Army: service of tax-
    payers in, 23
Confederates, in Oregon, 26, 27
Congress of Industrial Organizations
    (CIO): feud with AFL, 115
Connor, Edwin M.: on FDR, 162n17
Constitutional amendment: for
    income tax, 79, 100; in 1936
    election, 110
Constitutional convention, Wash-
    ington, 38
Copeland, Henry J., 107, 114
Corporate license tax, 59
Corporation income tax: of *1931*,
    73, 74, 75; of *1951*, 120, 122

Costigan, Howard, 110–11
Coulson, H. A., 31
Cowles, William H., 64–65
Cowlitz County, Washington, 21
Coxey's army, 40
Credit cards: use in gasoline stations, 92
Culliton, Helen, 92
Culliton, William M., 4, 92; sues state over income tax, 93, 96, 99, 100, 124
Culliton-McHale lawsuits, 93, 95
Cunningham, Ross, 123, 124
Currency reform, 41
Custis, Vanderveer, 57
Customs duties: as means to finance government, 7–8

Daily Journal of Commerce, 101
Davis, J. H., 74
Dawson, W. C., 114
Deady, Mathew, 28
Democratic Party, Oregon, 27
Democratic Party, Washington: controls 1934 legislature, 105; electoral success of, 3, 113; endorsements of income tax, 88; influence of farm groups on, 120; schism in, 114; splits on income tax, 41, 115; victories in 1932, 86
Denny, John, 12
Denny, Robert, 102
Depression: of 1837, 8; of 1894, 40
Dill, C. C., 94
Dilling, George W., 52
Direct tax: application to states of, 9
District assessor, 10, 11
District collector: duties of, 10–11
Dole, Edwin L., 12

Donworth, Charles T., 124
Doolittle, William H., 40, 42
Dootson, John T., 121
Drumheller, Joseph, 113
Duggan, Fred S., 113
Dyer, E. S., 12

Earthquake, Portland, 26
Eastham, A. B., 50
Eaton, C. N., 114
Eckstein, Nathan, 59
Economy, Washington, 90, 110; during depression, 64; post-war growth of, 119
Eighteenth Amendment: repealed, 101
Eldridge, Wesley, 122
Election of 1860, 141n7
Election of 1864, 142n16
Elliott, George M., 59
Elwick, Andrew, 81
Equalization, tax, 60
Evans, Daniel, 125, 126
Everett, Washington: bank failures in, 40; effect of panic on, 147n11
Excise tax, national: in Oregon, 31; in Washington, 18; jokes about, 10
Excise tax, Washington: court defines, 123–24; passed by 1933 legislature, 100
Express companies: taxes assessed on, 59
Extraordinary session of legislature, 124

Faculty taxes, 130n4
Failing, Henry, 32
Falconer, J. A., 48
Farmer-labor coalition: in Oregon, 69

Farmers: on constitution tax provisions, 38; move to Republican party, 120; on tax issue, 39, 78, 114, 118; tax liability of, 21; as taxpayers, 22

Farmers' Alliance, 38

Federal deficit, 17

Federal income tax: amendment, 47–51; of 1894, 37–46; Washington filers, 95

Federal spending: importance to Washington, 54

Fessenden, William Pitt, 140n78

Finch, D. B., 23

Finley, Robert C., 124

Firemen's relief and pension fund, 102

First National Bank of Port Angeles, 63

Fisher, O. W., 95

Food: exempted from sales tax, 126

40–mill limitation, 86, 111, 118; draws support away from income tax, 92, 99, 112; fails in 1924 and 1926, 60, 61; initiative proposed, 82–83; lawsuit challenging, 102; passes in 1934 election, 105; passes in 1936 election, 111, 112–13; passes legislature in 1938, 116; passes in 1940, 119; praised, 117; support for, 81, 87; upheld by Supreme Court, 102

Fourteenth Amendment: relationship of income tax to, 6

Franchise privilege tax, 66, 67

Franenthal, J., 21

Frazar, Capt. Amherst Alden, 29

Frazar, Thomas, 29–31

Freeman, Roger, 121

Friedman, Lawrence M., 44, 96

Frost, J. E., 51

Fuller, Melville, 45

Galbraith, Thomas S., 68

Galliher's hotel, 13

Gallatly, John, 76, 88

Game department: law establishing, 82

Gardner, Booth, 126

Gasoline tax, 59, 106

Geraghty, James M., 97; and Jensen case, 5–6, 109

Ghent, J. A., 50–51

Gibbs, Addison C., 27, 142n10

Giddings, Edward, 19

Gill, Hiram, 52

Goldsborough, H. A., 11, 13; compared to Oregon counterpart, 30; financial troubles, 14

Goldsborough, Commodore Louis M., 11

Gose, M. F., 61

Goss, Albert S., 61, 156–57n23

Government bonds: Civil War, 8

Government employees: oppose 40–mill limitation, 112

Graduated income tax: Grange support for, 80

Grady, Thomas E., 124

Grange: and income tax, 74, 114. See also Washington State Grange

Grange News, 110; on court decision, 98; on 1928 tax initiative, 65

Great Northern Railroad, 40
Griffiths, Austin E., 89
Grooms, William, 31
Guthrie, William D., 45

Hall, Charles W., 73, 79; files amicus brief, 93
Hall, Dorsey, 68
Halleran, Martin P., 107
Hamilton, G. W., 93, 100
Hamilton, Richard, 91–92
Hamley, Frederick G., 124
Hanna, John W., 93
Harlan, John, 45–46
Harlin, Robert H., 59
Harris, Joseph Pratt, 105
Hart, Louis F., 59
Hartley, Roland, 62, 74, 89, 113; proposes 1931 budget, 74; reacts to income tax veto, 78–79; reconstitutes tax commission, 62–63; signs 1929 privilege tax bill, 67; signs tax proclamation, 4, 90; tries to eliminate tax commission, 76; vetoes 1931 tax bills, 75–76
Hart tax committee (1921), 59
Hastings, Fred W., 76
Hay, Marion, 51, 89
Hedges, T. S., 90
Heifner, Charles G., 66
Henneford, Henry H., 104
Henry, Ed, 116
Herman, Henry E. T., 89
High School Teachers' League: endorses tax initiative, 81
Hill, Daniel, 120

Hill, David B., 42
Hill, James J., 40–41
Hill, Knute, 67, 88, 99, 113
Hill, Matthew W., 123–24
Hindley, Harold R., 52–53
Hodde, Charles, 81, 96, 99; as house speaker, 120; on income tax after 1932, 118
Hoffman, David M., 108
Holcomb, O. R., 88, 97–98
Horton, Dexter, 22
Hotels: license fees on, 11
House Rules Committee: kills income tax bill (1929), 66
House Ways and Means Committee: favors income tax, 41
Howard, Rebecca, 20–21, 139n75
Howe, Samuel D., 19
Hubbs, Paul K., 12

Income: definition of, 109
Income tax: as excise tax, 124; constitutional amendment for, defeated, 105; corporate as wedge for, 120; declining support for by county, 105; difficulty in getting constitutional amendment for, 79; favored by Democrats, 113; federal filings in Washington, 57–58; graduated, 68, 74–75; legislature passes amendment for, 102; passes house, 103; phases of, 6; in Populist platform, 37; questions about, 116; proposed provisions for, 80, 108; states without, 128n5; suit against, 92–93, 108; tariffs attached to, 41; votes split on 40–mill and, 117

Income tax, federal: Civil War and, 7–9, 15, 18; collection system established, 43; legality of *1894*, 42; opposition to, 41–42; passes Congress, 37, 41; rates, 41; ratified, 47–55; as regional issue, 47–48; as socialist issue, 42–43; unconstitutionality of *1894*, 45; Washington filers, 43

Income tax, Oregon: as alternative to property tax, 70; passes, 57, 69; support for, 71, 72

Income tax bills: *1929*, 65–66; *1931*, 73, 74, 75; *1951*, 121, 123; *1970*, 125; *1973*, 125–26

Income tax constitutional amendment (*1936*), 110; cost questioned, 111; loses, 112–13

Income tax initiative of *1932*, 3, 86–87; becomes law, 3; constitutionality debated, 96–98; filed, 82; found unconstitutional, 5, 93; Grange support for, 79; legal challenges to, 4, 90–91

Income tax initiatives: *1938*, 118; *1942*, 119; *1975*, 126

Inheritance tax, 59; attempt to repeal, 64

Initiative process, viii, 82

Initiatives, 47, 112; *I 69* (*1932*), 80, 83, 85; *I 130*, 115; *I 314* (*1975*), 126

Internal Revenue Act, 26, 28

Internal Revenue Bureau, 5, 143n23

Iverson, Lyle L., 123

Jackson County, Oregon, 26, 32–34

Jacksonville, Oregon, 29

Japanese empire: threat to Pacific Coast, 54

Jenner, Earle, 90–91, 95, 97, 98

Jenner, T. M., 95

Jensen, George A., 108

Jones, Fred K., 68, 77

Jones, John R., 91, 102

Jones, Walter L., 86, 88

Josephine County, Oregon, 33–34

Kitsap County, Washington, 12

Klemgard, Gordon, 113

KOMO radio, 95

Ku Klux Klan, 70

Labor unions: coalition with farmers, 104–5; and Grange, 114, 115; support for income tax, 70, 110

Ladd, W. S., 32

Laman, J. D., 19

Landon, Daniel, 51

Landon, David, 73

Land sales: as finance for government, 7–8

Lane, Joseph, 26, 27

Lane County, Oregon, 28

Langlie, Arthur, 120–22, 124

Lawyers, 23, 24

Lease, Joseph E., 68

Ledyard, S. F., 12

Lewis, C. H., 32

Lewis, Clancey M., 101

Lewis, Fred W., 62

License fees, 11

Lilly, Wilmot H., 68

Lincoln, Abraham, 13

Lindsay, J. W., 66

Liquor commission, 101
Liquor laws, 102; debates over, 50
Liquor outlets: state control over, 101
Lister, Ernest, 89
Livengood, Lester, 61, 77, 115
Locke, Phil S., 51
Loyalty: correlation of taxpaying
    with, 27

Magnuson, Warren, 94, 113
Main, John F., 89, 97
Maine, 22
Mallery, Joseph A., 124
Manuals, self-help tax, 29
Manufacturers' Association of
    Washington, 101
Maples, Herman M., 108
Maritime industry: strike in, 114
Marsh, Arthur, 94
Martin, Clarence D., 5, 97, 104;
    appoints commission on liquor,
    101; appoints tax commission,
    95; elected governor, 86, 88; and
    income tax, 115, 117; line-item veto,
    107; recall urged, 108; refuses to
    veto sales tax, 107; returns to stop
    special session, 114; seeks advice on
    tax initiative, 91–92; on Supreme
    Court decision, 109; wins reelec-
    tion, 113
McBroom, Fred, 62, 76, 90
McClellan, George B., 28
McCormick, S. J., 29
McGregor, Peter, 59
McHale, Earl, 4, 92, 93
McInnes, Donald, 62, 76–77, 90
McKinley tariff, 39
McMicken, Rupp, and Schweppe, 123

McMillan, David, 113
Mellen, William A. K., 31
Merchants: as taxpayers, 22, 36
Metcalf, Ralph, 76, 114
Meyers, Victor, 114
Millard, William J., 89, 96–97
Miller, W. W., 12
Miller, William H., 68
Mill levies: by county, 60, 87
Mitchell, John R., 89, 96–97
Moore, Marshall F., 17
Moore, Philip, 14, 19, 136n44
Morrow, P. Frank, 103
Moses Taylor (steamer), 14
Multnomah County, Oregon, 31, 32

Nash, Louis, 165–66n59; on 40–mill
    limitation, 83
National debt, 131n7
New England natives: in Oregon, 34;
    in Washington, 22
New Order of Cincinnatus, 103
Newspapers: closed for Confederate
    tendencies, 27; on Initiative 69,
    83–84; support for 40–mill limita-
    tion by, 112. See also specific names
    of newspapers
Nichols, Ralph D., 50
Northern Railway Act, 40
Norton, M. K., 101

Oakley, Annie, 109
Oakley, Frank D., 59
O'Brien, Ross G., 19, 139n73
Occupation licenses, 11
Occupations: in Oregon, 32;
    in Washington, 22
Olney, Richard, 45

Olson, O. H., 67, 124–25

Olympia, Washington, 13

Oregon: income tax debate in, 69–71; rural-urban population in, 69; statehood, 34; taxation in, 25

Oregon Agricultural Society, 29

Oregon Grange Bulletin, 70

Oregonian: comments on corruption, 14; income tax act published in, 26; opposes income tax, 70

Oregon State Grange, 69

Oregon Volunteers, 30

Ostrander, Dr. A., 16

Palmer, E. B., 94

Panic of *1857*, 8

✓Panic of *1893*, 39

Parker, Emmett, 93, 96, 97

Patriotism: taxation and, 29

✓Patrons of Husbandry, 38

Penitentiary: built with tax proceeds, 18

Pennoyer, Sylvester, 46

Penrose, S. B. L., 59

People's Advocate, 146n1; on banks, 43, 45; calls for Supreme Court impeachments, 46; on *1894* income tax, 44

Personal net income tax, 106, 107

Personal property: census estimates of, 21

Petrain, Joseph, 22–23

Pickering, William, 17, 17

Pierce, Walter M., 70

Plehn, Dr. Carl C., 64

Politics: tax issues in, 35

Pollock, Charles, 45

Pollock case: compared to Culliton case, 97

Polson, Alex, 59

Population: post-war boom in, 119

✓Populists: elected to legislature, 40; and income tax, 43, 46, 47; platform, 37, 41

Port Angeles, Washington, 14, 15

Port Townsend, Washington, 12

Portland, 69; city directory, 28; tax share paid by, 32

Power, Inc., 123

Powers, John, 120

Preston, Harold, 93

Preston, Thorgrimson, and Turner, 93

Price supports: Grange interest in, 110

Production for Use, 110, 113

✓Progressives, 47, 55

Prohibition, 82, 101

Property: defined, 91, 97

✓Property tax: reduction in, sought, 64, 68; connection to income tax, 74; in *1920s*, 57, 58; reform sought, 90, 92, 116; system in the *1890s*, 38

Protectionist legislation, 39

Public power initiative, 61

Public utility district initiative, 114

Puget Sound Iron and Steel Foundry, 49

Pullman strike, 40

Quotas: troop and tax, 129–30n2

Racine, Samuel F., 96

Railroads: assessments on, 59; grievances against, 38; tax opposition from, 60

Real estate industry: opposition to tax by, 77; taxes of, 79

Recall: instituted, 47; of Hartley, 63–64

Rector, L. J., 12

Referendum: income tax in Oregon, 70; instituted in Washington, 47

Relief, 99

Remington Arms Company, 40

Republican Party: allies with Taxpayers' Association, 61; Civil War effect on, 35; farmers identify with, 120; and income tax, 48, 76, 117–18; platform, 61

Republicans, silver, 42

Residence, taxpayer, 23–24

Revenue Act of 1935, 106

Revenues: in Oregon, 31–32

Reynolds, Charles A., 88

Reynolds, John M., 98

Ritz, Philip, 22

Roberts, John L., 49–50

Robertson, W. W., 59, 65, 88

Robinson, Herb, 126

Rodbury, W. D., 96

Roderick, David M., 121

Roderick-Dotson tax bill, 121, 122

Roosevelt, Franklin D., 86, 88, 162n17

Rupp, John N., 123

Rural: defined, 127n4

Ruth, A. S., 51

Rydstrom, Arvid, 50

Salem, Oregon, 69

Sales tax: bill introduced for, 5, 94; constitutional, 109; established, 66; increase predicted, 125; increasing importance of, 119; legislative support for, 74; opposition to, 59, 70, 79, 100, 107; provisions, 106; removed from food, 121, 126; suit brought against, 108

Savage, Charles W., 31, 34

Savings and loan institutions, 66

School fund: income tax for, 92

Schools: in Portland, 29

Schwellenbach, E. W., 124

Seattle, Washington, 15

Seattle Argus, 80; opposes Initiative 69, 85

Seattle Central Labor Council, 81, 100

Seattle Jaycees, 92

Seattle Post-Intelligencer, 110

Seattle Real Estate Board, 61; pays for 40–mill initiative drive, 83

Seattle Star: on Initiative 69, 84, 85; strike against, 114

Seattle Times, 98, 103; endorses income tax, 125; on income tax forms, 98; opposes Initiative 69, 84

Secessionists: in Oregon and California, 27

Selwin, Edwin, 65

Senate, U. S.: elections to, 53

Seward, William, 9

Shank, Belt, and Fairbrook, 120

Sheldon, Charles, 97

Sherman Silver Purchase Act, 39

Showalter, N. D., 68

Sinclair, Upton, 110

Silver coinage, 39

Skamania County, Washington, 21

Slavery, 26; in Oregon, 141n6

Smith, Victor, 14, 135–36n41, n44

Snohomish County, Washington, 21

Smithson, John, 49

Snohomish County Tribune, 84–85
Sparks, John G., 11–17 passim, 19
Spokane Chamber of Commerce, 92
Spokane Insurance Association, 77
Spokane Realty Board, 77, 81, 111
Spokane Spokesman-Review, 83
Springer v. U.S., 149n28
Squire, Watson L., 40–42
Stamps, revenue, 30
State auditor, 58
State Bankers' Association, 67
State Board of Equalization, 58
State Federation of Taxpayers' Asso-
    ciations, 61, 77
State Rail Commission, 38
State Tax Commission, 73, 76, 98;
    abolished, 59; appeals tax decision,
    4, 93, 109; duties, 59; Henneford
    appointed to, 104; legislature
    strengthens, 58; prints income
    tax forms, 95; sued, 93; supports
    constitutional amendment, 104
Steilacoom, Washington, 10
Steinart, William J., 88–89, 97,
    109
Stevens, Hazard, 19
Stevens, Isaac, 19
Stevens, Thaddeus, 8
Stevens County, Washington, 21
Stewart, A. T., 143n22
Stewart, Grant, 103
Strikes, labor, 115; against *Seattle Post-
    Intelligencer*, 110; against *Seattle
    Star*, 114
Sugar: tariffs on, 39
Supreme Court of the United States:
    upholds income tax, 43

Sutton, W. J., 76
Suzzallo, Henry, 62, 63
Swayne, Noah H., 43

Tanner, W. V., 94
Tariff bill, 39, 41
Taverns: license fees on, 11
Tax Advisory Committee, 73
Tax assessments: in Oregon by
    county, 145n37; printing of, 15
Taxation: as voluntary contribution,
    24
Tax commissioner, federal, 10
Tax deductions, Civil War, 15
Taxes: avoidance in Washington, 21;
    bill of *1951*, 121–22; Confederacy,
    131n5; delinquencies, 116–17; guide,
    96; law, 10; reform, 56–72 passim;
    relief, 98–99; returns, 10; rulings,
    30; tokens, 108
Tax Investigation Committee, 67,
    77; holds hearings, 68; supports
    income tax bill, 73; supports tax
    initiative, 80–81
Tax limitation initiative (1924), 60
Tax notices, Civil War, 7
Taxpayers: demographics of, 19–25;
    Oregon, 31–34, 35; regional origins
    of, 22–23; Southern-born, 34;
    Washington, 18–19
Taxpayers' Economy League, 65, 77,
    78
Tax Reduction League, 78, 105
Taylor, James, 100
Teachers: oppose 40–mill limitation,
    112
Thurston County, Washington, 21

Thurston County Superior Court, 90, 93; tax law challenged in, 4

Tilley, M. R., 14

Todd, Charles H., 103–4

Todd, Hugh C., 50–51

Tolman, Warren W., 88–89, 97, 109

Troy, Smith, 123, 180n22

Twohy, D. W., 59

Unemployed Citizens' League, 82; radicalism of, 99; urges veto of sales tax, 107

Union Trust Company, 40

United Farmers of Washington, 115

University funds, 173n34

University of Washington, 63, 106

Urban residents: support for income tax by, 118; views on taxes, 99

Urban-rural: conflicts, vii, viii; on tax issues, 3, 66

Vetoes, 76

Villard, Henry, 41

Voluntary tax paying compliance, 25, 36

Voters' Information League, 60, 78

Voters' pamphlet (1932), 80

Wages: in Washington, 75

Waitsburg, Washington, 38

Walker, R. M., 9

Walla Walla, Washington, 13, 21

Wanamaker, Pearl, 67, 171n13

War of 1812, 8

Washington Athletic Club, 92

Washington Commonwealth Builder, 107, 108, 174n38

Washington Commonwealth Federation, 99, 107, 110; endorses income tax, 115, 116; loses Production for Use vote, 113; and schism in Democratic party, 114

Washington Education Association, 60, 94; endorses tax initiative, 81, 82; opposes 40–mill limitation, 83; supports income tax, 64, 115

Washington Farmer, 65

Washington Mutual Savings Bank, 67

Washington Parent-Teacher Association, 64; endorses tax initiative, 81

Washington Realty Boards: supports income tax, 64

Washington Savings and Loan League: endorses 40–mill limitation, 111

Washington State, viii, 38; population growth in, 43–44; revenues received by, 106

Washington State Assessors' Association, 101

Washington State Bar Association, 89

Washington State Federation of Labor: endorses tax amendment, 82, 110

Washington State Federation of Women's Clubs: endorses 40–mill limitation, 111

Washington State Grange: active after WWII, 119–20; angry with court decision, 98; changing view of income tax by, 110; congratulates members on tax, 91; continues support for income tax, 64, 104;

Washington State Grange *(continued)*
counties with large membership
in, 87–88; educating voters, 81; electoral success, 85; endorses 40–mill
limitation, 83, 111; endorses tax
committee plan, 68–69; formed,
38; income tax as victory for, 4;
introduces income tax (1935), 106;
leaders, 61–62; leads on tax questions, 78–79; membership, 164n40;
opposes sales tax, 79, 100; seeks signatures for tax petition, 81, 82; support for income tax erodes in, 105
Washington State Labor News: council, 82; on 40–mill limitation, 83;
on income tax, 81
Washington State Legislature: passes
federal income tax amendment, 48
Washington State Supreme Court,
3; decision appealed to, 93; invali-
dates 1951 act, 124–25; rules on bank
tax law, 67; strikes down 1951 tax
law, 123
Washington State Tax Commission:
in court, 123; orders valuation
increase, 63; reconstituted, 62.
See also State Tax Commission
Washington State Taxpayers' Association, 107; on 40–mill limitation,
82; local chapters, 78; officers, 78;
opposes income tax, 115, 116;
opposes constitutional amend-
ment, 111; opposes Langlie tax,
120; organized, 78
Washington Taxpayer, 78
Washington Taxpayers' Council,
56, 60
Washington Title Insurance Com-
pany, 90
Washington Titlemen's Association:
endorses 40–mill limitation, 111
Weaver, Frank P., 124
Willapa River Pilot, 75
Williams, Gail M., 108
Wilmer, F. J., 65–66, 73
Wilson, James, 40, 42
Wilson, John L., 40
Wilson-Gorman tariff bill, 42
Wirt, William, 11
Wright, Charles, 109
Wright, D. F., 4, 93, 109
Wright, Edgar J., 98
Wright, General, 27

Yakima County, Washington, 21, 88
Yantis, George, 88, 100; files amicus
brief, 93; praises legislature for tax
measures, 108

Zioncheck, Marion, 83–84, 88, 113